D0853578

Totally Wired

Also by Andrew Smith

Moondust: In Search of the Men Who Fell to Earth

Totally Wired

On the Trail of the Great Dotcom Swindle

ANDREW SMITH

London · New York · Sydney · Toronto · New Delhi

A CBS COMPANY

First published in Great Britain by Simon & Schuster, 2012
A division of Simon & Schuster UK Ltd
A CBS COMPANY

1 3 5 7 9 10 8 6 4 2

Simon & Schuster UK Ltd
1st Floor
222 Gray's Inn Road
London WC1X 8HB

www.simonandschuster.co.uk

Simon & Schuster Australia, Sydney
Simon & Schuster India, New Delhi

A CIP catalogue record for this book
is available from the British Library

ISBN: 978-1-84737-449-3

Typeset in Palatino by M Rules
Printed and bound by CPI Group (UK) Ltd, Croydon, CR0 4YY

Contents

For H C E

'You are not the kind of guy who would be at a place like this at this time of the morning. But here you are . . .'

Bright Lights, Big City
Jay McInerny

Prologue

One day in the mid-1990s a group of young people woke to find themselves lords of a new realm called cyberspace. Money was showered upon them to start businesses and instruct elders in the ways of an 'online' world they saw coming, and many became rich beyond their wildest dreams as 'dotcom' technology stock prices spiralled to a dizzy peak. Between 1995 and March 2000, all rules of sound finance – of the 'Old Economy' and old society it served – were abandoned and the unthinkable appeared to be happening: twenty-somethings were taking over. And unlike the imagined youth revolutions of the 1950s, 60s, 70s, 80s, this one was remaking society *for real*.

But no. Three months into the new millennium and with pundits claiming the technology boom could roll on forever, investors, as if waking together from a trance, looked down and panicked and in one of the most spectacular financial crashes ever seen, fled the dotcoms until by the end of the year the entire sector had simply ... vanished. Most 'tech' workers had been paid largely in company stock, now worth nothing, and the failed revolution's leaders became hate figures as public and media ire settled on them. Three *trillion* dollars were lost to the economy in what became the signature event of the 1990s, while the dotcommers melted away to nowhere, apparent victims of their own hubris and greed.

The internet was a joke. Was *over*. Those five weird years might never have happened.

As someone with no financial expertise, I'd watched all this happen with a mixture of bewilderment and disbelief; a sense that none of the received explanations convinced. Could the young multimillionaires really have blown enough money on first class travel and thousand-dollar office chairs to sink their businesses? Why had their elders invested so heavily and unconventionally in something they didn't understand – and how was it possible for so many bright people to surrender sanity at the same time? Had the dotcom boom been a con-trick or pre-Millennial delusion? As many times as I returned to it, the official story of events failed to add up.

Increasingly my attention was drawn to the activities of one man. Joshua Harris had been one of the first (if not *the* first) internet moguls in New York. An early online evangelist, he'd founded a successful net research company in the mid-1980s, then ditched it in 1994 for a flamboyant web media and TV portal called Pseudo.com, based in an imposing former warehouse at 600 Broadway on the edge of SoHo.

Almost immediately Pseudo had become the social and creative hub of a downtown district known as Silicon Alley, where web businesses were beginning to gather. The media called him the 'Warhol of the Web' as bacchanalian parties and art events drew revellers from all corners of the city and were reported across the world. By decade's end, Pseudo employed 300 people and was regarded as the leader in its field, but in a mystifying twist, Harris's view of the online drift appeared to have darkened. Despite having been one of the earliest apostles of a networked society, he took to dressing as a grotesque clown called Luvvy and, leaving Pseudo in the hands of managers, turned his attention to a series of extravagant and increasingly dangerous-looking social experiments, seemingly designed to explore his vision of an always-on, totally wired future.

New York thrummed with extravagant parties and events in the final years of the twentieth century, but Harris's were different. In December 1999 he enticed almost a hundred people into a disused warehouse on lower Broadway for a month-long happening called *Quiet*, during which they were fed all the food, drink, drugs and skewed entertainment they could want, a scratch community streamed live to the world in an atmosphere of permanent night, prodded and pushed until personalities frayed and the event was shut down on New Year's Day by the Federal Emergency Management Agency, who imagined Harris to be running a suicide cult. Later, the net mogul wired the entirety of his Broadway loft with webcams and microphones and announced that he and his girlfriend Tanya Corrin would live online for 100 days in a project called *We Live in Public*. Before the time was up, however, the couple split in acrimony and web watchers saw Harris lose the bulk of his fortune to the crash and then shatter like a pane of glass. He fled to an upstate apple farm he'd bought during the boom, where he remained, licking his wounds, 'laundering my head' in his own words, for six years. Friends and former colleagues who visited took to calling him 'The Colonel', after Colonel Kurtz, the star officer who melts upstream and goes rogue in Francis Ford Coppola's adapted film masterpiece *Apocalypse Now*.

I thought about Harris often as the web evolved and moved into the mainstream of society during the first decade of the new century. Business-focused books had dissected what came to be known as the dotcom bubble, but my own feeling that those five amorphous years between 1995 and March 2000 were about something broader and more interesting than a straightforward economic bubble never lessened. And over time it became clear that of all the tragic, comic, barely credible facets of that period, the one that couldn't possibly have arisen at any other time was *Josh Harris*. How and why did a rich, successful businessman go so luridly AWOL? And how was his trip related to the fate of the dotcoms he spearheaded – and to the data-driven world we are still in the early stages of making?

For several years I struggled to persuade publishers that these questions were worth asking. Then, in the summer of 2007, just as others were beginning to see what I thought I saw in Harris and the dotcoms – something bizarre and unhinged, but *exemplary* – the internet pioneer surprised everyone by reappearing, this time on the West Coast, fronting an organisation called Operator 11.

The word was that he'd finished laundering his head and was ready to get back on the grid. He'd sold his farm and acquired a Hollywood sound stage, around which he intended to build a website which effectively offered users the means to run their own web TV station, using clips, chat, live feed and an ability to invite video or webcam-equipped audience members on to shows at will. Programmes or whole channels could be devoted to individuals, families, organisations or any topic from the environment to games to sex to cigars, to be aggregated in one place and surfed at will; a logical amalgam of MySpace, YouTube, Facebook and reality TV, but more subtle and sophisticated than any of those entities on their own. By year's end, the site was up and running and claiming 6000 users, and although the shows seemed to consist mostly of people chatting aimlessly, the possibility existed that they would learn and evolve . . . until, early in 2008, I began to notice the same faces and then shows repeating, as if the site was freezing up like a bird dying in the cold. Curious as to what had happened, I sent some emails; tried to call; watched in bewilderment as the site seized into an eternally looping ghost site, one of thousands which litter the web, mostly relics from the first dotcom age, wreckage of Web 1.0.

After weeks of surfing and calling with no result, a rumour reached me that Harris had sold up and vanished. And this time nobody seemed to know where he'd gone. It was as if he'd pixilated away into nothing.

Over the next few months I heard enough stories to make me despair of ever finding the former mogul. He'd gone to ground in Mexico, Spain, Paris, Malta; was lying low in Baja California or hiding in New York; had been admitted to a mental hospital or sailed off in a boat or was on the run from the FBI, IRS, CIA, AmEx, FedEx, the Stay Puft Marshmallow Man . . . name it and I'd heard it, or something like it. There was almost nowhere Harris couldn't be placed.

Until at the death of June one of my now-despairing queries bore fruit, when a young online journalist who'd interviewed Harris for a piece about Operator 11 back in 2007 told me he'd received an email from its missing founder the previous week, with a comment about the New York Mets' ongoing travails.

'We're both fans,' the journalist explained when I called. 'We kind of bonded over that.'

A chuckle and hint of pride.

He didn't know where Harris was but offered to forward a message, which I composed apprehensively, explaining my interest in the first dotcom boom and his part in it, before hitting 'send' and preparing to wait. But not for long, because to my surprise a reply arrived the very next day; a cryptic little story relating to my last book, which was nominally about the men who walked on the moon. The heading in the subject bar was 'a party circa 1975'. I opened it and found:

andrew.

i was attending an adult party at my best friends father's house (my friend lived with his very stricken MS mother).

we playing pool, just kids knocking balls around the table.

my friend points out Buzz Aldrin sitting on one of the pool room chairs . . .

i vividly remember his vacant eyes . . . that were still out in space circling the moon and earth . . .

I smiled as I read and only afterwards marked two details which pulled me up: first, that the name in the 'from' column of my inbox was given not as Joshua Harris, but as mjluvvy – so Luvvy lived; second, that after agreeing to meet and suggesting sooner rather than later, my correspondent signed off with the words: 'Josh Harris. Sidama, Ethiopia.' I imagined him laughing as he typed.

BOOK I

Bikers and Drag Queens

1

Addis Ababa, Tuesday 15 July, 2008

The city seems to roll on for ever, a bruised carapace of concrete and dust and patchwork shanty settlements. At times the road south is more theoretical than real, three-quarter collapsed into craters that would swallow a four-by-four whole, around which lorries and buses creep like lines of ants. Our Land Cruiser crashes through potholes with the ballistic rattle of machine-gunfire, as—

Eucalypts jut from hills.

Traffic screams.

People swarm everywhere.

Our descent reminds me that Addis Ababa is a mile high. Last night I was light-headed and couldn't work out why.

I can hardly remember how I got here: after making contact, everything moved so fast.

Harris advised me not to call, citing a 'mysterious buzz' on his line. The internet scarcely works in Ethiopia, he added, but emails could be sent slowly and painfully between one and three in the morning. He was in the deep south on the shores of Lake Awassa, not far from the lawless Somali border – eight bone-splintering hours' drive from Addis with no alternative means of travel. Asked why he was there, he told me he was editing a film on game fishing, which answered my question not at all.

My hope that he might find himself somewhere more accessible in the near future was quickly dashed. 'i'm pretty much strapped in here ...' he wrote. '... off the grid you might say LOL ...'

The only way I could be sure of meeting or even speaking to Josh Harris, who had a history of disappearance and unpredictability, would be to travel to Ethiopia. He offered me a couch in his rented 'compound', promising that, 'I don't get many visitors here so if nothing else i am sure to be extraordinarily chatty ... three squares a day prepared by my cook ... the dally is not recommended ...'

Our exchanges were easy, expansive at first, his messages contracting into short phrases and sentences linked by ellipses ... thoughts drifting together like clouds. But containing wit, a glimpse of dry humour. Getting to him might be expensive, but my trip was unlikely to be dull.

When I said I'd go he seemed pleased, promising to find me a vehicle and reasonably drug-free driver, pricey at two hundred euros or so, but the safest way to negotiate what would undoubtedly be the most dangerous part of the journey ('even with a good driver expect some white knuckles'). I'd need to buy bedding for the couch, although there was a basic but clean hotel down the road if I preferred. The one favour he asked was that I carry with me 'a few clothes I need muled in ... which got hung up at customs in spain'. He would get his friend Vicente, who ran an art gallery in Madrid, to ship them over.

We settled on a date three weeks hence and I set about making plans, booking flights and arranging jabs.

*

The stuff started arriving a week or so later, first in a trickle of packages containing books and clothes, then as a torrent of clothes and books and boots and caps; of socks and shades and DVDs; trinkets, gadgets, underpants, a Frisbee – all bought via eBay and Alibris, never Amazon, and all addressed simply to 'Josh Harris c/o Andrew Smith'.

At first, the porters at my girlfriend Josie's north London apartment block, which had seemed a better destination than my Norwich flat for 'a few clothes', found the deluge amusing. But as the date of my departure neared and the flow of goods increased, I noticed a progressive tightening of smile as I tried to sneak past the reception desk unnoticed. 'Ah, *Andrew*,' I would hear announced in my general direction, 'your friend has been busy again!' Always in that tone reserved for children and their imaginary playmates.

Meanwhile, Josie, having noted my prospective host's use of the word 'muled', grew anxious that I was being used to run drugs and even I began to wonder whether setting me up to rot in an Addis Ababa jail could be classed as an 'art project', thereby making a useful addition to the Harris CV while also being agreeably tax-deductable. When I complained to him (only half in jest) that there was going to be no room for my own clothes in my suitcase by the time I left, he assured me that I didn't need much, as his housekeeper could do my laundry. A bunch of clothes arrived from Spain in a cat food box. His concern that I might wear his new underpants prior to delivery seemed genuine.

Silicon Valley in California is most readily associated with the technological changes wrought in the 1990s.

I visited the Valley a number of times during those years and my overriding impression was surprise that somewhere so close to San Francisco could be so dull and devoid of colour – all clogged, smogged, ten-lane highways and Lego-brick offices standing bland insult to the poppy-washed hills. The first time I went, I called a reporter from the *San Jose Mercury* to ask where the Valley people kicked back, and wondered whether to believe him when he cited Fry's Electronics superstore as the social hub of the place. But it was true, even if the young men you found there tended to stare at their sneakers and shuffle away like crabs the moment they were spoken to. A trio of workers from Women.com ('The empowered women's guide to health, beauty, business, parenting & relationships') looked gloomy when I mentioned this experience: they were outnumbered sixty to one in the Valley, they said, but couldn't get a date because the men were more interested in programming and making money. As one 33-year-old told *Time* magazine at the peak of the tech boom in 1999, 'For most people here, relationships with the opposite sex are simply not time-effective.' If this was the future, I thought, we're done for.

Then there was New York. While the coder cowboys of the West frotted circuitboards at Fry's, a group of switched-on bohemian ex-slackers in lower Manhattan formed companies with names like Razorfish, Nerve, DoubleClick and disinfo and made it their business to design the websites, magazines, alternative news sites and TV portals that would form a New Media, attracting huge sums in investment on the basis that 'eyeballs' – meaning viewers – would be manna to advertisers, and that first-movers would have a potentially insuperable advantage in establishing the brand identity everyone craved in this new realm. Where better to hand over the twentieth century to the twenty-first than New York?

New York . . .

In the eighteen months leading up to the Millennium, billions of dollars in fresh investment flowed into the downtown tech district, driving stock prices skyward and making not just the founders, but often swathes of staff at its companies very rich indeed – at least on paper, in terms of shares and stock options.

It must have felt *magical* to have that constantly inflating promise of plenty in your pocket, backed by a vision of the wired world you were creating. Ten per cent of the staff at the 'digital recontextualizing' company Razorfish were reckoned to be millionaires, including an unspecified number of first-come secretaries. One legend had 'Fish co-founders Craig Kanarick and Jeffrey Dachis making an ice cream van man an offer he couldn't refuse in order to *buy* the van for his staff on one of those hot-hot New York summer days. As Kanarick's future wife, Marisa Bowe of Word.com, remarked, 'Just a few years ago, we were dance or literature majors. Now we live in a strange world where it seems every tenth person has won the lottery.'

So Harris wasn't the only one doing crazy stuff. The second half of the 1990s marked one of the highest times this highest of all cities had ever seen, with the downtown district of SoHo turned into a perpetual partyland, where the pressures of dotcom life could be sloughed off with art, music, drugs, drink and the eternal dance of sex – not to mention the thrill of what its people, the *digeratti*, were making ... nothing less than a new society, in their own enlightened image. Even a brief visit to end-of-century Manhattan felt like being plugged into the electric mains, in what now presents as a last mad fling of the old New York, gateway to a more clenched era.

The key for me was that in the years between then and now, Josh Harris's prognostications had come to look eerily prescient. In particular, MySpace, Facebook, YouTube, Second Life and other user-generated 'social networking' sites had given people the opportunity to project themselves into cyberspace, which had begun to elide with the physical world in a way that made differentiation start to look arcane. Psychologists said that children were losing the impulse to remember facts, knowing they could Google them at will from any location, along with the ability to read facial expressions, the subtle messages which so often reveal more than words. With so much media, so much *information* coming at us, we were all losing the will to concentrate on a single stimulus. I didn't know whether this was a good or a bad thing, but it was clearly important and interesting. And Harris had predicted – perhaps *demonstrated* – much more than this. We were being asked to evolve in a very short space of time. Our minds were changing.

I've noticed that people speak of him in the way characters in Fitzgerald's *The Great Gatsby* speak of Gatsby – as a kind of cipher or spectre, someone they simultaneously know and don't know at all. The only thing everyone seems to agree on is that he's one of the smartest people they've ever met.

On the long flight to Addis, I stayed awake and read, watched, got a feel for the rhythm of Josh Harris's life over the previous eight years.

As late as 26 January 2000, just two months ahead of the crash, *Business Week* was presenting Pseudo.com as the leader in its field, a viable business which had just raised another $18 million in capital from the likes of Intel and the Tribune Company. Harris, fresh from his extraordinary performance in the pre-Millennial *Quiet* experiment and – as always – hard to disambiguate, was quoted repeating the mantra from that event: 'Andy Warhol was wrong . . . people don't want fifteen minutes of fame in their lifetime, they want it every night. The audience want to be the show.'

Even as recently as 1999 – still five years before Facebook and the others – this was a startling thing to say and none of the reporters who relayed these or similar words seemed to grasp the extent of their meaning. As Harris seemed to realise. 'Three years ago, people thought I was a complete idiot – they couldn't figure out what webcasting was,' he reportedly concluded. 'I know I have a hit here. Now I'm just going to leverage it.'

More revealing was a cover story David Kirkpatrick wrote for *New York* magazine during the preparations for *Quiet* in December '99, for which he followed Harris and his band of Prankster-like cronies as they gatecrashed a panel discussion at Sotheby's, pretending to film the vainglorious proceedings while running porn tapes in their viewfinders and worrying security staff with their dearth of respect for event, audience and exhibits alike. Afterwards, the Pseudo grandee treated his crew to sushi and saké, settling the $800 bill flinchlessly as someone lit a spliff and waiters pretended not to see. 'Let's face it,' he said, 'that panel was a big fart. We were the only ones doing anything interesting. We were running the gallery.'

Back at Pseudo HQ, a crowd drawn from Pseudo's near-three hundred staff (average age 'about twenty-seven') gathered on the sixth floor to watch the launch of a new show. That morning Harris reportedly showed Jeffrey Katzenberg – partner to Steven Spielberg and David Geffen in the DreamWorks SKG production house – around the place. He'd taken a meeting with Silvio Berlusconi the week before.

The piece began:

> Josh Harris, Chairman of Pseudo Programs Inc., lives in a SoHo loft big enough to house a fleet of double-decker buses. A grid of steel tracks hangs from the ceiling for lighting equipment and cameras; the entire space doubles as a television studio, with a control room in back ... the 350-square-foot bathroom – also equipped for cameras – includes a sauna with two showers, a pull-cord spritzer for a quick cold rinse, and a three-tiered bench that could seat a football team. Three showerheads are directed at the top row of the bench; Josh Harris likes to shower lying down.

As founder of Pseudo Programs, 'the oldest and largest producer of television shows for the Internet', Harris was 'a major player in the race to define the post-television future of broadcast entertainment – an area of intense interest on Wall Street and in Hollywood'. The company's Chief Operating Officer, Anthony Asnes, a patrician 37-year-old with a background in business consulting, admitted that Pseudo's niche programming was 'rather like a tree falling in the forest', in the sense that few people had access to the high-speed net connections necessary to download the company's videostreaming software, and many corporate firewalls blocked it. Even so, he claimed that 400,000 users downloaded at least one Pseudo show per month, probably overnight – probably *through the night* – while they slept. Among the most popular 'channels' were 88HipHop, the gaming destination All Games Network, and an electro music forum called Street Sounds. Others were Cherrybomb (erotica 'from the female perspective'), the Space Channel (space news, sponsored by OMEGA Watches), Parse TV (for hackers) and ChannelP (spoken word, poetry, performance art). The front door was always open, so anyone could walk in at any time of day or night: an impressive roster of regular guests across the shows included everyone from Eminem and most of his big-name rap contemporaries to star NFL quarterbacks and commentators; to astronauts, DJs, art personalities, socialites and former Warhol faces such as Taylor Mead, Quentin Crisp and Anthony Haden-Guest. Levi's sponsored a show which followed three college kids as they traversed America trying to survive on the fruits of e-commerce alone – Marco Polos of the information age.

Underlying all of this was a feeling on Wall Street and elsewhere that fast net access and broadband were 'just around the corner'. And that, in the words of Dan Sullivan of Pop.com, the online entertainment company whose most prominent founders included the aforementioned Katzenberg, Spielberg and fellow

Hollywood director Ron Howard, 'Josh is one of the smartest people we've come across in the netcasting space ... he has empowered all kinds of different artists to create new kinds of programming – the first generation of Internet-bred actors and directors.' According to Jerry Colonna, one of the most storied venture capitalists in New York, Josh was 'one of the brightest guys in Silicon Alley. He may seem like a lunatic sometimes, but there are a lot of bigger lunatics that have raised a lot more capital.'

What would it feel like to be the focus of all this expectation? I can't begin to imagine. Harris sounds disarmingly surprised as he tells Kirkpatrick: 'They need me. They all need me. They know they want to do something on the Net, but they don't know how.'

At the time, few people would have understood the significance of a jarring rejoinder Harris attached to his explanation of the company moniker. Pseudo reflected 'the many different faces you can have in the online world', he said. Then: 'we call it "Programs" because we are conscious that we are in the business of programming people's lives ... we are the good side of Big Brother. We know that is going to happen, and instead of saying it is scary, we embrace it.'

This was mid-December, 1999, with the apocalyptic spectre of a computer-freezing, havoc-wreaking 'Y2K' bug the most prominent news story and media commentators discussing a more general anxiety among the populace, which was being called 'pre-Millennial tension'. Yet four months later the story had been wrenched volte-face with a severity that still makes my breath quicken, muscles tense. New Yorkers had long regarded the dotcom kids with a phlegmatic mix of scepticism, distaste and envy. While stocks were flying and pension funds flush, the Wonka-themed parties tended by Oompa-Loompas, the company cruises and junkets to Vegas and drug-fuelled art orgies, the lobster-decked ice sculptures and youthful optimism-bordering-on-monstrousbloodyarrogance were overlooked. But when stocks began to plummet, invested savings disappear and pension funds wither, anger was quick to rise. Just as water finds a crack, anger finds a target, and in Harris the search for a villain couldn't have been easier.

With a few exceptions, such as Jeff Bezos of Amazon.com, the faceless techies of the West escaped personal opprobrium, but the celebrity CEOs of the East now learned what a dangerous game they'd been playing. Harris was by no means the only one to become a dilettante-charlatan-huckster overnight in the eyes of the media (usually with a smug implication that the writer pointing the finger had known it all along), but he was the one whose Broadway loft and yacht-sized bathroom suddenly rankled most.

Vanity Fair began its long purgation with the founder of 'Silicon Alley's flashiest dot-com, a feverish man-boy of 39', noting that with investors some three trillion dollars poorer, '"dot-com" is starting to take on the distinct ring of a punchline'. Replacing the bacchanals of yore were 'Pink Slip' parties, named for the redundancy notices dispensed by American employers, while the *New York Post* ran a new section tracking dotcom casualties and websites such as Netslaves and Fucked Company stoked the crucible atmosphere. E-workers who had imagined (and in some cases *lived*) a new corporate ethos based on freedom and trust and transparency were furious not just at losing their jobs, but at their dreams of escaping the nine-to-five world being whipped away without warning – thanks to what looked like and was presented as managerial carelessness, *staggering* hubris. *The New York Times* reported former Pseudo staff busking in the subway or accepting charity beer in bars, wistful for the old days of '80-hour weeks' in a place where 'employees smoked marijuana for lunch and snorted cocaine for supper'.

Binding the articles was a tone of betrayal: the dotcom kids had partied on the promise of a future which hadn't materialised and even the riches had been an illusion, just sheets of paper with numbers and notional values, share certificates worth pennies apiece now if anything at all. Former Pseudo Art Director Steve Fine's 290,000 stock options, passport to plenty in December '99, were historical curiosities by mid-2000 . . . souvenirs, essentially. Certificates of lost innocence.

Neither was the Old Media's response surprising. As Razorfish's Craig Kanarick reminded the *Silicon Alley Reporter*, he and his peers had led with a punkish 'Fuck you, Mr Big Company, you don't know what you're doing!' so it was hardly surprising that Mr Big Company should enjoy the humbling when it came. Every single report reheated Harris's boast to the blow-dried CBS TV reporter Bob Simon on a hostile *60 Minutes* programme that, 'I'm in a race to take CBS out of business – that's my focus. That's what my bankers are telling me to do . . .' and even the online evangelists at *Wired* magazine documented the fall with a piece called 'Bratitude Adjustment'. At the London newspaper I worked for as a feature writer, the word 'internet' was banned from print for a time and when I interviewed Amazon's Bezos at the company headquarters in Seattle at the end of 2000, it was in the context of a share price which had plunged from over $400 to under $20. Wags called his company amazon.toast.

Yet for all the disillusion and contention that Pseudo had always been 'more about buzz than product', there appears to have been widespread sadness among those who'd invested emotion in it, who'd 'drunk the Kool-Aid' in the parlance Alley workers borrowed from the countercultural 'acid tests' of the 60s. One ex-manager said, 'I think it will be a badge of honour to have worked here,' while a news report claimed defiantly that, 'They imagined a world where programming wasn't just spoon-fed to the viewing public but instead involved the viewers' active participation.'

The next flurry of media interest arrived when Pseudo became the first big Alley company to run out of cash and go bust, in October 2000. As I rifled the cuttings, I wondered how many people noticed at the time that Harris now referred to Pseudo in the third person, and had been doing so since *Quiet* had been closed down the previous New Year's Day. In interviews he was philosophical about the loss, remarking that, 'It could have been worse. It could have been acquired ... and it would have been bastardized on the way out. This way ... it died in its sleep. Or put to sleep.'

The commentator and academic Clay Shirky, a dotcom veteran himself, has since cited the closure of Pseudo and the webzine Word.com as marking the end of Silicon Alley as an ideal; the death of its *soul*. Downtown had lost its rumpled talisman. Hidden in the acres of *schadenfreude*, though, was regret, a poignant sense that one era had ended and another opened on a city more braced and dour, as if the previous decade had been but a hallucination. No one imagined that this atmosphere would endure, much less become permanent.

When Harris and Tanya Corrin popped up a month later with their experiment in networked living, *We Live in Public*, some kind of line had been crossed. *Wired* magazine's announcement that 'Jupiter Communications and pseudo.com founder Josh Harris is pretty sure you want to watch him having sex' was rendered ironic by an unflattering photo and the London *Independent* barked, 'Josh Harris: Turn for the Weird' – though both ran sizeable features, as did the London and New York *Observer*s. The only way to understand the project at the time, it seems, was as an attention-seeking stunt, *Big Brother* writ small. And yet a week before flying to Ethiopia I'd stumbled across some web footage of Harris in 1998 looking dishevelled but trim and animated, contrasting sharply with an image of him in his underpants towards the end of *We Live in Public*, blank as a slate and shockingly bloated by comparison, suggesting that *something* happened inside the loft.

More shocking still was a half-hour film one of the world's great filmmakers, Errol Morris, made about Harris as part of his brilliant *First Person* documentary cycle. *First Person* employs the conceit of an 'Interrotron' machine to light the inner lives of a range of unusual people, from the crime scene cleaner to a former CIA spy and master-of-disguise, to a zoologist on the trail of the elusive giant squid and a man with the highest IQ ever recorded, who nonetheless works as a nightclub bouncer. Harris's turn comes in *Harvesting Me*, which was recorded towards the end of *We Live in Public* and shows him talking – lucidly – about what's billed as his 'TV addiction' but sounds more like an eccentric theosophy.

The film opens with sepia images of an apple farm. The subject's disembodied voice a low, even drawl. 'I'm not able at this point to explain why. I'm recognising what the drug has truly done to me. My emotionality is not derived from other humans, but rather from ... Gilligan.'

Gilligan? Anyone who grew up in the US understands 'Gilligan' to mean the children's TV programme *Gilligan's Island*, an often surreal farce about a group of boating daytrippers who run into a storm and end up stranded on a desert island – perhaps the most ubiquitous kids' show ever made, repeated every day after school for decades. The show's creator, Sherwood Schwartz, also came up with *The Brady Bunch*, clever valediction to the American nuclear family, but *Gilligan* is his more authentic legacy . . . with a character, I now remembered, called Lovey, like Luvvy the clown. There was a smile on Harris's face as he addressed the Interrotron, and at first I assumed he was joking. In the next breath I was robbed of this thought.

'That's both deep and heavy. I've been programmed by

somebody else's dreams. That's who I am. It's a very scary, scary thing.'

Spoken like a taunt, as though he's teasing. CCTV-style shots of him stalking alone through what must have been his loft: huge and opulent-looking, with a projected TV screen covering one wall of the lounge, cigar abutting his lips like a gun barrel. Footage from *We Live in Public*.

Soundbytes. An astonishing claim that Harris 'cast' Tanya Corrin as his girlfriend for *We Live in Public*, despite my understanding that they'd been together for at least four years. And now I saw the difference between his project and *Big Brother*, because while TV viewers voted for evictions, they remained passive in all other respects – whereas the *WLIP* screen was devoted half to picture and half to chat, allowing audience members to communicate directly with the subjects and each other … making them part of the show. Perhaps the *essence* of the show. They found Harris's keys if he'd lost them, he said, and scolded if he forgot to wash his hands after a pee.

'They understand my life better than I do. They're objective while I'm not. Big Brother isn't a person, as it turns out, it's the collective consciousness. After a while you just wash your hands, it's not worth the trouble.

'It's not that living in public is going to be imposed on us. It's that we're going to be conditioned to ask for it. Fourth quarter of 2004 I'll roll out the consumerised version of *We Live in Public*. And I'll charge them for recording their lives to disc.'

Again I was taken aback. This was early 2001, three years before Mark Zuckerberg and his Harvard pals chanced upon the idea for Facebook; *five* years before it became generally accessible and *Time* magazine gave their person of the year as 'You'. And Harris was talking about social networking of a far more ambitious kind – more Facebook, MySpace, YouTube, Twitter and reality TV rolled together. Seven years on, it was clear that he'd been right. He'd predicted Mark Zuckerberg … should be as famous and rich as Zuckerberg by now. *Shouldn't he?* Jason Calacanis, a dotcom millionaire who's been around from the start and is cited by *Fortune* magazine as 'one of the eight bloggers all businesspeople need to read', has described flashing a photo of Harris on to a screen at a podcasting conference and asking whether anyone knew who the man in front of them was.

Nobody did.

'It's ironic,' Calacanis says, 'because a lot of what people are trying to do today ... Josh did in 1996. He's one of the ten most important people in the history of the internet and nobody knows who he is.'

And yet Harris appeared to be presenting himself as a *warning*. As I sat in the dark cabin at 35,000 feet on my way to another continent, unable to turn off the malfunctioning video screen in front of me, I found myself wondering: 'What happened to him?'

Errol Morris ends *Harvesting Me* with a haunting image of a young boy gazing steadily into the lens while Harris intones: 'I'm still in the loft. It's still on.'

Which means Corrin has already left and he's on his own.

'I understand what you gotta do to make a masterpiece. I'm not there yet, but I'm building up to it. There's probably five or ten more years to go. Then I'm maybe free. I'll go live on the orchard and have a family. I might be a late bloomer in that respect. If I make it that far.'

Within a month of sitting for Morris, Harris was gone. Six years later he would sell the orchard at a huge loss in order to construct the short-lived TV multiverse, Operator 11. It occurs to me that five or ten years from the time Harris made these pronouncements is pretty much ... now. And that I'm not on my way to an orchard in upstate New York, I'm on my way to Ethiopia.

*

Hours pass as we barrel south, watching the sun rise and arc back to a land that is suddenly loamy and lush emerald green, as far from boiling dust and strangled traffic and Do-They-Know-It's-Christmas expectation as could be. At intervals into the distance, mahogany stick figures trudge behind horses and ploughs as though knitting the earth into a deep collective trance. We hit a whole village of Rastafarians, which Harris has flagged as a sign that we're close. In the same message he claimed an affinity with the Rastas owing to their shared reverence for the late Ethiopian Emperor Haile Selassie, but I couldn't tell whether he was joking or not, and when I asked he changed the subject.

Of course, curiouser than any of this is the contents of my luggage, because nestling against my few t-shirts, couple pair of jeans, jumper, toiletries and notebooks are a beige North Face jacket and pair of heavy Blackhawk military boots, some army trousers, shirts and a pair of Ray-Ban Aviator shades.

Headphones, a Leatherman and torch.

Two packs of dental floss.

Three tins of English tea ('not bags'), one *Avid Xpress for Dummies* video editing workbook and.

The complete fights of Muhammad Ali on twenty-two discs.

One box of twenty-five Serie D No. 4 Partagas (Habana) cigars, costing £250 and the subject of much agonizing, with Montecristo #4s preferred in the first instance ('my one extravagance', Harris had confided, a trio of servants clearly falling under the rubric of 'necessity'), plus those two pairs of red Calvin Klein jockey-style pants (lightly worn) and a large bag of toys for the kids at the local orphanage.

Sunscreen.

And a switchblade knife. Repeat: switchblade knife. Collective introduction to the Harrisonian notion of 'leverage'.

But it doesn't end there. Weightiest and most amusing of all if you don't have to carry them are the books, which arrived in a dog-eared paperback flood the week before I left. These were: *On the Road, The Last of the Mohicans* and *The Beach; The Time Traveler's Wife, The Purpose Driven Life, Women in Love* and *The Rainbow* . . .

The Decline and Fall of the Roman Empire and *War and Peace.* (*War and Peace!*)

Kerouac, Tolstoy, Lawrence: a list any English teacher wishing to punish a class of recalcitrant schoolboys would applaud (add *Pride and Prejudice* and it's definitive) – to the extent that as I sit juddering in the back seat I wonder whether this is part of a performance. Whether the show has already begun.

With the abruptness of a train striking a tunnel, we're in the town, passing an enormous Christian church fronting a busy roundabout circled by trucks, bikes, scooters, old Toyota cars and people carriers, then clattering down the main street, watching Lake Awassa loom and fill our windscreen, dark and brooding and still. Square concrete buildings line the street, devoid of frill or flourish, host to cafés, restaurants, shops selling bright clothing, jewellery, food, radios, old cathode ray TVs . . . an internet café, white stucco hotel and pavements teeming with people – most notably straggling armies of children who play or wander aimless and unattended, lords of a parallel universe no one else seems to see.

It's impossible at this stage to know how much of what I've read and been told about Harris is true. There was a touch of awe in the voice of one British Silicon Alley veteran, a winner in the dotcom lottery thanks to the well-timed sale of his website towards the end of 1999, as he told me that, 'Josh wasn't just a little bit ahead of his time, he was *way* ahead of his time.' But how much of this is retrospective myth-making? *Story-telling*? An early Pseudo artist-employee who knows Harris as well as anyone speaks of there being 'a kind of reality distortion field around Josh . . . and people would get kind of addicted to that.' Perhaps he was ahead of his time. Or perhaps he's a clever showman who fooled a lot of greedy or gullible people.

Now a deserted boulevard: broad as the Champs-Élysées, flanking the lake, lined with stone or breezeblock walls and houses behind, many hidden, others tottering upwards, paint-flecked and part-built, bristling corroded rebar.

A pair of gates, opening; bungalow, tree in the yard, three or four people . . . a tall Ethiopian man in a military-style cap, small smiling woman . . . and another, younger and anxious-looking. Dogs yelping and a command of 'Hesh! Hesh!'

And there he is in front of me.

Josh Harris.

Slim, almost gaunt. Dressed for the bleachers at a Mets game.

He smiles. I smile back.

I turn for my bags, but they're already gone.

A small, square room, functional in the fast-fading light: coffee table and two chairs, no TV. Windows to the walled yard and dogs barking, hyenas crying on the other side . . . the kind of music Mingus and Beefheart spent the whole of their lives trying to find and which more than anything else I'll take away with me, to remember for the rest of my life. Harris hears it too, tells me that every three months or so the authorities poison the dogs and a cold eerie silence descends, until the underdogs on the outskirts move in to replace the dead ones and the pitch-black blues of the African night starts up again. Their leap in status also a death sentence.

'That's Ethiopia. That's why I love it here. The thing about life in deep Africa is that every day is a life and death experience and your senses get sharp. You know, New Yorkers think the world's ending if they can't get dinner reservations at the right restaurant . . .'

That distinctive lopsided grin, as if perpetually tuned in to some cosmic joke only he can hear. Hint of goofiness in the voice. I ask him why he's here and we're off.

2

I wake early, having spent the night warring mosquitoes. Light streams through the window; the air is cool, my bedclothes bunched on the floor. No sound or movement. No sign of Josh. A funny moment to wonder for the first time what the fuck I'm doing here.

I'd imagined us easing into each other's company, but last night was as disorientating as any I've experienced – a trippy torrent of names and events and incidents related in long elliptical sentences, full of cryptic allusions and hints at more under the surface, zagging thought-trains which ended only by crashing into each other. At one point I tried to take notes, but gave up almost immediately, because what I was writing seemed so bizarre. More than once I wondered whether he really had lost his mind in the datastream, as I struggled to connect the Broadway scene-maker to the man sitting in shadow opposite ... only for him to snap into focus like a trap, leaving my callow theories about what happened in New York during the last years of the old millennium painfully exposed. Within half an hour I understood how little I knew, and how different to expectation this project would be.

'It depends how far you want to go down the rabbit hole,' he said. 'I can take you as deep as you want to go.'

The lopsided grin.

I went to bed both wired and exhausted, and woke feeling as though my brain had been steeped in syrup . . .

Jeans and a t-shirt. Wander to the yard. Dogs bark and Josh's cook Kelemework appears from nowhere to hiss 'Hesh! Hesh!' at which the pair fall silent and slink away. Samara and Tony Blair, named by the staff, who wonder why I laugh so hard at their assumption of Blair to be American like Josh. The latter dog replacing a recently dead animal named after that other well-known American, Princess Diana.

A big, warm smile.

'Mister Andrew. You like tea? Coffee?'

Before me a modest lawned yard, probably twenty metres deep and thirty broad, with a porch looking on to it. The house has three bedrooms – one used as an office, another as a store room filled with video gear, lights and tripods – but no integral kitchen: Kelemework cooks and cleans from an adjacent shed, next to Abraham the guard's tiny guardhouse. The third member of Harris's household, Filagot, gardens along a border by the front wall to the outside world. She turns and smiles, while birds flutter in the trees and spider monkeys peer down from the tin roof. In a far corner a pair of giant tortoises rehearse coitus with the grim intensity of porn stars, as if imagining themselves the show.

'Don't forget that this is the oldest culture in the world. There's fifty thousand years' worth of continuous culture here and they know it.'

Harris is still smiling as he tears a piece of toast with his teeth. We're on the porch, sharing a breakfast of fruit, toast, honey and silty local coffee, and I'm surprised to find him relaxed and voluble, last night's manic intensity a seeming world away. A different person.

He loves to talk about Africa, which runs as deep as you let it; which he discusses as though it were a giant game, even when it sounds uncomfortably real. Being *faranji* – an Amharic word which seems to fall somewhere between 'foreigner', 'whitey' and 'asshole' – he claims to have been targeted for extortion by a local gang, who painted his house then hiked the agreed price with menaces, up to and including rumours of an impending raid on the compound. I think he might be joking when he mentions the Somali border and a black market Kalashnikov as a means of protection ('Only 500 bucks down there – not bad, uh?'). But then I also think he might not be.

We part, he to edit, me to explore, read, puzzle till six, at which time we've scheduled dinner and a first recorded download session. I go for a stroll along the broad road to the front of the property, which defines an upscale district known as the Canadian zone, so named for the overseas water specialists who once populated it. Interspersed with the houses are several aid agency compounds, wire-fenced and with an air of siege about them, tense guests of a Marxist government which no longer welcomes them. A few white faces in Land Rover Defenders: the only setting in which you ever see white faces.

I duck into the hotel Harris mentioned and have a macchiato coffee, the national drink inherited from the Italians, who occupied Eritrea to the north and Somaliland to the east but failed to take Ethiopia, which covets its hard-won status as the only African country never to have bowed to Europe. People look you directly in the eye and even street-dwellers dress with care, and as I turn into the main street and children crowd round I'm unsurprised to detect a nebulous hostility, yet still shocked to feel it settling on me. Being this visible, this clearly *other*, weighs like an extra force of gravity. Again I wonder why a former web impresario would choose to live in these circumstances.

*

'They think of us as these rich, mannerless oafs, and when they see you coming, they see ... an opportunity.' Harris laughs, delighted by my first real taste of Ethiopian street life. 'They want something from you, even if they don't know what it is.'

Chicken, fries, fruit, tea. Light fading in the living room as plates are cleared away and I set my recorder on the coffee table between us, notes at hand, ready to follow Harris into the warren of his mind, through a conversation which quickly presents as another muddle of stories and names and relationships I can't possibly connect right now. One moment he's building a full-scale boxing gym in an old warehouse, the next funding an Austrian art group to build a balcony half-way up the World Trade Center, claiming to have seen an office-light 'bull's-eye' on the side of the building in the middle of the night; to have been surveilled by government agents post-9/11 as a result. Equally destabilising is his renewed claim to have 'cast' Tanya Corrin as his 'fake girlfriend' in advance of *We Live in Public*, with an insistence that he never loved her at all.

And I sit captivated, but thinking: 'He's flipped. Paranoid. Or playing with me.'

Always feeling himself an outsider in Silicon Alley, he nonetheless copped the best piece of real estate, 600 Broadway, at one of New York's wildest canyon junctions, where downtown Broadway meets Houston on the fringe of Greenwich Village, gateway to SoHo – a totemic pile of mortar and brick with a landmark DKNY mural on the side (a panoramic view of the city from which Liberty thrusts like a goddess) yet still with an air of louche decay. Perfect mid-90s New York. And yet he insists that the day his first $2 million in cash arrived was 'the worst day of my life', while the Pseudo parties are elevated in his mind almost to the level of philosophy, occasionally attaining a kind of sacredness ...

I try to focus on issues surrounding the Bubble at the centre of his story, but can already feel the questions I brought slipping away from me. Throughout, the sense is of trailing in Harris's narrative wake as his world reorders in real time, a feeling I'll grow used to but find discomfiting now. Tales begin with the disclaimer 'This is all hearsay, but fairly reliable,' putting me in mind of *Tales from the Thousand and One Nights*, which begins 'It is related – but Allah alone is wise and all-knowing . . .'

As if everything is just story.

More Pseudo characters: Missy Galore, Janice Girlbomb, Jess Zaino and V. Owen Bush; Gompertz, Galinsky and JudgeCal; EQ, Uzi, T-Bo, Feedbuck and Mangina . . . names from a comic book, speaking of that old New York shuffle – of invention and reinvention, a place where backstories vanish and everyone is but *now* or nowhere.

And watch the soundbytes fly.

'You took the deepest part of downtown New York and just collectively blew their minds . . .'

'Money doesn't show up with nothing attached to it. The freedom of money is illusory . . .'

'I'm Googling real-time . . .'

'It's just a download deal . . .' (meaning our idea of 'reality')

'Compared to art, business is easy – you just have to read the man . . .'

I quickly see that he's selling himself as an artist these days and divides the world into 'artists' and 'civilians', with the latter deserving some protection, the former *de facto* fair game for experimentation and manipulation in the name of 'art'. He shows me a letter he's written to *The New York Times* but not yet sent, in which he claims that Pseudo.com was 'a fake company' – an art project all along.

Again I'm taken aback. A fake girlfriend *and* a fake company? So what was real in his eyes: what *is* real?

Is this approach to the world representative of the dotcom boom as a whole? And if not, how did he end up running a company that attracted tens of millions in investment, employed 300 people and sprawled across SoHo? We keep returning to *We Live in Public*, the 'work' of which he is evidently most proud, but which also seems to have coincided with, perhaps to have *precipitated* his dissolution. If that's what this is.

I'm entertained: there's a thrill to this 'real-time Googling'. But the bearings I brought with me are already starting to fade. The mazey crossword-clue syntax, long lists of alien names and insane events and improbable gossipy stories that sound like revenge fantasies; sexual jealousy; some weird personal theosophy . . . a persistent feeling that, for all the extraordinary things he patently *has* done (and I'm nowhere near appreciating the extent of this yet), Harris might actually have lost his mind, or be in the process of losing it while I sit and watch. Nothing here is as expected.

* * *

Light streams through the window: the air is cool, my bedclothes bunched on the floor. No sign of Josh, just a tinny clatter above my head, as if an army marches across the roof. Jeans and a t-shirt, outside, squinting into the sun, a family of larger monkeys than before gazing down. One has a baby clinging to its abdomen: strong arms for such a vulnerable-looking creature. Eyes intelligent and watchful, as if waiting for something.

Josh is earlier this morning, probably also woken by the monkeys.

'Morning! So those guys are back, huh?'

Yesterday's same unlit cigar juts from his mouth. A castanet clack in the corner of the yard attests that the tortoises are busy again. Josh likes animals, is trying to learn the Ethiopians' unsentimentality towards them, but I can see he struggles as we play a game which involves throwing pieces of banana between two trees, then watching the monkeys monkey the dogs, one descending to the lawn as a decoy while the other swings down and grabs the banana, climbing to safety before Tony or Samara can grab a piece of its flesh. The trick, Josh tells me, is to balance the prize and jeopardy as evenly as possible. Offer the monkeys something they want, then see what they'll do to get it. I smile and he smiles back, knows what I'm thinking; and the thing is, I know he knew even before I thought it. Am I starting to enjoy myself?

We chat over breakfast, he growing cagey when I start to probe his childhood and family background. He lived here for two years between 1970 and '72, before a Marxist coup and civil war forced Americans out, and he has happy memories of the place, because it was one of the few periods during which his itinerant father was consistently present. Josh is about the same age as me, which would have made him between nine and twelve when he lived in Awassa. So he's returned to the place he felt safest as a child, I suggest, and he chuckles.

'It's uses and gratifications.'

'Uses and gratifications?'

He smiles and rolls his still-unlit cigar between thumb and forefinger, looks me in the eye.

'OK. That's what we'll do tonight.'

We break up, he to edit, me to wander, read, think, feeling more at home. My host, I now feel sure, is sane: something odder and more interesting is going on.

A macchiato at the hotel, then the lake and the same queasy feeling of being watched and assessed, which I do my best to face down, not sure whether I'm the dog or the monkey in this game – or whether it's a game at all. Couples smile and nod pleasantly as they stroll the dirt trail along the shore; young men sell gnarled fish cooked on makeshift grills, looking well-enough fed but still with some unquantifiable hunger in their eyes. For a second time since I've been here, I notice a young man with sculpted features and shoulder-length dreads, dressed fit for hip

Hoxton or Williamsburg, who looks at me with enmity in his eyes and mutters something to a companion as I pass. The back of my neck prickles: I slow down, then speed up and head back to the compound, unnerved by the lakeside's stark mix of beauty and menace.

I return to find Josh hard at work in the office, editing his film, *Tuna Heaven*, which turns out to stem from another eccentric trip . . .

Another story . . .

Some months after *Quiet*, in the summer of 2000, the net mogul hired a massive deep-sea fishing boat out of Turtle Bay in Baja California. He filled the boat with New York sophisticate friends and took them far out to sea in search of tuna, offering a prize to whoever caught the biggest fish, with the aim of seeing how primal these Gotham hipsters would be prepared to get and how their relationships might change, all driven by a question: *is it OK to kill the fish for fun?*

I watch and see that there *were* changes. An Argentine-born artist named Alessandra, who comes across as open and sweet, sets out stroking the beautiful creatures and ends up with bloody handprints on her shirt like trophies – where Tanya Corrin, the 'fake girlfriend' from whom Josh had recently split, revels in dominating them from the off. Last night Josh made me laugh by insisting that, 'People fish like they fuck,' but today he extends this dictum to, 'People fish like they really are,' adding that the fish have personalities; there's nothing neutral about gaffing a tuna with its full-moon eyes staring horror at you.

More curious than the film is the sight of Josh watching it. As the rough edit unfolds, I slowly become aware that he's watching the women, and Corrin in particular, with special avidity – a fascination bolstered by his claim that she arrived on the boat wearing an engagement ring, while refusing to say whose it was. As he tries to leverage me into solving the mystery for him,

I can't help noticing that for a 'fake girlfriend' he hasn't been with for seven years, Corrin seems to exercise him greatly and I struggle not to laugh aloud as we watch her wrestle a giant tuna, working a pole with ecstatic, almost carnal enthusiasm while he shifts in his seat and grows ever more agitated at the sight. There's a note of real Freudian torment to his admission that, when the day of reckoning came, Tanya had indeed caught the biggest fish.

The fake girlfriend line is already getting hard to swallow and I'm curious as to why he's so resolute in playing it.

That night pasta, fries, fruit, tea. Kelemework clears away the plates and Josh leans back, an arm over the corner of his chair. Escalation.

'Uses and gratifications,' he announces, examining his cigar and grinning.

'Uses and gratifications,' I parrot.

The story that follows is far more coherent than last night and has me gripped for the next hour: his own personal creation myth.

Uses and gratifications turns out to be one of the earliest sociological theories of mass communications, though it is still discussed and debated today. In essence, it holds that we are not passive consumers of media, but use it creatively, to fulfil specific practical or psychological needs of our own. The idea that media might brainwash or turn us into *Brave New World*-style automata, as feared in the early days of radio and television, is thus dismissed.

Josh's own narrative version of uses and gratifications starts with his childhood in California. His mother Roslyn worked with delinquent girls for the California Youth Authority in Camarillo, a taxing job which left little energy for her own children when she got home. With seven youngsters to raise and a husband who had a habit of disappearing unannounced – once for six whole months, leaving his family's house to be repossessed – she would arrive home in a frayed state, able to relax only after a couple of Martinis. Her elder children eventually learned to be somewhere else at this time of the day, leaving Josh, the youngest, to absorb whatever anger or resentment she felt when she got home. For a couple of years, he and his youngest sister were sent to stay with their doting maternal grandparents in Iowa, a loving interlude in an otherwise troubled early existence. But when Ted Harris returned from another mysterious absence, he insisted his children be recalled and the process of alienation began all over again. Josh would soothe himself with the ensemble teleplays of *Gilligan's Island* and *I Love Lucy*, deriving his emotional sustenance from them. He now calls them 'low-tech virtual reality' – a telling description, intended to convey the extent to which they were real and necessary to him, while also drawing a parallel with the modern realm of cyberspace. The way he extends the theory is both mad and ingenious. He smiles while he talks: I'm never sure whether he's playing with me or being deadly serious.

'It wasn't John F. Kennedy or Marilyn Monroe that had the most influence on American culture and society,' he begins, 'but rather it was Sherwood Schwartz, the creator of *Gilligan's Island* and *The Brady Bunch*. Who I am is much more like Sherwood Schwartz than it is like my parents. That's how it works.'

For Josh, the world Schwartz created, an extension of the writer's psyche, was as real, was *more* real and desirable than the real world. He reminds me of some of the storylines, about radioactive vegetables and gender-swaps and S & M dungeon-caves, saying: 'His [Schwartz's] psyche was basically being projected out to kids of our generation. It might be the earliest example of virtual propagation: we're kind of his children – though not just his, cos we also had a mosaic of other people doing the same thing. Maybe for our generation that was the first demonstration of what happens with virtual reality. Just *low-tech*.'

He laughs, adds a theory of his own, which he calls the Spectrum Theory of Communications, holding that over time the 'filters' which allow you to distinguish virtually-derived emotion from that produced by interaction with people in the material world degrade. As he puts it: 'It defeats that software patch, that fundamental software program. In modern terms it's a *virus*.'

He adds that with TV, at least in the US when he and I were kids and there was no BBC or HBO, you always knew that an advert would be along soon, usually at a moment of high tension, so you never *completely* gave yourself to the emotion.

'So if you watch enough it starts flattening out your emotionality, top to bottom. It's like a sponge that loses its elasticity. If you're watching the final episode of *M*A*S*H* and Hawkeye is killing the chicken, you know that a commercial is coming on soon, so you can never, even in the most acute situation, allow yourself to be fully involved – because you know you're going to be cut off.'

'So . . .'

'So your range of emotionality gets compressed, loses its elasticity. To me, that was always the main effect of uses and gratifications. And then I evolved from that to the next logical thing . . . I'm watching this TV for five hours a day and while that is on I am in that world – that world is as real to me as the physical world, in fact sometimes more real. Well, it's not a very efficient mechanism for putting you into that world. It's the best we have even to this day, but it doesn't take much imagination to understand that you can make that world more efficient than broadcast television. Which is the combination of the interactivity of the net and video. Which is sort of where I got to with Operator 11 . . .'

He stops and grins. As in the Errol Morris film, Josh appears to be presenting himself as a warning.

'Of course, you and I were raised low-tech,' he says, knowing that we were raised in the US at about the same time.

'By Gilligan, you mean?'

'You're a Gilliganite.'

He weaves a hilarious Biblical fantasy about a Second Coming, in which Steven Spielberg becomes Moses and TV the burning bush, ending with the proposition: 'So any way you look at it, the parallel is ... Gilligan is Jesus Christ. I know it all, like I got the window. I spent six months looking in that window, thinking, "Now I see how it's gonna come down." In fact it's all there in *Launder My Head ...*'

A Pseudo computer animation from the early 1990s, featuring a collection of TV-headed people and to which he ascribes a far fetched, almost mystical significance.

'I saw it *all*.'

'Saw what?' I think, not yet knowing that my next few years are going to be taken up with finding out.

We move on: another parade of names and yarns and aphorisms and me again struggling to keep up and make sense of what I'm hearing, of the New Year's Eve party which got out of control and the pre-Tanya *sort-of* girlfriend who wound up in Bellevue ... hoping it does make sense in some tangible way and that he's not just crazy. Keats once declared that 'A man's life of any worth is a continual allegory,' but until now I've never seen anyone *try* to live in such a way.

He doesn't seem a very music-driven person, but says that the musician he 'always resonated with' was the icy Velvet Underground singer Nico, especially on her classic *Chelsea Girl* album. 'For me, the Velvet Underground wasn't about Lou Reed, it was about her,' he declares, a line I confess to wishing I'd thought of.

I learn that some of the Pseudo artists followed him to the farm and that he had trouble getting rid of them in order to have time on his own. On Awassa, he says: 'I came back to the one place I felt at home. I kind of want to get Pseudo and all that scene off my back. I got a psychic load you can't imagine ... I just want to move on to the next phase.'

We've been talking for three hours and it's dark: the night chorus riffs outside. I decide to hit the hotel for a head-clearing beer, but after half an hour the place shuts and I'm forced to return home, with Abraham following at a discreet distance.

Josh is fiddling with *Tuna Heaven*. I tell him about my curtailed drink and he unexpectedly asks whether I'd like some Scotch, promising, 'I've got some pretty nice stuff ... it should be good.' So we go back to the living room and start on the Dalwhinnie, sparingly at first, then in larger draughts, while he entertains me with the story of a filmmaker acquaintance whose next project was set to receive funding only if a certain AA-list star signed on to play the lead; who by way of sweetening negotiations asked Josh to take three or four women friends to the star's suite at the Four Seasons for a private party. Such was the man's draw that in the event Josh took eight Pseudo employees, then watched, fascinated, as in some subtle way one of the women was chosen for the candle-strewn bedroom and the party broke up.

He hated the experience, disliked the star and left with the void of a pimp in his soul, while the movie got made but flopped. Despite these feelings, he laughs as he pours more Dalwhinnie – until in the blink of an eye his mood darkens and the Four Seasons is revealed as the locus of yet another unspecified betrayal by the 'fake girlfriend', leaving me no option but to observe that his hurt sounds ... *real*. With him blustering back: 'Oh, don't confuse emotional entanglement with the performance. I cast her and she played the part well. And part of the performance was that I had to stay true – anything else would have seemed inappropriate, out of character ... sort of like Truman cheating on his wife.'

Another reference to Peter Weir's remarkable 1998 film *The Truman Show*, story of a man who doesn't realise that the totality of his life is a TV show, and which I'm increasingly noticing Josh to discuss as though it were a documentary. Again I feel lost, but I'm starting not to mind.

I wake covered in mosquito bites. Light streams through the window: the air is warm, my bedclothes bunched on the floor. Eleven a.m. and no sign of Josh, no monkey clatter, no idea what day it is. Must be ... what?

Friday?

He rises smiling at twelve and as per our ritual we chat happily over breakfast, rehearsing things we might talk about later. The groove is becoming clear: our days start easily, casually, then intensify, with Ali a release valve at the end. Last night it was the storied second title-fight against Sonny Liston, in which Liston fell to a 'phantom punch' no one at ringside appears to have seen.

I walk the half-mile into town, past the plank-and-plastic cigarette huts and wire-fenced NGO compounds and pairs of young men combing the pavement like perambulating couples, who give the impression of perpetually seeking something that isn't there.

Awassa bustles and for the first time I notice clear signs of affluence – the jewellery and dress shops, electrical emporia and restaurants; sharp-dressed men and women with hair piled high under scarves. Wealthy Addis Ababans holiday here, so there's money, but what strikes me now are the hundreds of children on the streets, who play games with stones against the curb and sleep in dusty ruined buildings, nothing but each other to rely on, and then not usually for long. Life expectancy for a man in Ethiopia is fifty-three years, so God knows what it is for these kids, many of whom have been born with HIV, pretty walking ghosts sent into the world to die.

They smile and hold out their hands: the guidebook says not to give money, but it's hard to resist. Then you do and are suddenly surrounded by dozens and wondering how to choose who to give to and whether you'll be causing fights, and then adults crowd round too, some with disfigurements, twisted features and grotesque tangles of would-be or once-were limbs. And suddenly everyone's looking at you, smiling hopefully. So you decide not to do that again, at least overtly. Many of the children wear frayed English Premier League football shirts, the most common name on the back being 'Rooney', as in Wayne, poster-boy for brattish, irrational consumption and vapid excess – for a world which, from where I'm standing right now, is demonstrably madder than anything the likes of Josh Harris could hope to invent. And the maddest thing of all? Within a couple of days I'll have grown used to it; within a month I'll be back in England and it'll be just another story to me.

Fish, fries, fruit, tea, our tenebrous room, me on the couch, he on the chair. Another story. Further escalation.

We've been shooting the breeze about books, film, TV, so it's later than usual when Josh says: 'So, back to Gilligan. Let's suck it off with Gilligan and the Second Coming. What the fuck did he send down?'

Send down? I thought the Second Coming was hypothetical. A metaphor. I also think 'Let's suck it off with Gilligan' is an unfortunate phrase.

He smiles.

'Well, if you look at *Launder My Head*, the second episode, part two . . .'

The six-minute computer animation again, which I've now seen, with TV-headed people perched onstage in an amphitheatre, chorusing gnomic refrains like 'We're here to tell you how we tell you how to live/ We're your conscience, we are not conscious, launder my head, launder my head . . .' An impressive feat of programming for its time, achieved using relatively primitive computers, but ultimately just an early 3D animation. A curio.

He pauses, as if deciding how much to offer, says: 'See, for me, I got all of this ... for whatever reason, I got the job.'

He looks me directly in the eye and I say: 'Sorry, Josh. What job?' But he ignores the question and carries on.

'Because those characters in *Launder My Head*, to me, are ...'

Something beatific in the eyes.

'*Them*.'

Them? I'm confounded. I can't explain why, but a little shiver runs up my spine. Again I ask what he means.

'I mean they're *real*.'

He looks me in the eye again and I suddenly feel very alone, a long way from home. Is this the effect he wants, I wonder? I wait for a sign that he's joking, but the sign doesn't come as he returns his still-unlit cigar to his mouth, laughs in a way that momentarily pulls me up. I ask once more, 'Josh, are you telling me you think these creatures actually exist outside of your imagination?'

Am speechless as he leans back and grins: 'So ... how do you like them apples? Like, I got you down the rabbit hole, man. I told you there's a rabbit hole. *How far am I going?*'

A full-on laugh. Nervous glance. There's no way not to ask: is Josh mad? If so, was he always? With these questions begin the deepest, strangest four-year period of my life.

3

That night a gun-blast shook the compound. Dogs erupted and a woman screamed; howls shrilled the air as if voiced by the darkness itself.

We leapt from our seats and ran into the yard, where moonlight poured on to the lawn and Abraham stood, listening. A scan of the visible space revealed no movement: on the other side of the high wall there was shouting, a palette of rustles and clangs and whispers; then people talking as the background noise faded and the night stilled and nature retreated to the shadows again, waiting for the next rupture in the fabric of the human swathe. Satisfied that we weren't under attack, Abraham cracked the door to the street and slipped through. We went inside.

The timing of the gunshot incident was so perfect that much later I would wonder whether Josh had staged it, at a point where I was already spooked by a turn in our conversation. As so often with him, that evening's narrative had begun with a party.

In marked contrast to most of the other events we talked about, this one wasn't a big production featuring classical dancers or fashion shows or the world's largest bong: rather, it was a small gathering of a dozen or so people in his private chambers, all of whom had signed up to try a powerful psychotropic drug called dimethyltryptamine, or DMT. First studied by a Hungarian chemist who had been refused access to LSD by its Swiss developers, Sandoz Laboratories, on the comic grounds that psychedelics might be dangerous in the hands of communists, DMT produces a short, sharp, very intense trip. Writing for *The Face* magazine in the mid-1990s, I came across numerous rave-scene clubbers who'd experimented with the drug, more than one of whom appeared never to have recovered. DMT has never been a recreational turn; this one's for serious psychonauts and tends to produce an almost – or even *actual* – religious sense of awakening. Some people think it persuades the brain that it's dying, which, if true, would lend the experience a special poignancy.

Josh named the seekers who were present in his chambers at Pseudo HQ that night, ready to be led into the bedroom in pairs and guided through their trips by the perhaps-less-than-propitiously-named 'Brian the Evil Shaman'. These included at least one other dotcom celebrity CEO, a writer, a filmmaker, a videographer and various Pseudo employees. Like anyone who'd partied or done business in New York in the 1990s, Josh had spent a great deal of time around people who were high on illegal substances, but according to just about everyone who knew him then, he was unusually abstemious; never drank much or took hard drugs as a matter of course. But that night wasn't a matter of course.

Others came out of the bedroom with accounts of soaring into space, meeting Egyptian pharaohs or alien creatures or in one case their own aborted child. Everyone was shaken and when Josh's turn came, the first thing he saw was all of Brian the Evil Shaman's equally evil ancestors – 'and it was like, *I see who you are*' – before moving on to a place where he found his mother and the fake girlfriend waiting for him, although in this peaceful upland he had become their father.

En route to the two women, however, something more profound had happened, when he ran into a group of creatures he calls the 'Ticklers': geometric figures, constantly reconfiguring through three dimensions, 'and looking at me'. Afterwards, he moved on to other 'journeys', but it was Ticklers that seemed significant.

'That's why I was there,' he told me. 'And when I first got out, the first thing I said to Brian was, "The thing I'm going to wonder for the rest of my life is whether that was a trip or a journey." Now I see it as a business trip – ha-ha!'

The vision Josh described was typical of the DMT experience, right down to the form of the creatures he met. Infinitely more fascinating to me was his interpretation of what he saw as he asked, rhetorically: 'But what was the business trip all about? The thing I realise is that, as I understand it, what these things were doing was . . . they were . . . recording me.'

'Who were they?' I asked, not sure how far to commit to this narrative turn.

'Well, it's not *who*. I'll never know that. I can't get to it. But I know one thing: they were trying to harvest me. Me in particular. I'm a tasty harvest. I'm like a truffle – hee-hee-hee . . .'

He proceeded to link this to everything else we'd been talking about, in ways which I found intriguing and ingenious, forming a Grand Narrative in which everything he'd ever done, even the painful parts, made sense and had value. Around a metaphor which posited us as 'beakless chickens in a chicken factory', he had the Ticklers harvesting our psyches, uploading the information we are composed of as much as atoms to a giant ethereal hard drive when we die – much as we have begun to upload ourselves to cyberspace, a parallel dimension in which we are *nothing but* disembodied information: a sphere no less ethereal and no more tangible to most of us than that of the Ticklers; in which Josh, with his determinedly à la carte psychology, is a particularly rich source of energy.

Thus *Gilligan* represents the food used to fatten us; *Launder My Head* Josh's scripture; *Quiet* an attempt to show what society could become as everyone becomes their own show and connections proliferate, while relationships grow more tenuous. And *We Live in Public* becomes his attempt to live in this perma-wired, always-on, screen-mediated future where distinctions between 'real' and 'not-real' come to seem not just problematic, but *incidental* as physical and imaginative space elides, perhaps one day to become indistinguishable. As – a queer thought – may already be happening for him.

Even *Tuna Heaven*, the Ethiopian Emperor Haile Selassie (who Josh claims to have met as a child) and the apple farm, a place so beautiful that no one who visited can understand how he let it go, are drawn into this idiosyncratic personal theology, this whole improbable mix of Judeo-Christianity and *The Truman Show*; of Philip K. Dick, *Field of Dreams*, *Gilligan's Island*, Aldous Huxley and *The Matrix*.

'So now I have a better appreciation of the expression "Jesus saves",' he smirks, able to make me laugh even while doubting his wits. 'I mean, I was getting saved to disc.'

We're being 'fattened up' on 'electronic calories'. Either a wonderful metaphor, a coping mechanism for disappointments too profound to face ... or evidence that I was indeed sleeping in the next room to a madman, I found myself thinking. Then the gun went off.

The rest of my ten-night stay passed in a convivial haze. The night of the gun-blast, we unwound with Ali versus Foreman, the famous Rumble in the Jungle fight from 1974 in which the master, having spent years in the wilderness after refusing the Vietnam draft, faced a hard-hitting opponent he could never out-slug in Zaire. Shaken by a first-round battering he knew he couldn't sustain, Ali improvised a counter-intuitive tactic of leaning against the ropes and inviting the other man to swing at him, either ducking out of the way or covering his face and allowing punches to fall painfully but harmlessly on his torso or glove-padded head. We watched enthralled as Foreman grew frustrated, swung harder and with ever more venom, and eventually tired, allowing Ali to step forward and finish him in a fierce eighth-round hail of blows.

The highlights for me, though, were to do with punches not thrown: with Ali's decision to pull a valedictory right as Foreman fell, so – in the writer Norman Mailer's words – 'preserving the aesthetic of the moment', and with his trainer Angelo Dundee's post-bout observation that, 'You spend a lot more energy in missing a guy than you do in hitting him.' The media dubbed this the 'Rope-a-dope' fight, playing to Ali's characterisation of Foreman as a mindless brute and afterwards Josh chuckled, 'That's the way I like to work, too,' adding to the disorientation I felt over our earlier conversation. Was I his dope? My half-suspicion that he'd been messing with me still begged the question of 'Why?' Either possibility – he *believes* or *he manipulates* – seemed extraordinary, and I wondered if this was what the ex-colleague had meant by there being 'a kind of reality distortion field' around Josh . . . which people, having experienced, don't want to surrender? Only after I'd left Awassa would I be stunned to notice that his later *New York Times* stories were nearly all written by Jayson Blair, the rogue reporter who brought the paper to its knees with a slew of extravagant fabrications.

Time collapsed. Some mornings I'd get up or return from an early walk to find him pacing the lawn, the same cigar he'd opened on my first morning stuck to his lips as if by superglue. He seemed to have relaxed, post-Ticklers, and the *Arabian Nights* stories grew into something I looked forward to, playing games with myself by trying to figure how each would fit into the larger Grand Narrative, usually falling hopelessly short of the mark. One night began with a declarative, 'The trial of Alfredo Martinez!' then opened, fabulously: 'So, Alfredo, he could do Basquiat better than Basquiat . . .'

And I listened, confused but rapt as he teaselled a yarn about Martinez, a bear-like Pseudo artist who had been assistant to the New York painter Donald Baechler, selling one of his own works to a collector for $35,000 under the pretence that it was by art hipster Jean-Michel Basquiat. Typically of Josh's narratives, the collector was revealed to be a gangster. Another night we turned to his father, who worked for the Ethiopian Livestock Development Company, Elidco, but is suspected by Josh of having been a CIA operative. Although these Le Carré-esque expositions are of marginal interest to me in themselves, most of the details I'm able to check later turn out to be either true or surprisingly plausible. Interspersed with entertaining digressions and conceptual inventions such as his notion of 'the corporate drive-by' and of humanity, or *somebody*, 'goosing the growth' of evolution with the arrival of cyberspace, and with declarations like 'if I ran Starbucks, I'd give 'em the coffee and sell the social experience' and 'the difference between us and later generations is . . . *remote control*', each would be followed by the potted drama of another Ali fight.

Our days grew closer, too, to the point where I knew I was distracting him from his editing tasks, which all but ground to a halt. We took a donkey-cart ride to the fish market, in reality a lake-edge outcrop where dozens of fishermen, many just children, stood surrounded by marabou stork whose ravenous black eyes seemed to summon the end of time, selling tilapia and catfish they'd caught with wooden poles for ten birr a time, or about forty British pence. On the way home we passed one of many half-constructed houses on which work had clearly ceased.

'And you know what?' Josh asked. 'The guy killed this 150-year-old tree to build this.'

Days blurred.

One morning we woke to find a beautiful mantled guereza monkey perched in one of our trees, large and jet-black with a skunk-like white stripe down his back and penetrating African eyes. We went to play, Josh videoing while I proffered banana, until the animal startled me by reaching beyond the fruit and grabbing my hand with his own, which was so shockingly soft and human. The monkey had sharp teeth (and a tiny erect penis like a carved wooden mushroom), but made no move towards me: when we told Kelemework about the incident, she explained that he'd been curious, wanted to know what my skin felt like. All while the tortoises were humping away in the background, or perhaps just trying, because as the days passed I grew to appreciate how difficult their task was, and that their problem boiled down to lack of *leverage*. They should have a word with Josh, I thought.

That same day I returned from exploring Awassa's crazy backstreets to find myself face to face with the dreadlocked aggressor I'd encountered around town, who sat opposite Josh and glared as I walked in. I'd forgotten: in an effort to solve his gang problems, Josh had called a 'trial' and this was it, with a stoned-looking policeman acting as magistrate and Abraham doing his best to translate. Startled, I sat down expecting the worst, but was soon impressed by the even-handedness of proceedings, calmness of debate, efficiency of such localised justice – until, after three hours of discussion, the policeman summed up in Josh's favour, muttered something about carrying out further investigations, then took the disputed 650 birr . . . and handed it to the gang leader.

What was there to do? We burst into laughter, then all hugged in the shoulder-barging Ethiopian style, with Josh promising to hold a friendship-promoting traditional coffee ceremony at some point in the future. The *faranji* had been played, but saw the humour and had enjoyed the drama, just as he did the next day when we donkey-carted into town for a meeting which to nobody's conspicuous surprise failed to happen. Still, the sight of him crossing the road in the huge boots and combats I'd brought from England, sporting Aviator shades and a log-like cigar and looking like a narcotics agent or long-lost fifth member of the A-Team, will remain with me for the rest of my life – one of the funniest things I have ever seen. Seldom can two grown men have had more fun, and to my astonishment no one asked us for money.

With a jolt I realised that I was enjoying the distortion field, would miss it when I left.

Repeatedly I demanded to know whether he'd been deploying metaphor or talking in literal terms about the Ticklers, the hard drive, the bull's-eye on the World Trade Center – reminding him that people back home would think he'd lost his mind. Each time he smiled and said variously: 'You know, I'll take my chances with the 15-year-olds'; 'I'll let you decide'; 'Why is it harder to believe than a crucified guy coming back to life?'; and lastly, finally, 'I don't ask you to believe it, I only ask you to believe that *I* believe it.'

He did open up and show self-awareness once he felt safe, confessing sadly that, 'I always wonder whether I'll ever throw another party,' and offering, 'You know it's all very well to put $40 million into your work, it's the cost of a mid-budget movie, but that last million ... man, that *hurts*'; later, 'I've learned to trust the gut and that's why ... I'm broke in Ethiopia!' More consequently, he talked in detail about 'the day I cracked' at the end of *We Live in Public*, which in every sense seems to represent a zenith, a nadir, a crescendo he's spent every subsequent moment trying to process. Either the act of living in public was innately destabilising, or it was destabilising, *traumatic* for him at that point in time. One of my jobs would be to find out which it was and whether he was rationalising when he said: 'Well I knew all this before I came into *We Live in*

Public, but I had to understand. With *We Live in Public* I went where no one had ever been before, because I wanted to see where ... I wanted to see where we're gonna end up. And I mean, I *saw it*.'

In *One Thousand and One Nights*, a cuckolded king, after dispensing with his wife-queen, resolves thenceforth to take virgin brides for one night only, arranging to have them executed in the morning. The king thus becomes a kind of Islamic Golden Age Rod Stewart – bad news for the city's virgins, until the eldest daughter of the vizier charged with procuring the young brides steps forward with a plan. Clever Shahrazad marries the king and begins a different story every night, leaving him sufficiently intrigued to stay her death another day in order that he might hear the end of the story. And when I look back on the Awassa nights, I'll fancy to see a similar process: a collection of tales, brilliantly told, *outlandish* but impossible to ignore.

Mischievously encouraged by my host, I took the bus back to Addis – one of the most terrifying experiences of my life – and spent an unreal evening in the sauna and thrumming bar at the Hilton, where the bulk of pan-African business seems to get done and the first sip of my gin and tonic tasted so good that I wanted to cry, suddenly aware of how spent I was. Of how exhausting the absence of boundaries and at least a semblance, even illusion, of certainty can be.

I'd been hoping to go away with some of my initial questions answered, like how and why Josh Harris, with the world at his feet, had thrown it all away; how his trip related to the fate of the dotcoms? – but now saw that I was taking home more questions than I'd brought, not the least of which was whether Josh Harris was a huckster or a fantasist ... or something else entirely, the like of which I'd never encountered before. The only things I felt sure of were that his journey from Silicon Alley to Awassa *was* tied to the more general fate of the first dotcoms and that if I could make sense of what had happened to him, I would learn what or who had killed them. With a sense that the 'reality distortion field' was about more than him alone.

I walked the mile back to my B & B with the last thing he said spinning through my head.

'You know, you were asking what was the truth,' he'd offered with the usual paisley grin. 'Well, the truth is what happened.'

But what *did* happen?

I was going to have to return to the beginning, I realised. But first I would have to *find* the beginning.

* * *

When the Europeans came to Manhattan Island, the thing most remarked upon first was the sweetness of the air. There was much discussion among the British and Dutch as to the source of this pleasantness, although the meadows bright with wild-flower and strawberries; the reed marshes and woodlands full of cherries and of pear, hazelnut and apple trees provide one obvious explanation. Where Greenwich Village and SoHo are now, there was a trout brook; to the north a pond with streams trailing off to the Hudson and East Rivers, clattering with so many ducks and swans that settlers had difficulty sleeping. Those settlers' rhapsodic descriptions of this new Eden invariably focused on its bounty – on the oyster-lined bay patrolled by whales and porpoises and bubbling with sturgeon and tuna and trout and striped bass you could scoop out of the water with your hands, and on the fecundity of the wildlife; of the beavers, bears, foxes, otters, elk, deer, raccoons and occasional mountain lion, turkeys tall as a man. Running diagonally north-west to south-east was a pathway worn by the native Weckquaesgeek tribe, an early trade and information superhighway which the Dutch eventually knew as 'Breede Wegh', but the British Anglicised to 'Broadway'.

Thus, everything that would come to define New York for the rest of the world was there from the outset. In a history of the city from 1809, Washington Irving even notes the alleged presence of unicorns in those early days, fully three and a half centuries before sightings became common again in the Greenwich Village of the 1960s. When writers try to capture the place in words, they often resort to elemental imagery, as if the playbox skyline were a miracle of nature, independent of human will and outside the normal pattern of behaviour or event. Which is perhaps what Warhol meant when he observed that, 'Living in New York City gives people real incentives to want things that nobody else wants.' Yet for all this, my favourite summation of the place remains with Fitzgerald and Gatsby, whose narrator Nick Carraway crosses the Queensboro Bridge into the metropolis with the words, 'New York had all the iridescence of the beginning of the world.'

Iridescent was no longer a word anyone used to describe New York as the 1980s limped into the 90s. Office space languished empty as businesses failed and bankrupt city authorities slashed services until a trip down Broadway or to the fetid subway became a piss-parade of misery; a sideshow of hawkers, squeegee men, porn-sellers and panhandlers working in shifts, with crack dealers prowling parks and drunks shitting in doorways. Mugging and homelessness moved beyond the reach of anger or pity and into the realm of comedy, as the talk show host David Letterman drew laughs with gags like 'New York now leads the world's great cities in the number of people around whom you shouldn't make a sudden move' and his rival Jay Leno with 'The crime problem in New York is getting really serious: the other day the Statue of Liberty had both hands up.'

When New Yorkers are joking about something, you know it's serious. A *Time* magazine cover from 1990 bewailed 'The Rotting of the Big Apple' and *The New York Times* employed the lyrics from 'Hold On', an excoriating state-of-the-city address from Lou Reed's lauded *New York* album, as an op-ed piece.

With an irony that would grow familiar enough to seem banal by the second decade of the twenty-first century, only the banking sector, which had precipitated the crisis via a stock market crash in 1987, escaped the recession. Two running gags in Brett Easton Ellis's brilliant 1991 satire of the city, *American Psycho*, concern the sheer, numbing scale of the homeless problem and the equally numbing, rococo absurdity of the dishes served at celebrity-cheffed restaurants whose tables are conferred with the solemnity of knighthoods. Only in the 90s could 'carpaccio of tuna' be misheard as 'cappuccino of tuna' and seem entirely plausible.

How had this socio-economic malaise come to pass? As an economics virgin, the first thing to strike me as I pile into the research is how little I understand about this demented province which bosses so many aspects of my life. Luckily, the second is how little *economists* seem to understand it, given the tendency of their analyses and predictions to be either wrong, irrelevant or wrong *and* irrelevant. On the question of New York's early 90s nadir, however, there does seem to a broad, plausible consensus, which already looks important to an understanding of what's to come – and of the world we find ourselves in now. It runs as follows:

In 1975, the US Securities and Exchange Commission, those Keystone Kops of the finance world, decided to allow commissions on stock market transactions to become negotiable, where previously they'd been tied to fixed rates. Before long, profits at Wall Street brokerages were down as clients renegotiated fees, until it was clear that another profit engine had to be found. Enter [stage right, twirling moustache] the 'hostile takeover'.

Up to the 70s, one company bought another by approaching management and/or owners, agreeing a price, signing contracts and shaking hands. Now Wall Street pointed out that where a target company was publicly traded (meaning that *shares* of ownership, – of *stock* – in them could be bought and sold on the market), a predatory firm could bypass management and workers by appealing direct to the venality of shareholders, hoovering up stock at an inflated price. Worth noting is that a company's best defence against hostile takeover was to nurture a share price so high that it failed to present a bargain ... and thus did share price move to the forefront of the business mind. Nasty stuff, we might think – until we get to the mid-80s heyday of the 'leveraged buyout', next to which hostile takeovers looked less Wall Street than *Sesame Street*.

The philosopher René Descartes once argued for the existence of God on the grounds that perfection is intrinsic to the definition of an Almighty and to not exist would be a flaw: therefore He must exist. Schopenhauer called this argument 'a charming joke' and in logical terms it has much in common with the leveraged buyout, one of those exquisitely improbable high finance devices that sound like a joke until you find yourself wriggling on the end of it. Here, one company borrows enough money to buy another, using the target company's assets as collateral for the loan, thus making the victim organisation responsible for the typically huge loans used to conquer and then emasculate it. Given that target management and workers were often violently opposed to such deals, this process was like making an innocent convict build his own scaffold, hang himself, then come back from the dead to pay for the rope. It allowed small, badly run organisations to buy large, well-run ones at very little risk to themselves, so long as they could borrow enough money to persuade shareholders to sell out. Cash was often raised through the ruse of selling high-risk 'junk bonds' to third-party investors.

The *$25 billion* leveraged buyout of RJR Nabisco in 1988, which (in a near-billion-dollar shower of bonuses and fees for lawyers, bankers, brokers and executives) resulted in the destruction of a venerable company by a predatory upstart, represents a curious sort of watershed and cast a shadow over the decade that followed. The late-80s story which lingers longest in my mind, however, is of a well-heeled investment adviser named David Herrlinger who, after bidding $70 a share for a company called Dayton Hudson, watched the stock price skyrocket before confessing to a nonplussed *Wall Street Journal* writer that the source of financing for his generous offer was 'still undecided'. Asked whether his offer was a hoax, Herrlinger replied: 'I don't know. It's no more of a hoax than anything else.'

The bull market which would define the 90s thus began in 1982 and after sixteen years of flat *bearish* attrition, its market riders were in no mood to apologise for the wealth it could bring. As industry contracted and unemployment rose to a post-Depression high, economists arrived to explain that extravagance among the few was not just a right, but a moral duty underpinned by the so-called 'Laffer curve', which purported to imply that if you lowered taxes for the rich, they would be motivated to get richer still and so boost the economy for everyone. Around this theory rose the Christmas cracker science known as 'Reaganomics', named for the actor-turned-president whose wife Nancy did her bit for the poor by spending a reported $25,000 on frocks for her husband's first inauguration, rising to $46,000 for the second in January 1985. A triumphalist celebration of the Statue of Liberty's 100th birthday in July 1986 subsequently featured the largest assembly of ships since World War II, the largest firework display and perhaps the campest entertainment ever created, in which twelve thousand performers (including two hundred Elvis impersonators and three hundred jazzercise dancers) filled a twenty-tier stage laddered with five waterfalls. Not only were the Reagans' faces projected on to the statue: a caterer moulded Liberty's image out of sixty pounds of chopped liver and no one even thought to ask . . . 'Why?'

That's the kind of decade the 80s was. As unemployment hit 3 million in the UK, groups like Duran Duran and Wham! flaunted their new wealth in videos of them sailing yachts or skiing, while Robin Leach, presenter of *Lifestyles of the Rich and Famous* on American TV, signed off with 'may you have caviar wishes and champagne dreams' and glam soaps *Dallas* and *Dynasty* monstered the ratings. Ever on the money, the author Tom Wolfe coined the word 'plutography' to mean 'the graphic depiction of the acts of the rich' and satirised both New York and the decade in one of its best novels, *Bonfire of the Vanities*, which among other things gave us the term 'Masters of the Universe', in reference to the Ivy League patricians who ran high finance back then. According to US Census Bureau figures, income flat-lined for the bottom half of the population in the 1980s, but rose by almost 20 per cent for the top 5 per cent. All the same, when Wolfe wanted to impress us with the affluence of Sherman McCoy, his main protagonist in *Bonfire of the Vanities*, he thought 'an eight million dollar fortune' would suffice. Mark this.

By 1988 the predatory M & A (Mergers and Acquisitions) business accounted for 50 per cent of profits on Wall Street, but by 1987 the leveraging had already gone too far. That winter, with members of the public piling into the stock market for the first time since the early 70s, shares were trading at twenty times company earnings, a level not seen since the pre-slump stock bubble of 1973. The market had gained 200 per cent in value over the previous five years: parents were enrolling 10-year-olds in 'money management' camps in the expectation that the run would continue indefinitely, as some analysts predicted it would.

Until on Monday 19 October, the market teetered and collapsed, with the Dow Jones Industrial Average shedding 508 points (22 per cent of its value) in a single day. One of the buzz-words of the boom was 'yuppie', standing for 'young, upwardly-mobile professional' (latterly 'young *urban* professional') and predictions of his/her demise began almost immediately, accompanied by reams of gleeful jokes, two of my favourites being:

> What's the difference between a pigeon and a yuppie?
> A pigeon can still make a deposit on a Mercedes.

And:

> A highway patrolman approached an accident site and found that the whole side of a white BMW had been torn off, taking the driver's arm with it. The injured yuppie, a stock broker, was in shock and moaning, 'My car, my car . . .' while the officer tried to comfort him, soothing, 'Sir, help will be here soon, but I think we should be more concerned about your arm than your car' – at which point the driver looked down at where his arm should have been and screamed, 'My Rolex! My Rolex!'

In the wake of Black Monday, the *Daily Telegraph* in London banned the word 'yuppie' from its pages; Burger King stopped selling croissants. The phrase 'go for it' all but disappeared and the concept of 'cocooning' – staying in to watch *Twin Peaks* rather than going out and spending money – entered the lexicon. With faultless timing, Prodigy, one of the first public online service providers, launched regionally a few months later, at a time when young people were being squeezed. In a wryly sympathetic essay entitled 'The Short Happy Life of the American Yuppie', the *New Yorker* writer and editor Hendrik Hertzberg explained why the yuppie had been shown so little mercy, observing that:

> He became the collective projection of a moral anxiety. We loaded on to him everything we hated about the times we

> had been living through – everything we hated about what we suspected we ourselves might have become. We made the Yuppie the effigy of selfishness and self-absorption, of the breakdown of social solidarity, of rampant careerism and obsessive ambition, of the unwholesome love of money, of the delusion that social problems have individual solutions, of callousness and contempt toward 'losers', of the empty ideology of 'winnerism' and the uncritical worship of 'success'. Then we strung the little bastard up.

The yuppie was a synecdoche, a piece that came to represent the whole, and was assumed, like the times that gave rise to him/her, to be gone for ever. Hertzberg ended his piece with an assurance that the 1990s would be as different from the 1980s as the 30s from the 20s or the 70s from the 60s – just as the *Wall Street Journal* writers Bryan Burrough and John Helyar felt able to conclude at the end of their bestselling *Barbarians at the Gate: the Fall of RJR Nabisco* (published in 1990) that the age of Wall Street excess was over and the 'casino society' dead. You'd have been forgiven for imagining that a new Age of Aquarius beckoned . . .

And yet the remarkable thing about Black Monday was its legacy to Wall Street. *Nothing*. While Main Street America agonised over lost jobs, crumbling house values, shrunken or vanished investments, Wall Street shed 15,000 jobs and offered a few high profile hostages to prosecution (like Michael Milken, the former 'Junk Bond King' whose 1988 earnings exceeded the US spend on AIDS research) then carried on as before. The conditions that led to the crash remained intact. In 1960, an average of three million shares of stock were traded on the New York Stock Exchange each day, with 12 per cent of the listed shares changing hands over the course of the year and shares typically held for eight years before being sold again. By 1988, however, the number of shares changing ownership on a typical day had increased almost *70-fold* to 200 million, with 95 per cent of listed stock changing hands that year and most shares held for only a few hours. More tellingly still, the value of trades in stock index options and futures, bets on whether particular groups of stock would move up or down, *outright gambling* in other words, was five times that of simple trades in shares.

All of this was abetted in the beginning by the new Chairman of the Federal Reserve, Alan Greenspan, a native New Yorker who considered Wall Street an essential driver of the economy and would guide the nation's finances accordingly. He took office in August 1987 and cut interest rates twenty-four consecutive times from spring '89 onwards, injecting Federal Reserve money into the economy by purchasing Treasury Bonds (long term investments with a low but guaranteed yield of interest) from banks, so vastly increasing the supply of cash available for banks to lend. The effect of this was to create a huge pool of cheap money to be borrowed and spent by companies and the public, with saving coming to seem progressively more ludicrous – a situation economists classically associate with consumer price inflation, as prices climb to meet increased demand. But that's not what happened on this occasion. Instead of buying goods and services, Americans bought houses and *stock*.

So instead of consumer price inflation, there was asset price inflation.

And the 'Market' began to rise.

4

Over in the Village, no one cared about stock prices. If you stood on Sixth Avenue and watched the taxis slide past, you could imagine the city stretching away for ever, but New York has always been about incomers and the most recent influx had reason to rue their timing – as indeed they had at every turn up to that point. Mostly born in the mid-late '60s, their childhoods had been coloured by the petrol crisis, Watergate and post-Nam angst. Perpetually shadowed by recession and parented by the first generation for whom the Pill was available and divorce almost mandatory, they must have felt a rare flash of optimism as they left for college or the big city in the mid-1980s with the US economy soaring and pundits declaiming that the boom could go on for ever, with anything seeming possible and elders' best advice being the (in retrospect rather vague) 'Just do it!' ... only for normal service to resume in the form of a financial crisis timed to meet their graduation from arts or social science programmes with dazzling precision.

Generation X: billed as the first generation to reach adulthood with broadly lower expectations than their parents, whose battlecry, as articulated by house band Nirvana, was 'Nevermind'.

To affluent uptowners, downtown's East Village was a ghetto

and SoHo, the rectangular pitch south of Houston (hence *So-Ho*) and north of Canal, remained a hard-bitten neighbourhood rather than the gigantic open-air designer mall it would become. As the 80s became the 90s and the city's depression dragged on, career paths were few for young New Yorkers, but downtown rents were low and what the author Douglas Coupland dubbed 'McJobs' plentiful. Prospects for the future looked bleak, but the present was not so bad once you found a way to get by: with the Democrat Mayor Dinkins distracted by crime, homelessness, racial tension and drugs – and wondering where future revenues would come from with almost 9 per cent unemployment – there was a slackening of pressure to conform. Unencumbered by career, property, fidelity to an employer or employer's pretence to give a shit, if ever a generation arrived prepared for the world that awaited, this was it. And lurking in its midst was a handful of smart, artsy bohos who'd seen something almost no one else had; something that appeared as powerful to them as the taming of fire must have to their hominid ancestors a million years before. The internet. Or, more precisely, *cyberspace*. A tunnel you entered only to find the end-light fading until it no longer mattered at all.

These were the Early True Believers and they were in the process of finding each other.

Urban myth holds that the internet began as a military project, but this is not true. In fact, cyberspace was conjured from the opposite impulse in the same remarkable moment as NASA and the American space programme.

In October 1957, the Soviet Union shocked the world by announcing that it had sent the first human-made object into orbit around the Earth. The Sputnik satellite was a basketball-sized orb with a trailing array of silvery antennas and it caused panic in the US, where the CIA spent days trying to decipher its inscrutable 'bleep' and commentators schooled on B-movie sci-fi raised the prospect of an orbiting bomb or death ray, or a sinister device that would mesmerise Americans and compromise their will. In fact, Sputnik's bleep really was just a bleep and the sinister device already existed, being commonly known as 'television', so the satellite's only negative effect was a tendency to send automatic garage doors into spastic fits as it passed overhead – irritating, but short of catastrophe. Yet the panic didn't abate.

Any way you look at him, President Ike Eisenhower was an incredible man. As Supreme Commander of Allied Forces in Europe during World War II, he orchestrated the D-Day landings from London (you can still see the cylindrical top of his HQ, effectively an upside-down thirty-storey skyscraper in Chenies Street, off Tottenham Court Road) and from 1953 to 1961 became one of the most independent-minded presidents the US has ever had. Although a Republican, he maintained and then expanded most of the Democrat's New Deal programmes and harboured an affection for scientists which ran as deep as his suspicion of his own military commanders. The phrase 'military industrial complex' was coined by him, as a warning, and so when this self-interested coalition of commanders and contractors tried to hitch public fear to its own wagon and win military command of space and science, Ike – to their fury – outwitted them by entrusting both domains to civilians. Early in 1958, he created the space agency NASA, followed by the Advanced Research Projects Agency, or ARPA, to oversee science.

The latter fell under the aegis of Defense Secretary Neil McElroy, who as head of Procter & Gamble was credited with pioneering not just the 'soap opera' and notion of marketing his company's own brands – Daz, Bold, Tide – as though they were rivals, but the company's ground-breaking 'blue sky' research department, in which bright people were given time and money and near-complete freedom to follow their muse. This type of research and development was any scientist's dream and the model for ARPA, whose annual budget reached $250 million within a few years. By 1964, the US was spending an extraordinary $13 billion, or 3 per cent of Gross National Product annually on research and development, a Cold War-inflated figure which dwarfs today's allocation. Like the lunar programme, the internet as we know it now could only have arisen at this particular time, out of these particular circumstances.

It happened like this.

In 1961, Air Force cutbacks resulted in an embarrassingly expensive, bespoke IBM Q-32 computer being stranded at a contractor's headquarters in Santa Monica, California. In perhaps the most rarified game of pass-the-parcel ever played, the Department of Defense kicked the machine over to ARPA, who suddenly had the task of finding someone who could both run the machine and think of something to do with it (no mean feat in the days when only a few computers existed in the world). The person they chose, perhaps the only person they could have chosen in that moment, was a man with the fabulous name of J.C.R. Licklider – or 'Lick' to his friends.

With fifty-plus years of hindsight, the notion of computers as *connectors* looks obvious, inevitable, but in the 1950s and 60s it was neither of these things. The pioneers considered computers to be about fast maths or the fringe future dream of artificial intelligence: any notion that machines might one day revolutionise the way humans related to each other – that these manly-looking assemblages of tape spools and circuitry were actually about *relationships* – would have seemed obscure to scientists and sci-fi fans alike. But not to Lick. As always in these instances, he was standing on the shoulders of others, most notably Norbert Wiener, a home-schooled polymath whose refusal to join the nuclear bomb-building Manhattan Project caused him to be regarded with suspicion by US authorities, but whose work on the complex problem of aiming anti-aircraft guns during World War II (before him, they were fired primarily to bolster morale among the public) led to an interest in communication and the way information moves through networks. The discipline Wiener thus founded, 'cybernetics' – from 'cyber', meaning 'pilot' or 'helmsman' – had a limited impact when he first applied the term in 1942, but found purchase in the 1960s, when complexity and 'non-linear' ways of thinking became fashionable. Especially radical was his concept of 'feedback', where the products of a process start to *feed back* into the process itself and change or accelerate it. If this becomes continuous, a 'feedback loop' is created: we often hear this concept applied to theories of global warming.

Lick was a polymath, too, at a time when this was unusual. As a professor at the Massachusetts Institute of Technology (MIT) he was first to advance the idea that computers might be more than fancy adding machines; that they might one day become 'extensions of the whole human being' and even help save humanity, making citizens better informed and more globally attuned. In 1960, he wrote a seminal paper entitled 'Man–Computer Symbiosis', whose influence was narrow but profound among those who 'got it'. Three years later, in a memo to ARPA colleagues, he summoned the idea of an 'Intergalactic Computer Network' and became the first person to use the word 'online' in this context. Lick had taken the ARPA job on a promise of complete freedom, and quickly changed the name of his department from Command and Control Research to the Information Processing Techniques Office, routinely dismissing military proposals for research as 'asinine kinds of things'. He set up a network of the best university computer departments and focused on advanced research into computer graphics and language, and ways of optimising use of the expensive machines through 'time-sharing'. Before long, there arose the idea of linking machines together so that researchers could pool information more easily. The communications writer and academic Howard Rheingold, in noting that there was nothing intrinsic to computers that would enable them to 'connect people', credits Licklider and those who fell under his spell with steering them in a networked, cybernetic direction . . . 'which I think puts them in line with the Enlightenment thinkers', he adds.

The first person known to have wondered why ARPA's network of computers couldn't talk to each other was Bob Taylor, who arrived from NASA in 1961. In later life, Taylor grew impatient with the various urban myths ascribing development of the internet to the military (most commonly as a supposed means of communicating in the wake of a nuclear strike): on the contrary, what he found in Lick's office was an avant-garde committed to the ideal of 'interactive computing'; of turning the computer into an extension of the mind and body, a magnifier of human potential rather than the replacement more commonly envisaged in books like Isaac Asimov's *Foundation* series and movies such as *2001: A Space Odyssey*. Taylor approached Charles Herzfeld, ARPA's director from 1965 to 1967, with the notion of tying computers into a remote network and, according to him, the conversation ran:

Herzfeld: Is it going to be hard to do?
Taylor: Oh no. We already know how to do it.
Herzfeld: Great idea. Get it going. You've got a million dollars more in your budget right now. Go.

Science may never see such days again. On 29 October 1969, three months after the first moon landing and two after Woodstock, a student programmer from the University of California, Los Angeles (UCLA), tried to send the word 'login' to another computer at the cutting-edge Stanford Research Institute (SRI), but the system crashed before he reached the third letter – meaning that the first communication to pass between two computers was 'lo'. By the end of November, the link between the UCLA and SRI machines had become permanent. Early in December, two further 'nodes' were added, at UC Santa Barbara and the University of Utah. The 'ARPAnet', begetter of the internet, was born.

Yet nothing about the network's shape or ethos sprang inevitably from the science: crucial to its development is the fact that while Licklider, Taylor and others were pushing the hardware, another programme was running in the background, even if this one depended on substances other than silicon and retrospectively became known as *The Sixties*.

The two programmes, counterculture and computer revolution, elided on 9 December 1968, when in ninety minutes of what seemed pure science fiction even to a packed crowd containing most of the nation's computing experts, a quietly spoken man named Doug Engelbart stood under a twenty-two-foot high screen in San Francisco's yawning Brooks Hall auditorium and – to gasps and applause – not just explained, but *demonstrated* the future. By all accounts, not a soul left with the vision of the future they'd brought, which is why Engelbart's presentation is often referred to a little unpoetically as the Mother of all Demonstrations.

How had this come to pass?

As a 20-year-old Naval radar technician in 1945, Engelbart had been influenced by the work of Vannevar Bush, the brilliant wartime intellectual and scientist who had organised the Manhattan Project, then grown concerned for the destructive power he had helped unleash. In an *Atlantic Monthly* article from 1945, entitled 'As We May Think', he sketched ideas for interactive computers and what amounts to an internet, all in the hope of making the world's collective knowledge accessible to everyone, expanding the pool of wisdom. By the early 1950s, Engelbart agreed that computers were key to solving society's increasingly complex problems – not as all-powerful thinking-machines which could give us answers, but as communication devices which could foster understanding. He took a doctorate at UC Berkeley in order to learn everything he could about the brave new realm of computing, then moved to the SRI and in 1962, while the Cuban Missile Crisis threatened to lay waste the entire planet, wrote a ground-breaking paper entitled 'Augmenting Human Intellect: A Conceptual Framework'. With a generous grant from ARPA, he established the Augmentation Research Center, or ARC, based at the SRI.

At the 'Mother' demonstration in San Francisco, Engelbart used the world's first mouse (a wooden box with two wheels underneath) to show off the first user-friendly graphical interface and ARC's 'oNLine System' of hypertext links, connecting electronic documents through cyberspace. For almost everyone there, this would have been the first sense that there was such a thing as cyberspace, or that a computer's resources might empower an ordinary individual. The established industry, led by the behemoth IBM, saw no purpose to 'personal' computing and would remain hostile to the idea right into the 1980s.

A mere year before the birth of the ARPAnet, Engelbart's view of the coming age was as stunning as it was heretical, even if few people outside or *inside* the auditorium would grasp the full implications of ARC's work for another twenty-five years.

It shouldn't be surprising that Engelbart and Lick turned out to be in tune with a younger generation: after all, the drivers of their thinking had been Hiroshima and the Cold War; a sense that humanity needed to find ways of channelling empathy and intelligence if it was to survive a so-far traumatic century. And that technology, whether in the form of computers or LSD, might have a role to play in this quest. Precisely the same imperatives were playing on the counterculture, in other words.

In their book *Where Wizards Stay Up Late*, Katie Hafner and Matthew Lyon tell of an ARPA contractor arriving at the house of a Licklider-hired computer engineer on New Year's Eve, 1965, only to find himself in uncharted waters. 'It was like going to the Addams Family house,' he said afterwards. 'They were in bare feet. The women were wearing tight-fitting clothing. I showed up with a tie on and had to take it off.'

Such stories abound on the East Coast, but are even more plentiful in Engelbart's manor at Stanford, where office parties frequently consisted of driving to the beach, dropping acid and staying the night in sleeping bags. Stanford had become an unofficial centre for psychedelic adventurism after student guinea pigs were paid to drop acid, mescaline, DMT, psilocybin, ecstasy and other groovy substances as part of the CIA's infamous MK-ULTRA research programme – a charming twist on the convention whereby one pays one's dealer rather than the other way round. Among the first Stanford scholars to discover this wheeze and spread the word was Ken Kesey, then a graduate creative writing student, but soon to be hailed as the author of *One Flew Over the Cuckoo's Nest*. As later detailed by Tom Wolfe in his classic *The Electric Kool-Aid Acid Test*, Kesey and his hairy group of Merry Pranksters held parties and staged 'acid tests' at which Kool-Aid would be spiked and a band called the Warlocks, later known as The Grateful Dead, would jam for hours and hours ... and hours ... usually with a clutch of computer students and researchers among the wigged-out revellers. When one of these researchers took Kesey to see the Augment team's computer system, the author is reported to have sighed and said: 'It's the next thing after acid.'

A thought which, for better and worse, would become embedded in the fabric of the modern internet.

* * *

One of the young computer enthusiasts present at Engelbart's Mother of All Demos – he actually worked as a camera operative – was a 29-year-old seeker named Stewart Brand, whose influence on the evolution of the net is still felt today.

Brand arrived on the San Francisco scene with an unusual background. After an expensive private education, he studied biology at Stanford before joining the Army, which he credits with teaching him both discipline and organisational skills. He then returned to the Bay Area in 1962 to study art and photography, and was introduced to LSD by a psychology postgrad, who also took him to see the computer centre, where a group of researchers were playing a first, primitive video game called *Space War* just months after it had been created by hackers at MIT. Years later, he would explain that, 'What I saw was an epiphany for me; something really strange and different was going on.

'And remember,' he added, 'this is well before all the drug stuff.'

Brand shared Engelbart and Licklider's cybernetic view of material reality as a complex information system. He was also persuaded by the inventor Buckminster Fuller's belief that trying to change human nature through politics was futile; that the best way to improve behaviour was via the tools we use to engage each other and our environment. Or, as Brand puts it now, 'New tools make new practices and better tools make better practices.'

The young Army vet saw, or thought he saw, parallels between the altered state delivered by hallucinogens and the SRI programmers' absorption in the radically new virtual reality of cyberspace. Why? Because on an intellectual level, the nascent counterculture was about accepting everything as connected (an orthodox notion to the Eastern mind, radical in the West) and here were two powerful experiences that suggested such 'one-ness'. Neither was this the dope-addled whimsy we tend to assume with hindsight: with the planet teetering on the brink of nuclear annihilation in the early years of the Kennedy administration (1961–3), an acceptance of such one-ness implied a refutation of the idea that you could blow up half the world while leaving your own patch intact, or inflict misery on other cultures without some of that misery rebounding. At that point, cyberspace, which wouldn't have a name until William Gibson coined it in his 1982 story 'Burning Chrome', was more metaphorical than actual, but its promise was not lost on those who glimpsed it. The universe through the screen looked exciting.

Although patriotic and politically conservative, Brand became a key figure on the San Francisco scene. He co-organised the epochal Trips festival in January 1966, immediately after LSD was outlawed, and agitated for NASA to capture a photo of the whole Earth as seen from space; he even appears in the opening pages of *The Electric Kool-Aid Acid Test*. But as the Vietnam War dragged on and an Aquarian Age neglected to dawn, disillusioned heads and freaks began to give up on wider society and head for the hills to establish communes. Estimates have between 10 and 20 million people involved in this migration, making it the biggest in US history – a claim which seems improbable to me until I remember that at least two of my teachers from a San Francisco suburb joined in, and that remnants of the communities they formed remain scattered across the country like spent roaches.

Brand decided to serve this surge by setting up one of the most influential emanations of the 60s underground, the *Whole Earth Catalog*, an open forum for discussion combined with pages and pages of ads for things these new communards would need. The *Catalog* began on six mimeographed pages, but within three years was selling over a million copies, aimed at 'bringing people into direct communication with each other as equals'. Given what he'd seen of Engelbart's work at

Stanford, Brand was careful to ensure that the *Catalog* engaged with the nascent technology underground, as expressed in Free University courses on 'How to end the IBM monopoly' and the information technologist Ted Nelson's geek manifesto *Computer Lib*.

'There was this tiny, tiny unknown subset of longhairs who were hanging out with computers,' Brand explained later, 'who had very little to do with politics and nothing to do with drugs – they had a *way* better drug. And their world was getting better and better and better, and that was not true of politics and not true of drugs. Which reinforced the idea that this was where the action was.'

In 1972 Brand wrote an article about these people for *Rolling Stone* magazine ('Fanatic Life and Symbolic Death Among the Computer Bones') which cemented his sense that 'the real action is here'. And still hardly anyone noticed: the first pop-cultural references I can find to the birth of the ARPAnet – an event of far greater long-term profundity than the lunar landings – are in Colum McCann's panoramic novel of New York, *Let the Great World Spin*, and Thomas Pynchon's playful, California-set *Inherent Vice*. Both published in 2009, *forty years after the fact*. In the latter, Pynchon's stoner private dick, Doc Sportello, visits a friend who works with the ARPA computer at Santa Barbara.

> 'Wow ... so when they gonna make it illegal, Fritz?' Sportello asks.
>
> 'What. Why would they do that?" replies his friend.
>
> 'Remember how they outlawed acid as soon as they found out it was a channel to something they didn't want us to see? Why should information be any different?'

A year after *Inherent Vice*'s publication, the remarkableness of the fact that no one *did* make it illegal or at least impose centralised control, despite efforts by the Clinton administration in the early 1990s, was illustrated by WikiLeaks' releasing thousands of US diplomatic emails and a series of broadly based hacking attacks on financial websites.

I also can't help noticing Pynchon's inclusion of multiple conversations about Gilligan.

The hippies came back from the boondocks, often chastened by their attempts to create and maintain harmonious new societies from scratch. Many got involved in the San Francisco Bay Area's growing computer underground, forming organisations like the People's Computer Company and Homebrew Computer Club, and ultimately Apple (whose Stephen Wozniak was a founder member of the Homebrew Club).

Through the 70s, processors got cheaper and machines smaller. Some were sold in kit form, like the Radio Shack TRS-80 and Altair 8800, which boasted just 256 *bytes* of memory (roughly one ten-millionth of the memory in my low-end Apple laptop), but cost just $395 and drew so many orders that the small manufacturer from Albuquerque, New Mexico, couldn't keep up. In 1977, Wozniak and Jobs launched the Apple II to such enthusiasm that bumbling IBM, tech's own Elmer Fudd, was forced to reverse its previous stance and ramp up its own production of PCs. When the Apple Macintosh arrived in 1984, it was accompanied by a dramatic TV ad directed by Ridley Scott and based on George Orwell's *1984*, in which IBM was cast as Big Brother and Apple the rebel liberator. The slogan at the end read: 'On January 24 Apple Computer will introduce the Macintosh. And you will see why 1984 won't be like *1984*.' Back then, anyone suggesting that Apple might one day be the largest corporation on earth, or that the CEO of this largest corporation, Steve Jobs, might one day cite dropping acid as 'one of the two or three most important things' he had done in his life – as the *New York Times* writer John Markoff claims in his entertaining history of the personal computing industry, *What the Dormouse*

Said – would have been considered one chip short of a motherboard.

With the appearance of personal computing, pressure grew for a more democratic online network. The ARPAnet was accessible only through machines belonging to Department of Defense contractors: websites cost upwards of $100,000 per annum to maintain. Plans had long existed to pass the network into private hands, but the established telecom companies saw no future in owning the internet: AT&T reportedly formed a committee and debated the issue for months, only to reject it as 'incompatible' with their existing business interests. Not until 1981 did democratisation begin in earnest, with the National Science Foundation (NSF)-funded launch of CSNET, a network connecting university computer science departments. In 1986, CSNET was superseded by a more general academic network called NSFNET, which quickly established itself as the backbone of the modern internet; a spine to which the various public and private networks could connect.

The first online business transaction is said to have involved a quantity of dope shipped between students at MIT and Stanford circa 1971, but legal commerce was officially banned by the NSF until 1991. There were still no pictures or graphics and there was no surfing, because browsers were not yet conceived of: neither was there a way of moving seamlessly between sites and networks, because there was no organising mechanism. All the same, this early online idyll seemed magical to those few who had found it, usually by word of mouth, and the first people to recognise its social power were the former flower children. In 1984, Stewart Brand started the *Whole Earth Software Catalog* and the next year the *Whole Earth 'Lectronic Link*, known as The WELL and by most accounts the first *virtual* community of ordinary citizens.

The WELL was an early example of a BBS (short for Bulletin Board Service), on which members dialled into a central server using a local phone line and modem. Once there, you could upload and download free software created by peers, read news of interest to the community, post messages on message boards and chat real-time in a selection of themed chat rooms. Strictly speaking, this was not the internet: The WELL was not intrinsically connected to anything else and, because it relied on domestic phone lines, most users were local to the San Francisco area, a disproportionate number being 'Deadheads', meaning Grateful Dead fans. In essence, the BBSs functioned as mini-webs of their own, testing the idea of the self-organising online society and finding that it worked ... that people had a tendency not just to join, but to *immerse* themselves in these pulsating collections of mind, and that the lack of physical presence was not just acceptable, but alluring.

For some of these early colonists, the internet and BBSs were tools for finding people with similar niche interests or for exchanging information unmediated by conventional news media. Others, however, saw something more esoteric, even *spiritual* when they peered through the screen. Kevin Kelly, a former *Whole Earth Catalog* editor and digital evangelist who would edit the era-defining cyberculture magazine *Wired* when it launched in 1993, looks back at the shift from counterculture to cyberculture and says: 'What was attractive about that? It was virtual. For me it was like an out-of-body experience, which was always what it had been about for me – not LSD, but out-of-body experiences. And here was an out-of-body experience you could have whenever you wanted.'

A pause.

'And people would *respect* you and not consider you crazy.'

Nonetheless, the person who got around to naming this intriguing new space was not a geek or a scientist, but a writer, and his vision hinted at something more complex and ambiguous than conventionally imagined. In his 1984 novel *Neuromancer*, William Gibson saw:

A consensual hallucination …

graphic representation of data abstracted from the banks of every computer in the human system …

lines of light ranged in the nonspace of the mind, clusters and constellations of data. Like city lights,

receding.

5

The 90s began in a headlong rush of change and event. In the dying weeks of 1989, the planet's political chemistry was transformed by the fall of the Berlin Wall and end of the Cold War; three months later a vast TV audience watched Nelson Mandela stride free of Victor Verster Prison in South Africa after twenty-seven years' incarceration, knowing that the Apartheid system of governance through racial segregation was effectively over. Within a further year, US tanks were rolling through Iraq as part of the first Gulf War; in 1992, Americans chose to elect their first Baby Boomer president, the blow-dried sax-tickling arch pragmatist Bill Clinton, just as the nation pulled out of recession. The birth of the World Wide Web in 1990 went all but unnoticed.

In a curious, freakonomic sort of way, the development that would have the profoundest effect on New York – and on Josh Harris and the Early True Believers – was one of the most indirect: the fall of the Berlin Wall and subsequent collapse of Soviet communism. Work had begun on the wall in August 1961, a few months after Josh and I were both born, and it had stood as the most surreal symbol of a very real socio-economic schism ever since – between a system which trusted the Market to create and distribute wealth in a broadly rational, just, efficient manner (capitalism), and another which didn't, so placed these responsibilities under the paternal wing of the State (communism). Two decades and a credit crunch later, it's hard to keep a straight face when describing either ideal, but the point is this: for half a century, these two economic systems, for all their multifarious faults, stood as living rebukes to each other, provided an ideological challenge and, in the world of *realpolitik*, competition.

But the collapse of communism handed capitalism and its evangelists a sense of moral authority that was harder to reign in or resist. Did meddling busybodies – governments, regulators – really want to hamstring the triumphant Market and its all-conquering generals, demonstrably the *actual* inheritors of the earth (because where were the meek now)? Politics all but disappeared as Democrats like Clinton and social democrats like Chancellor Gordon Brown in the UK fell over themselves to laud the contributions of Wall Street and the City of London to their respective economies. For the next decade, oversight of the finance sector would be minimal. The academic Francis Fukuyama caused a sizeable stir with an essay and book proclaiming 'The End of History', meaning the end of our ideological evolution as a species: the decisive triumph of Western liberal democracy and its creative engine, the market. Even for those who thought the first two syllables of Mr Fukuyama's name a fair conceptual summation of his idea, the conceit was a hard one to challenge in the short term, and would get harder while people were making money and feeling rich. A perfect storm of hubris was gathering.

Then came the web.

A stone's throw from Wall Street, the Early True Believers had seen something almost no one else had. Early in 1989, Tim Berners-Lee, an English scientist working at the European Organization for Nuclear Research (CERN) in Geneva, taking note of the fact that all information on a computer hard drive, or network of hard drives – travelling as it does at the speed of light – is effectively equidistant, had proposed using *hypertext* to link sites and documents into a web of knowledge, allowing movement from one to another to another to another at the click of a mouse. Working with a Belgian colleague, Robert Cailliau, he spent two and a half years developing the necessary set of protocols and software tools, before releasing them to what there was of an online public on 6 August 1991. The following year, he uploaded the first photo, of CERN's in-house spoof doo-wop group, Les Horribles Cernettes – his choice an indication of how little moment he attached to the event.

Keep in mind that nothing about the web was inevitable and not everyone approved: the *Computer Lib* activist Ted Nelson, who'd begun work on his own global knowledge bank, Project Xanadu, back in 1960 and coined the words 'hypertext' and 'virtuality' not long afterwards, complained that the web 'trivialised' his team's original hypertext model by offering no management of contents or copyright, and that in mimicking the properties of an obsolete technology, paper, it lacked sophistication. All perfectly true. And as the *Hitchhiker's Guide to the Galaxy* author Douglas Adams pointed out, 'www' is the only acronym which takes longer to say than the name it represents.

Here's something important, though: the terms 'internet' and 'World Wide Web' (or web) are often used as though interchangeable, but they're not. The internet is a series of physical or wireless connections between computers, a *network*, whereas the web is a system of organising information within that network – essentially an *application*. It's quite possible – and in the early days was the norm – for a website or network to be on the internet, but not linked to the web (or indeed anything outside of itself). Access would be via a tortuous numeric 'IP address', which could not be searched or sleuthed online, so had to be known to the user. When Berners-Lee uploaded that first picture in '92, there were still only three Internet Service Providers

(ISPs) offering access to the web in the US, one of which was The WELL, while in the UK there was *one*. Berners-Lee had given the world something incalculably valuable: the ability not just to connect to the internet, but to *surf* it by clicking on links.

Not that more than a few thousand people did. 'Dial-up' connections via modems and standard phone lines were slow, unreliable and expensive, with drab, text-only pages taking up to half an hour to draw, often at the second or third attempt: pictures would pop up in a separate window, while sound and video were distant dreams. Officially, the public was still unwelcome, leaving a handful of hobbyists and hackers to prise open this new frontier, loosely policed by authorities which were unsure why anyone but uber-nerds would want to connect in the first place. Cliff Stanford, who set up the UK's first ISP, Demon Internet, in July 1992 and could boast only a couple of thousand members twelve months later, remembered the first year with amusement. 'The question we always got was, "OK, I'm connected … what do I do now?" It was one of the most common questions on our support line. We would answer with, "What do you want to do? Do you want to send an email?" "Well, I don't know anyone with an email address." People got connected, but they didn't know what was meant to happen next.'

All the same, there was a magic in sharing information and debate – mostly at night in the UK, when phone lines were cheaper – with people who could be anywhere on the planet; who, like you, shared a secret. Because the general public knew nothing about this new space, which was still hidden and hard to find.

Some early users came via wired subcultures. Jason Chervokas, a journalist who went on to found the New York listings site @NY, saw the net demonstrated at college, where it bored his peers but entranced him. Still the medium only properly made sense when he – a jazz buff – found a group dedicated to the

Blue Note record label on the Usenet network. 'I mean, there were record company guys, academics, musicians, fans, and really high-level discussion,' he says. 'It was obvious that this kind of community was going to grow.'

Perhaps because of the difficulty in connecting, the dominant ethos online remained countercultural: was less about what *was* than what *might be* – a vision of something better. The in-house wired journal in the US was *Mondo 2000,* which walked an edgy line between sci-fi-fed cyberpunk and slacker drug culture, and whose editor called himself R. U. Sirius. With what seemed like hyperbole at the time, Sirius warned the New York writer Douglas Rushkoff, one of the first to report back from the virtual frontline, to 'oppose it if you want . . . but you're already existing in relation to the datastream like the polyp to the coral reef . . . there's just no getting away from it.'

Re-reading *Cyberia,* the book Rushkoff wrote about his travels among the cyberpunks of America and 'zippies' (self-styled 'hippies with computers') of Britain in 1994, it's at times comically clear that he'd drunk deep of the cyber Kool-Aid himself. He lectures in media at New School university in Manhattan now. In an uptown diner, he'll shrug and chuckle when reminded of the book. 'What you have to remember is that nothing was happening for profit online then, and as a result, those of us who were there imagined the spread of the internet meaning the spread of a new co-operative global culture,' he reminds me. 'And people who were having these experiences online were having such a good time that they really wanted to spread the word around.'

When the Clinton administration tried to establish surveillance rights over all electronic traffic via a so-called 'clipper chip' which featured an access key known only to state authorities, cyberworld fought back by distributing a free encryption system called PGP ('pretty good privacy'), so rendering the Clinton plans unworkable. At the forefront of the fight was the

Electronic Frontier Foundation, co-founded by the Lotus software designer Mitch Kapor and former Grateful Dead lyricist and early WELL advocate John Perry Barlow. Overt commerce was still banned by the NSF, so software and content in this virtual idyll was for the most part free, posted by idealistic developers for the good of the 'online community' as a whole – and this ornery, anarchic tendency would remain, all the way through music industry crushing 'peer-to-peer' file-share programs like Gnutella and Napster in the late 90s, to Facebook and WikiLeaks in the new century. Online etiquette and protocols were difficult even for practised insiders to define. Of his own efforts, John Perry Barlow said: 'I'm trying to build a working scale model of a fog bank out of bricks. I'm using building material that is utterly unsuited to the representation of the thing I'm trying to describe.'

One of Pseudo's first freelance producers, Marc Scarpa, an art school grad who was born in 1969 and had been online since stumbling into his school computer room at the age of nine, recalls the hostility which greeted paid-for internet services like Prodigy and AOL and CompuServe when they arrived, explaining: 'I think the reason those early net guys were so against CompuServe was because to them the internet was a very Utopian environment, where you could exchange information and ideas for free with one another. And it was all hacker IDs; you would have pseudonyms. People were being clandestine and mysterious, I guess in part because there were so many folks engaged in what either was or became illegal activity.'

He remembers chatting with Apple's Jobs and Wozniak, who were known both as 'guys on the bulletin boards' and for peddling 'blue and black boxes' which enabled users to make free phone calls to most parts of the US. 'It was absolutely a counterculture. To be online felt special,' he concludes. 'One of the things you heard all the time was Stewart Brand's dictum that "information wants to be free".'

Usually overlooked is the fact that Brand had added 'and it also wants to be very expensive'. Either way, the coming Age of Information found a public voice in January 1993, when a politically conservative oddball named Louis Rossetto finally overcame several years of scepticism on the part of investors and published the first issue of *Wired* magazine. The galvanic thrill of that maiden issue is hard to overstate, with its cover blazing a promise from the English revolutionary turned US founding father Thomas Paine that, 'We have it in our power to begin the world over again.' Inside, Rossetto declared Paine a 'patron saint' of his new magazine, along with the brilliant Canadian media theorist Marshall McLuhan – summoner of the phrases 'global village' and 'the medium is the message' (not to mention my own favourite McLuhanism, 'the answer is always inside the problem, not outside'). Opposite the contents page, the proprietor's iconoclastic mission statement declared: 'It's finally time to embrace the future with optimism again, in the realization that this peaceful, inevitable revolution isn't a problem, but an opportunity to build a new and better civilization for ourselves and our children … Our first instruction to our writers: amaze us. Our second: report back from the future about what's coming.' Elsewhere he claimed: 'Mass media in the Twentieth Century destroyed community. It is single-handedly responsible for destroying neighborhoods and families and creating mass society.'

Wired was part of a revolution aimed at changing all that. And yet the remarkable feature of Rossetto's 'new society in wild metamorphosis' is that the internet wasn't central to it: his 'revolution' was digital *in general*, with the net scarcely mentioned until page 105, when a weary-sounding columnist described a virtual desert defined by bland sites and '*awful*' writing.

* * *

The Early True Believers of Manhattan benefited from the media's net-blindness through the first half of the 1990s. With little interest or interference from outside, these young New Yorkers, nearly all in their early twenties, had time and space to rehearse their ideas in peace – time and space that the popularisation of the web would, perversely, deny future generations. The continuing recession helped, too: the city had leaked almost half a million jobs and evolved no new industry since TV moved west in the 1950s, so lessening pressure to rush into a career. According to one proto-dotcommer, 'Anyone with half a brain who graduated when we did wouldn't have wanted to be part of that *Bright Lights, Big City*, asshole bankers in power-ties scene. And when we graduated, it was that or nothing.' Another, Rufus Griscom, later co-creator of the erotica site Nerve.com and an influential voice on the scene, likened the atmosphere to 'Prague before the Velvet Revolution ... there was something attractive about being an intellectual dissident, especially in the aftermath of the 80s. *Not* making money was a symbol of your integrity.'

As a breed the ETBs bore little resemblance to other early online populations. Most had degrees in the arts and social sciences from reputable universities, then found themselves in New York doing things their parents wouldn't have chosen for them, trying to survive in theatre or film or the visual arts, or playing in bands while slinging coffee or working bars. A few key players were veterans of New York University's Interactive Telecommunications graduate programme (ITP), run from a Greenwich Village loft since 1983 by the filmmaker and academic Red Burns. Generally born in or around 1966, the year work began on the World Trade Center, these downtown 'technobohemians' were classic Gen Xers, forged in the consumerist wasteland of the 80s and with their barely conscious hunger for something substantial to believe in disguised as cynicism. Also unlike other info-tech populations, they were natural communicators and frequently even female.

In fact, the early connectors were primarily women. Stacy Horn had been working as an analyst for Mobil when she was offered the chance to take a graduate degree, choosing Burns's Interactive Telecommunications Program because the word 'telecommunications' suggested a relevance to what she was already doing – despite there being none. Unable to believe her luck, by 1990 she was an enthusiastic member of the WELL bulletin board community, until frustration at not being able to meet her mostly West Coast-based online circle tipped her into action. She called her East Coast BBS Echo and laughs when asked if friends understood what she was doing. 'No!' she says. 'First of all, I couldn't get financing, because I couldn't convince *anyone* that the internet was going to be big. And not only would they not finance me, they made fun of me. And I still say I was not a visionary to see this: anyone who was online for two seconds saw the same thing. Everyone else who was already doing it '*got it*' – it's just that if you hadn't done it, it was very difficult to see.'

Horn points out that plenty of people were online by then, but most were men working in the fields of technology, maths and science.

> And I thought, 'Those people are already online: let me address the *other* people.' So the first journalists who wrote about us described us as this electronic salon of artists and writers and filmmakers and poets and stuff, which we weren't – *yet*. But the fact that they described us as that meant that I started getting phone calls from those people, saying, 'What's *this*, how do I get online?' And we grew from there. It was a small group, nearly all New Yorkers, and none of us cared about money – it was all about this wonderful world that we were going to build. More like a religion than anything else.

One of Echo's first members was a fresh-faced Californian skater girl named Jaime Levy, who'd been attracted to New York by the music of Sonic Youth and the East Village street-lit of Burroughs, McInerny, Easton Ellis, Tama Janowitz – a hedonistic association she would later rue. Drawn to NYU's film school by the work of recent graduates Spike Lee and Jim Jarmusch, she stumbled across details of Burns's ITP course at a library in San Francisco and a chill ran up her spine. 'And I just got on a plane and went out there and walked into the school without telling them, this *kid* walking into school and just saying, "Where do I sign up?"'

Burns arranged a scholarship and Levy was in. She began by specialising in multimedia, particularly the interactive CD-ROMs which allowed books and magazines to be presented electronically on home computers (and looked exciting until the web broke out), then found Echo and other ETBs like Marisa Bowe, according to whom, 'We bonded over being punk-rock techie girls, the only girls out there who loved nothing more than to be alone and online all night.' In a 'pre-Windows' environment, Echo acquired an almost mystical edge, being 'just text against this deep blue space background'.

Bowe went on to edit Word.com, an early online magazine and Silicon Alley talisman, while Levy became the first true Alley celebrity, an edgy web designer who was profiled in *Time* and *New York* magazine and on TV at a time when most websites (and their creators, for that matter) looked like they'd been styled by committees of Albanian fishermen. As these connections deepened and spread, Levy began to run 'Cyberslacker' gatherings in a borrowed Avenue A loft, bringing in DJs to play the tech-heavy rave sounds she heard on visits to London – Orbital, Underworld, The Future Sound of London, The Prodigy – while guests traded ideas and taught each other HyperText Markup Language, HTML, the framework for web pages. Named for the Gen X honorific 'slacker', no one present was dreaming of fortunes, but everyone was excited. One speaks of there being 'something about the hypnotic pull of the internet which turned us all into apostles', adding that, 'for the first two or three years there was nothing else I could talk about.' Another speaks of 'this poststructuralist wet dream', where 'you name something and it comes into existence!'

The Cyberslacker house joke was still, 'This is going to be bigger than CB radio!' On New Year's Day 1994, there were thought to be 623 websites and a tiny enchanted cadre of people with access to them. Something had changed, though, and was about to make itself felt in ways no one had foreseen. At the National Center for Supercomputing Applications in Illinois, a pair of students – without the faintest notion that they might be doing anything important – had designed a 'web browser' which would shrink the world more, and more rapidly, than had the airplane, the ship, the wheel.

They called their new tool 'Mosaic'. Cyberspace had found its compass.

The curious thing about cyberspace in those early days is that everyone who gazed into it saw something different, and yet the same – because everyone saw a version of themselves. Just as hippies saw *freedom*, writers *magic*, cyberslackers *meaning*, so switched-on members of the mainstream saw this new medium through the prism of their own dreams and fears. Thus lucky Bill Clinton's Vice President, Al Gore, whose senator father had played a major role in creating the interstate highway system in the 1950s, came into office championing the 'information superhighway', while the cable companies saw an exciting route to video on demand . . . the TV companies a threat . . . marketeers a fresh way to pester consumers, media conglomerates like Time Warner a newly efficient means of distributing the content they already produced.

And the real killer: in common with *Wired*'s Louis Rossetto, none of them saw the World Wide Web as essential to their online visions. Gore's worthy infobahn anticipated cable-style ADSL and ISDN technology, while Time Warner's autocratic CEO Jerry 'if he wants your opinion, he'll give it to you' Levin committed billions of dollars to building the corporation's own proprietorial net, to be known as Full Service Network. Remarkably, even the early online services like AOL, Prodigy and CompuServe failed to offer access to the World Wide Web until 1994–5, with Microsoft's MSN service treating it like the mad aunt in the cupboard until 1996, by which time Bill Gates's reluctance to embrace the web looked little short of *cute*.

Yet Gates's resistance, like Levin's covetousness, Gore's grandiosity, Rupert Murdoch's suspicion ('How are we going to make money from this?'), is easy to understand. Business was about ownership and control, and the web's design made these things impossible. In the language of cybernetics, it was 'distributed' rather than 'centralised', meaning that if you tried to censor or block a piece of information, the information simply routed around you. And nothing about this modus had been inevitable: had AT&T accepted their invitation to run the ARPAnet back in 1971 – effectively to 'own' it at an early stage – the nascent medium would have evolved differently. But when *they* looked at the internet, they saw something chaotic and disruptive, which threatened the value of the investments they'd already made. Indeed, as awareness of the internet grew in the early 1990s, Red Burns of the NYU's ITP couldn't help but revel in the confusion it caused, exalting: 'I think it's one of the most wonderful ironies of all time that, because of the Cold War and because of ARPAnet, we got ourselves a decentralised system that cannot be centralised … I can remember in the early days hearing men at conferences saying, "Who runs the internet? I want to talk to the man who runs the internet!"'

And why wouldn't they? Until September 1993, it was still possible to believe *anything* about the future form of the net.

That month, the University of Illinois students Marc Andreessen and Eric Bina released Mosaic on to the web. Motivated primarily by irritation with existing navigation tools, the pair had begun work on the project just months after Tim Berners-Lee uploaded that first picture, in December 1992, with dreams of money or fame no nearer their minds than a date with Cyndi Lauper.

Free to download and owned by the university rather than its creators, Mosaic was a 'graphical' web browser which allowed pages to be searched without recourse to lengthy coded 'addresses' and enabled colour pictures to be displayed alongside text instead of appearing in a separate window as before. Not only did Mosaic make the web friendlier and easier to surf on a current of curiosity and intuition, but uploading documents, images and web links became easy, leading to a more open, interactive experience and deeper sense of *connection*. A version for UNIX, the 'open source' computer spod's operating system of choice, appeared in April 1993, followed by adaptations for Apple Mac and Windows PC in September – at which point figures for web use start to rise,

RISE,

then *rocket*.

Between 1994 and 1997, statistics compiled by the research company Netcraft show the number of websites rising from 623 to over one million. The Silicon Alley key venture capitalist Jerry Colonna is typical in recalling his introduction to Mosaic as if it were a first sexual encounter or psychedelic experience. Tipped off by a fellow editor at *Information Week* magazine, he went to the company IT department, connected to the internet and downloaded his first browser, with which he 'looked at the whole internet in about ten minutes'.

And it was one of those moments where I said, 'Jesus, this is the future. This is it. Forget the deal we're about to do with

America Online – this is *really* different.' So while all these big companies were planning their proprietary online services, we started planning for a web-only edition for that fall. We launched in November of '94, and it was like a *comet*. I remember being at the COMDEX computer expo in Vegas at the time, and the theme song we picked for our show booth was 'It's the End of the World as We Know It' by REM. Just playing it constantly. And I remember the print salespeople coming up to us and saying, 'This is terrible, I can't believe you're doing this – you're giving our content away for free.' And I said, 'Either we do it to ourselves, or it's gonna be done. Just get used to it. Print is over.'

Two months later Colonna skipped out of the company to work with CMG@Ventures, the first 'pure-play' internet investment firm. Immediate problems were a) trying to explain to people *what this was* and b) finding anything to invest in. But that was part of the fun. And he knew it would change.

As to the cyberslackers, Jaime Levy had already begun to notice her parties being crashed by staff from Sony, Random House, Time Warner ... Old Media looking for a way into this shimmering New Media realm, straining to see a route to profit. As one of the few people who understood HTML ('How long does it take to learn? About an hour!'), Levy was suddenly in demand and was designing a home page for IBM in 1993 when a workmate drew her attention to Mosaic.

Within seconds she knew that this was what she and her cyberslacker friends had been waiting for. 'All at once you could create a website and anyone could access it. Now there was an open network, with colour graphics and the potential for adding music.'

'They showed it to me and it was like being hit by lightning: *finally it's here!*'

She quit her IBM job and set about preparing for the future.

6

Late in the day, New York brick acquires a wilting-rose blush, a *glow*, as if radiating twilight into the city. I see people scattering home or out into the night; a yellow rain of taxis gliding down Houston then jinking right into SoHo. And looming over the junction, the painted façade of 600 Broadway, windows dark, empty but for memory, cityscape mural a little faded now but essentially the same as the day Josh stood in this precise spot and gazed at the home of his new company back in June '94. He'd yomped in and offered 30 per cent more than the landlord sought for a still dirt-cheap long lease on the top floor, elated to find such a beautiful space in such a central location – even basted with dust and gunk as it was. Afterwards, while he lingered outside, a woman he knew but had always considered out of his league stopped for a chat and left seeming to look at him a little differently. He stared up at the window by Liberty's crown, *his* window from this point on, and felt something that in all his thirty-three years he'd never felt before. *Sexy*. As proprietor of Pseudo Programs, he would get suddenly better looking, a tougher truth to live with than you might think.

A week after I got back from Awassa, a bolt from the blue: the ex-Pseudo presenter and programmer JudgeCal was found dead in his apartment. He'd lain alone for ninety-six hours before his landlord forced entry to find a body that was already decomposed enough as to be identifiable only from tattoos. Word emerged like a point of light, then broadened and took on its own life, with cause of death and the whereabouts of Cal's family still unknown. Something poignant about the fact that, despite Pseudo having folded eight years previously, Josh was listed as next of kin.

Cal seemed to embody the spirit of Pseudo better than anyone. An intimidating presence to those who didn't know him, all spiky blond hair and body art and gruff cod-Brooklyn no-shit front, he'd fetched up in Manhattan in 1984 and taken his New York name from the British comic Judge Dredd, but beyond that no one appeared to know much about him – save that he'd been born Calvin Chamberlain and was estranged from his family. A friend and supposed former lover of the Blondie singer Debbie Harry, he knew everyone and could get you into any club in the city; had little formal education but was whip smart and good with technology. He was adored at Pseudo and as the point of light became a shaft, then a flood, there was an outpouring of email grief, screeds of names reeling through an online thread which multiplied and accelerated like a virus daily, many of which I remembered from my Awassa nights, others from articles in *Vanity Fair* or *New York* magazine . . .

. . . Robert Galinsky. Adeo Ressi. Jon 'Feedbuck' Buckley . . . Marc Scarpa, Tony Asnes, Janice Girlbomb, Missy Galore, Jess Zaino, Josh White, Mame McCutchin Betty Wasserman Michael Auerbach V. Owen Bush JeffGompertz JohnChristopherMorton SpyroPoulosNancySmithdavidbohrmanalexarcadiazeroboyand ymorrisjacquestege . . .

and on.

Josh copied me in and supplied a running commentary on the characters and nuances of their connections to each other, as if describing a TV soap. He seemed amused more than grief-stricken, incongruously detached given the nature of the event.

Only much, much later would it occur to me that the *relationships* were what counted for Josh: that the people, in themselves, might hold little interest for him. More than anything, he was curious as to the cause of death, refusing to believe it an accident, and when confidential news arrived that the cause was auto-erotic asphyxiation he was fascinated. It was Cal's ring he suspected Tanya Corrin of having worn on the *Tuna Heaven* boat trip.

Cal had presented a Pseudo show called *JudgeCal's High Weirdness*, in which he and sidekick Laura 'Thugz' Foy explored the darker reaches of the psyche and the web, treating them as aspects of the same thing. They got lips and nipples pierced live to camera and ran features on the likes of the 'Toecutter', who removed parts of his own body as performance (in this case part of a finger, separated with a hammer and chisel). They also held surprisingly candid discussions on subjects ranging from conspiracy theories to string theory to the Y2K bug and online porn, stuff you could never get even on cable TV. Cal's *New York Times* obituary notes that, 'Parts of Mr Chamberlain's life sound like scenes from a Jay McInerny novel,' but the truth is that McInerny, for all his brilliance, wouldn't have had the smarts to create a character like Cal, or a place like Pseudo. One experienced former producer laments that the company 'was on to something' with JudgeCal and *High Weirdness*: that if only they'd been able to survive long enough for the streaming technology to catch up with them, something special might have been achieved. The *Terminator*-esque vest he wore to report for Pseudo on the 2000 Republican National Convention, which was equipped with a webcam, headset and a keypad, is now held at the Smithsonian Institution.

David Bohrman, Pseudo's valedictory CEO and now Senior Vice President and Washington Bureau Chief at CNN, couldn't be more different from Cal as a person, but considered him talented enough to take to CNN. 'He didn't do it as well as he should have, and I just think he didn't want to be outed,'

Bohrman tells me. 'I don't think he had ever filed his taxes; he was sort of "off the grid" as a person, and he felt very uneasy being on real television. But at the convention, his interviews with people like Newt Gingrich were spectacular.'

Bohrman contributed money toward Cal's funeral (as apparently did Debbie Harry) and employed CNN researchers to find the Chamberlain family. He still thinks the work Cal and Pseudo did at the Republican Convention in 2000 was groundbreaking.

I watch the online assemblage gather and form little breakaway groups in an attempt to preserve Cal's dignity and keep some darker aspects of his life private. Suspicion greets post-Pseudo friends, whether from his beloved Burning Man festival or the art underground, some of whom are thought to have had a negative influence on him. There appears to be an unspoken assumption that Cal, for all his charisma and intelligence, never found anything to replace Pseudo – that his home and family were *there*; that this is true to an extent for them all and so in some nebulous sense, he died for them all. One of his last general communications appears to have been a round-robin email which read:

> All
> Thought you might get a kick out of this. Josh is at it again (or art it again . . . lol . . . did I really say that?)
> Josh Harris: 'Pseudo was a fake company.':
> http://www.boingboing.net/2008/06/26/josh-harris-pseudo-w.html
> hope things are grand on your end!
> Cal.

Josh, who persists in refusing to believe Cal's death pure accident, would wonder whether the 'fake company' article was a trigger of sorts.

In a famous essay entitled 'Here is New York', the *New Yorker* writer E. B. White claimed that 'No one should come to New York unless he is willing to be lucky.' Which is curious, because I think of New York as the one place on earth where you know for sure that luck will never suffice. By most measures, Cal was very lucky indeed. But still not lucky enough.

* * *

Josh Harris was the earliest of the Early True Believers, even if he wasn't quite *of* them.

Born on 5 May 1961, the day Alan Shepard became the first American in (physical) space, he came from a muddled middle class Jewish family on the West Coast and was recognised as a bright underachiever at high school until the final year, when his B grades abruptly became As and he landed a place at the University of California, San Diego (UCSD)'s rigorous Revelle College.

Although Revelle took a Renaissance approach to education, it specialised in science and engineering and Josh, ever the late developer, took a while to adjust. He spent his first year on probation and struggled all the way into the second term of his second year, at which point he found his way into a communications class and his mind seemed to ignite – to become agile and suddenly sure, and to see things his peers didn't; to *feel* the motion of the world around him. Up to then, life had been chaotic and unpredictable, but here was something he instinctively understood. Part-way into his course, he won a full graduate scholarship at the University of Southern California's Annenberg School for Communication for the 1984–5 academic year. Significantly, UCSD was one of the first nodes on the CSNET, the publicly funded network linking university computer science departments that didn't have access to the ARPAnet.

At UCSD a rebellious streak appeared, as Josh revelled in

his reputation as campus party planner and thorn in order's side. In the spring of 1981, he was barred from taking office as duly-elected student body president for having overspent his fifty dollar campaign budget by ninety-three cents, one of only two occasions on which he will admit to having cried. Later, when the university chancellor, Richard Atkinson, decided to sell a tract of land between the Revelle campus and a popular beach, forcing students to walk around it, Josh took revenge by starting a Greek fraternity system – an American college affectation which he, with his *National Lampoon's* worldview, detested only slightly less than Atkinson did. But that margin of extra tolerance was sweet. A year later, he launched a campus good-time journal called *The Koala*, after the unofficial university mascot. Both innovations were designed to be disruptive; destabilising to anyone covetous of convention or the status quo.

Then there was the postgraduate Masters degree at Annenberg, which Josh didn't finish. I was surprised to find one of his old teachers, Professor Bill Dutton, now working in England as fellow of Balliol College and head of the Oxford Internet Institute: still more surprised that Dutton remembered his former student so well after twenty-five years.

'Oh yeah – I do!' he exclaimed when I paid him a visit. 'It was so outstanding, because he came to me when the PC was just in its early stages. The Apple was 1979 or something like that. Same with videotex [the first public interactive information service, developed by the BBC]. And Josh put this all together with video conferencing. And for his course paper he wanted to do, not a regular exam or paper, he wanted to build a multimedia computer.'

'Really? In a serious way?' I laughed.

At which Dutton nodded, still smiling.

'Yeah, really. And I couldn't get my colleagues to go along with it. And I think that's one of the things that frustrated him with the university – you know, "It's got to be on an exam paper," and so on. I mean, here at Oxford I think it'd be even harder. Can you imagine substituting a project like that?'

I glanced out of the window, at the ancient stone walls and spires surrounding the institute. So he stood out even back then?

'Oh yes. He was a very creative and courageous young man, who had a real imaginative vision about where things were going. And it must have been very frustrating, being at university and having these ideas, which were well in advance of his contemporaries, then not being allowed to express them.'

Had the academic not gone on sabbatical to the UK as a Fulbright Scholar in 1985–6, he thought he might have dissuaded the department's star pupil from dumping his few possessions, selling his shabby '73 Volvo for $900 and flying to New York. There again, he concluded, Josh was never easily deflected once he'd made a decision: schools are hard to build for people like him.

New York burned bright-lights-big-city, pre-Black Friday excess in 1985, but not for Josh, who took a job at a market research sweatshop, working long hours for poor pay. After a year, he knew enough to leave and set up Jupiter Communications in his tiny midtown apartment, assembling obscure data and using it to write reports on how people were and would be using electronic media, until by the early 90s he was the New York media's go-to guy for intelligence on this little-understood field. Unlike the other ETBs, Josh wore a suit and ran a successful company, was in his late rather than mid-twenties; looked and sounded more like the journalists who came to see him than his pierced and excitable younger peers did. He noticed that the media moved as a herd and attention was cumulative ... that the more he talked, the more he was asked to talk; the more his company grew.

The research backed his preternatural sense of how our virtual selves might evolve, of what we'd do with the deep blue space behind the screen. In 1990 he produced a report on the French Minitel, a text-based online service accessed through phone lines and launched in 1982, five years after British videotex. By far the most versatile and successful pre-web online system, the Minitel supplied subscribers with dedicated, computer-like terminals through which they could buy, book travel, get news, exchange messages and, almost as an afterthought, 'chat'. Rehearsing many of the issues that would accrue to the web, Minitel's adult chat rooms sparked a debate about pornography and in 1986 students used it to co-ordinate a strike. Businesses sprang up, many of which were ill-conceived and destined to fail.

Josh's genius was to find the man in charge of statistical information about what happened on the Minitel – about what people *did* when they got online. No one had done this before, but Josh followed the thirty-odd franc per hour levies until he knew where each one went ... and the figures were unequivocal, confirming his weird intuition that by far the most time was spent not reading or consuming, but connecting to other people via user IDs known as 'pseudos'. Written up as 'Revenue Streams of Mass Market Videotex: A Case Study of the French Minitel System', the report sold well, with British Telecom being one of his most enthusiastic customers. It also established Jupiter Communications as the leader in its field, even though this was the last report he would write himself.

Through the Minitel, Josh had seen a different future opening up, one for which he might have been specially adapted. For a few months he felt as though the blood in his veins had turned to electricity. He began the task of recruiting senior staff to replace him at Jupiter.

* * *

Josh describes the four years between the Minitel report and the time he left Jupiter in 1994 as 'lonely'. He was now recognised as pre-eminent in his field; was regularly quoted on the finance pages of *The New York Times*, *Washington Post* and *Wall Street Journal* and was running a successful conference business on the side. The path ahead was clear. All he had to do was keep his head down and hang on for the ride. But he couldn't.

The Jupiter man had glimpsed something too extraordinary to ignore, try as he might. While other ETBs approached the new medium of the internet with spangle-eyed optimism, he saw something more nuanced and ambiguous. Or perhaps, like them, he simply looked into it and saw his own reflection.

He started going to the cinema on his own three or four nights a week, allowing the projector's crisp clack to charm him away from himself the way a snake charmer's flute charms a cobra, drawing him into classics like *Cinema Paradiso*, *Diva*, *Jules et Jim* and *The Grapes of Wrath* in the dark at St Mark's Theatre in the East Village – a place where his mind could wander . . . until one night while watching *Double Indemnity* for the third or fourth time, he fell to meditating on his own situation and had a series of revelations.

The first revelation was that the people in front of him were all dead in real life, yet still living on or through the screen; that they were in effect *ghosts* and that these ghosts were the only enduring life forms; that being seen and recorded for posterity was therefore 'a matter of life and death'. And in that moment he felt something extraordinary happen, as the screen became for him what the river Styx was to ancient Greeks – a bridge to the afterlife. He considered this thought for a while.

Then he went back to the movie.

He celebrated his thirtieth birthday alone, in a bar close to the SoHo tenement he lived in by then. As drinkers chattered and played around him, he decided that after five years of building a business, he wanted some art and fun. He threw a couple of

Jupiter parties, first a 'Cybercouch' night at the Couch gallery, into which he tipped a stash of weed, a brass jazz band, some video cameras (a big deal at this early stage of the digital revolution) and three Minitel terminals, so allowing guests to meet virtually as well as in the flesh. All very well, until it became clear that the event could never sing with the guests he'd invited, who saw money/business/*opportoonidy* in everything up to and including his spectral cyber-vision. So the people came, but didn't 'get it' and when a second event fell flat, channels clogged by techno-nerds and straight businessmen, he knew it was time to trust his gut and move out. The newly formed Fox Network invited him to produce a tech show, but the project became a farce as he went in search of talent and content, because he wasn't part of that world either and had no way of gauging who or what would work. He was going to have to find another way. And the way he found was *Launder My Head* . . .

Which is why on the first working day of 1993, January 4, Josh fished in his desk drawer for a slip of paper he'd stashed under a bundle of documents. Jupiter had doubled in size the year before, even while its proprietor's focus wandered, and the slip contained the germ of an idea he'd had one day at the company's newly expanded office: a jingle and simple visual trope based on a man with a TV head, face inside the screen, accompanied by an insidiously catchy tune and the words 'launder my head/launder my head/launder-launder, launder-launder/launder my head . . .' Stupid-sounding, but with meaning for Josh. When he tries to insist that the six-minute computer animation he produced over eighteen months with his first employee, a brilliant programmer named Jacques Tege, amounts to a manifesto or oracular *vision*, 'my life's work at least until the present' (at one point claiming that the TV people were sent by the DMT-induced Ticklers, like the Book of Mormon to Joseph Smith), I'm not prepared to take him seriously. Another piece of meta-narrative, as though a life may be *composed*, like a book or a film, cased in story the way spent uranium is cased in steel to make it safe.

All the same, finished two years before the ground-breaking release of the computer-animated *Toy Story*, *Launder My Head* now looks an intriguing cyber art period piece, with the TV-headed people singing the jingle between call-and-response chants like (leader) 'come form with me'; (all) '*con-form* with me'– and the leader very clearly sporting the face of Josh. Impressive for having been made on a pair of Commodore Amiga machines at a time when 500MB of disc space cost $20,000, one Pseudite recalls admiring *Launder* once his initial mystification had worn off, before adding with a touch of amusement: 'But I didn't think it was something to build a whole company around. I didn't think it was an ethos.'

Pressed on whether there might be some retrospective shading of Josh's memory as to the significance of *Launder* to him back then, the Pseudite stops smiling and furrows his brow, as though even he can't quite believe it. 'No. That really was how he saw it I think. From the start.'

Remarkable as it seems, in the short term Josh was right. He used the 3D animation to win a contract to write chat software for Prodigy, still the largest online services provider. He then used this deal to leverage another more speculative one, to create and manage a selection of 'Pseudo Channel' chat rooms – the name taken from the 'pseudos' used on the Minitel – in return for 10 per cent of the $2.35 an hour customers paid to access them, with earnings to be set against an initial $200,000 advance.

It was like taking candy from a baby. Prodigy was owned by IBM and Sears, two of the most uptight organisations in America. Even the company's own head, Scott Kurnit, called it 'the most conservative, by-the-book, bureaucratic company I had ever seen' and felt sure that, had he not taken the wrong shaver attachment on a business trip prior to his job interview and thus been forced to cut off his beard, he would never have been hired. Accordingly, Prodigy had chat rooms with names like Macrame, Stamp Collecting, *Connecticut* (and no idea why their business was failing), until Josh came along with his studied grasp of what people wanted online, and rooms like The Bar . . . Late Night . . . Cindy's Chamber . . . Married and Looking. One early employee laughs as he asks: 'I mean, where do you want to be? I don't want to be in "Connecticut" – I wanna be in *Mary's Parlor*!'

Before long, 25 per cent of Prodigy's chat traffic was going through Josh's channel.

The deal was done in May '94, enabling Jupiter Interactive and its first few employees to move into 600 Broadway a month later. Following a complaint from Jupiter Communications' new management, the corporate ident changed to Pseudo Programs. I'll hear myriad estimates as to the income generated from the Prodigy deal, ranging from $150,000 to $1 million a month, the lowest of which turns out to be inflated by a factor of *five*. For the time being, money would be tight – even if only Josh knew quite how tight. But the company was up and running and the process of recruitment could begin.

7

Spyro Poulos wasn't someone to mess with. His Brooklyn accent alone could anodise steel. He played in bands and did rant poetry and thought the preppy nerd who approached him after a show was 'fucking nuts', literally 'insane'.

It wasn't just the flannel shirt and coffee-stained sneakers (Josh Harris spilled coffee *everywhere*) – or the fact that no one wore chinos to a hip art joint in 1993. Or that his hair bore all the hallmarks of having been styled by his mom. Poulos thought the man looked like the world's largest 12-year-old but then spoke like the Wizard of Oz's drug dealer and appeared to be offering a surreal-sounding job at a company which as far as the poet could tell didn't *actually* exist. Curious but sure the cat was a time-waster, he chose the roughest East Village dive he could think of in which to meet for a further pitch.

Poulos knew nothing of the internet but was quickly entranced by what he heard the next night at Psycho Mongo's. Josh described a world of virtual communities and new media and a gradual loosening of humanity's ties to the physical world; a freeing of mind and a jolt to the species whose outcome no one could predict. He also offered something neither Poulos nor any of his friends had previously come into contact with – a job with a salary.

There was no getting away from the poet's quirkiness though.

He listened with growing amusement as Josh tried to impress him with talk of an English writer he'd never heard of, then watched his would-be employer try to chat up an attractive woman by lighting her cigarette, only to prove unable after multiple arm-flailing attempts to make his lighter catch. Trying to stifle laughter, Poulos grabbed the expensive Dunhill lighter and lit the cigarette: the next morning he got a call saying 'You're hired.'

All that remained was to work out what he'd been hired *for*. Poulos's job title was Producer, but he spent most of the first few months trying to figure out how to use Windows.

They came in distinct tranches and the turnover was brisk as Josh and his lieutenants set about trying to give his ideas physical shape. Of the first five Pseudites, who included Poulos, Jacques Tege and a performance artist called Gecko Girl, only Tege would last much longer than eighteen months, but even those who left early agree that they'd never seen such a pure act of creation before and are unlikely to again. As the artist Jeff Gompertz tells me, 'It was startup energy, before anyone knew that there would be more startups . . . it was really exciting.'

The new company took flight when Dennis Adamo arrived, shortly after the move to 600 Broadway. Adamo knew nothing about computers, but 'could sell ice to eskimos' in the words of a colleague: according to others he was 'a completely excessive human being' with 'a kind of full-on, "let's go", balls-out approach to things' – a well-connected New York University film school grad with strong links to the downtown art, spoken-word and club scenes. As the company's fourth paid employee and first Executive Producer, his most important jobs were to bring creative people in and translate his boss's often baffling ideas to them. He spent hours trying to understand what these were.

First encounters with Adamo were often memorable. The

video artist and producer Marc Scarpa recalls arriving to meet the Executive Producer one morning, only to find the place empty save for the newly recruited JudgeCal, who, despite his grungy presence, was a whizz with computers and proceeded to demonstrate some tricks on one of the 386 series PCs and teeth-grindingly slow but then-state-of-the-art 2400 bps modems. Adamo finally showed just as Scarpa was standing at the lift waiting to leave: Scarpa remembers him as wearing twin holstered cell phones and looking like he'd been up all night.

'Are you Dennis?' the visitor asked.

'Yeah. Who the fuck are you?' came the reply.

After an interval of shouting, Scarpa signed on.

Part of Adamo's interview process was to sit candidates in front of a screen and make them chat until they got laid, on the grounds that people needed to understand the dynamic of this new medium. 'You better learn fast or you're gonna be sitting there a while,' he would chuckle as he walked by. In the early months, he ran the place like a wired O.K. Corral. Yet somehow everyone seems to have loved him. His idea of Pseudo's mission was clear, being 'to populate Josh's ideas about the virtual world ... trying to emulate this virtual world, this thing which existed only in his head at that point, at our facility'.

Josh was on his own hunt for 'talent'. The actor-poet-presenter Robert Galinsky recalls him becoming a regular at Galinsky's Full-Frontal Theatre, where sketches and theatrical features would be followed by pasta and wine and an open-mic session at midnight, at which the net impresario would arrive with a flock of six to twelve crazies to perform music with instruments made of trash, or recite poetry composed of funny noises. Galinksy didn't know the other man at first – 'he was just this strange cat that would come in' – and thought him insufferably cocky when they did meet. Nonetheless, he agreed to collaborate on a coffee table book of early websites and when that came to nothing, was persuaded to produce a radio programme about the internet, which went out on WEBD 1050 AM from early 1995 and introduced most of the future Alley players to the public. Late-night recording sessions at a 9th Street studio would presage a ten-block march back to Pseudo, where shows would be encoded for the web. Staff recall a party-like atmosphere and the sight of Josh walking ahead, lost in thought, and never offering to help carry the gear.

People began to arrive out of the blue, because they'd heard of this bizarre semi-corporate outgrowth squatting at the gates of SoHo. Josh insisted on leaving the front door open at all times, meaning that anyone could ride the sluggish lift to the loft at any time of the day or night – and *did*. At first, staff would say, 'Josh, you gotta lock the door – this is New York City!' But he'd reply, 'No, you never know who's going to walk through … keep it open.'

So some days you'd arrive to find five blue-haired kids playing Hacky Sack or Frisbee; others there would be chair races or someone building mud sculptures in the middle of the floor. Spyro Poulos took to turning up early in order to get a jump on the day, but regularly arrived to see Josh pacing the loft as if in a trance, cigar in one hand and single malt in the other, looking as though he hadn't slept in three days and failing to acknowledge the new arrival at all. When eventually the producer cracked and asked in his delicate New York way, 'Dude, what the fuck?' the reply was '*Shhh*. I'm *thinking*.' Something Josh had been doing since childhood, pacing himself into a 'fugue state' of waking dream.

The atmosphere reflected the people. Most staff rejoiced in the freedom they'd been given but, being young, took it for granted. Recreational drugs and dope smoking were rife, and only when potential investors began to drop by and discipline crumbled were steps taken to set boundaries. Josh, always tending to sobriety ('He had enough insanity in his own head,' smirks an ex-colleague), took to sitting at the top of the lift from

10 a.m. and barking at anyone who was even slightly tardy for work: 'So tell us who you are and why you're late.' One newbie reports protesting, 'But it's 10.01!' only to receive a gruff: 'I don't care. Who are you? What do you do here? And why are you late?'

It was humiliating and effective. Pseudites arriving after 10.30 would be sent home and told to come back the next day – a punishment some found befuddling given that they would still be paid. But a day without Pseudo was punishment enough in Josh's mind and most of his people agreed, with eighty to hundred-hour weeks becoming the norm. Eventually, staff even undertook to refrain from smoking until any visiting grown-ups had left the building and the announcement 'Code Green, report to the fifth floor' rang from the Tannoy. This doesn't blunt one exec's recollection of being handed a memo stating whose job it was to procure ecstasy for a party. 'On paper! A memo!' she exclaims, before adding, 'So yeah, it was fun. But it wasn't just drugs. Josh chose really smart, fiery people. Everybody in that place was really interesting.'

From the off, no one was sure what to make of the Svengali in their midst. Adamo considered him unnervingly clever, but with something vacant, almost *robotic* about him ... 'always watching TV or listening to radio, away in his own world' and issuing 'blank stares' when intruded upon. And, just when you thought you understood him, something would happen to change your mind. For the first year, Josh and his programmers were compelled to spend a lot of time at Prodigy's headquarters in White Plains, New York, and fellow ETBs soon heard tales of him commandeering a wing of the building and changing locks to keep Prodigy executives out. Many of the more conventionally well-heeled ETBs thought Josh arrogant and odd, but they could see how astute he'd been with Jupiter and the Prodigy deal, and were soon making pilgrimages to the loft to see what was happening. Marc Scarpa shot a video exposing the boss's

Jekyll and Hyde professional life, with Harris as the conservative shinyshoe by day and Wired Piper at night, looking like an amused interpolator in both worlds. In *all* worlds. One day he might be arranging for himself and Tege to view ARPA-sponsored work at a Naval strategic facility in Florida – Tege never knew *how* – the next, organising remote sessions of the computer games Wolfenstein and DOOM in a bid to get straight-laced Prodigy programmers onside: nothing appeared to faze him.

Creative chaos reigned. As early as autumn '94, project boards detailed preliminary work on software for auction and gambling sites; on emoticons and webcasting channels and *Second Life*-style 3D environments with *Launder*-inspired TV-head avatars. Those lucky enough to be there were sailors on a new sea, a new *kind* of sea. One visitor arrived to see the loft floor covered in drawings of web pages, which staff were moving around intently, trying to imagine how their website might work and what it would look like. An extra frisson stemmed from the fact that everyone knew their immediate goals could change in an instant – as on the day Josh rushed from his chambers instructing artists and programmers to drop whatever they were doing and start work on a character called Marvin the Fry, an animated French fry who sat in the back of a cab wondering how much to tip the driver. A set of JudgeCal sketches show this to have been real, but a week later Marvin was nixed in favour of something else. Work on games and parties and some of the web's first viral videos were subject to similar vacillations. Creative staff were frustrated, but that was Josh.

Josh is Josh: a phrase you heard all the time, usually with a smile and roll of the eyes. Everything made sense. Everything made no sense. For the first year, it was impossible to know the difference and every day was its own unique invention.

New York was changing too. Six months before Josh moved into 600 Broadway, a Republican lawyer named Rudolph Giuliani replaced Democrat David Dinkins as mayor. One of the few people who could be variously described as 'the Emperor of New York', 'one of the most polarizing political figures since Richard Nixon' and 'a *heartless bastard*' (courtesy the *Village Voice*) without any of these epithets seeming unfair *to anyone*, 'Rudy' was elected on a promise to clean up the town and restore self-respect and he flew the traps like a whippet. Within months he was strengthening the police, chasing the homeless off streets and blitzing panhandlers, squeegee men, subway graffiti artists. He cleaned up Times Square and installed surveillance cameras in parks, closing them at night in a bid to inconvenience drug dealers. He also instituted an experimental but highly effective 'broken windows' policy, which involved tackling small crimes with the same vigour as major ones, challenging the impression that some districts were beyond law and hope.

Giuliani would push his luck with clampdowns on cyclists, litterbugs, jaywalkers and the drug-saturated nightclub scene (by mid-decade recognised as the most vibrant in the world). And yet by the summer of '95 New York crime had tumbled 16 per cent against a national fall of 1 per cent, and Police Commissioner William Bratton could point out that of 67,000 fewer crimes committed in the US that year, 41,000 were in New York, with the murder rate tumbling an unbelievable 40 per cent. The *Sex and the City* character Carrie Bradshaw joked that, 'There are no available men in their thirties in New York . . . Giuliani had them removed along with the homeless,' and at one point I would watch the singer Lenny Kravitz throw an expletive-rich fit at not being able to lock his bike to a lamppost – also banned – prior to an interview, but it would be hard to deny that by 1995 the place felt safer and more civilised than it had in 1990.

Giuliani's crime reduction came at a price though. The city's new figurehead had a monstrous ego (of which Commissioner

Bratton would fall foul) and his critics described him as sometimes vain, bullying and manipulative, with graffiti art depicting him as Hitler constituting a *genre* by the end of the decade and minority citizens resentful of a police force which targeted them disproportionately. Would the NYPD overstep the mark by rousting a black deputy mayor *twice* in one year? Possibly …

One of Giuliani's earliest and least controversial acts, however, had been to order a report on regenerating the downtown area, meaning that Pseudo and those Alley startups-to-come were about to acquire civic significance. The cat-and-mouse battle between Josh and the Mayor's Social Club Task Force would be a lively feature of the next five years.

As the first high-profile Silicon Alley startup, Pseudo was at the sharp end of the struggle to define this eerie new medium. Most fundamental of the conflicts was an ongoing schism between Big Media's proprietorial vision for cyberspace and the esoteric, unmanageable World Wide Web, which the latter was quietly winning. By '95, word of the web's pull had permeated even Time Warner's Old Media fortress to the south of Central Park, until CEO Jerry Levin had little choice but to trumpet a move into these anarchic badlands, burying his beloved Full Service Network as though it had never existed – though still with a presumption that the web could be dominated in the way of TV or print. On the other side of town, by contrast, an upstart New York New Media Association had formed with eight members, and three or four would-be venture capitalists turned up for a Cybersuds social event, to discuss ways of doing business without travelling west to Silicon Valley or falling prey to the corporations. Everything was up for grabs.

The problem for Pseudo was bandwidth. In 1994, before compression grew more sophisticated, sound files were huge and a few songs could take up most of the space on a PC hard drive. Through the web, a single such file could take hours to download and Pseudo creative staff were forever approaching techie colleagues with exciting material, only to be scolded that, 'It's never going to get up fast enough for anyone to see it . . . no one is going to wait for this material to load!' In stark contrast, Prodigy's system offered ample bandwidth, but was segregated from the web and accessible only through subscription. Worse, its corporate stiff-designed TOPS software was clunky enough for Pseudo programmers to cast its name as an acronym for 'Today's and Tomorrow's Obsolete Piece of Shit'. Everyone at Pseudo knew that a wholesale move to the web frontier was inevitable, but in 1994 the setting was too primitive. For the time being, all they could do was build and wait.

The tussle wasn't just between web culture and *big* business. The following spring, *Time* magazine described the furious online response to a husband and wife law firm from Scottsdale, Arizona, who'd used their own program to place ads on bulletin boards across the net. It may seem extraordinary that a *Time* article (headed 'The Battle for the Soul of the Internet') from 1995 should open its second paragraph with, 'The Internet, for those who are still a little fuzzy about these things, is the world's largest computer network and the nearest thing to a working prototype of the information superhighway' – but it wasn't then. The author went on to position the backlash against the law firm as 'the opening skirmish in a larger battle between commercial interests eager to make money on [the net], veteran users who want to protect it, governments that want to control it, pornographers who want to exploit its freedoms, parents and teachers who want to make it a safe and useful place for kids'. The piece concluded that, 'Just when it seems almost ready for prime time, the Net is being buffeted by forces that threaten to destroy the very qualities that fueled its growth.' It also quoted an adviser to Al Gore as admitting that censorship was impossible on this new frontier, with a Berkeley astronomer elaborating that, 'It's designed to work around censorship and blockage [because] if you try to cut something out, it self-repairs . . . it's the closest thing to true anarchy that ever existed.'

Back then, most of us expected the big battle to be between the state and big business on one side, with their hungers for control, and the individual's right to privacy on the other. The thing I never heard anyone suggest, and could never have conceived of myself, was that people might use the web to *cast off their own* privacy; to 'lose' it the way a teenager loses virginity. Or put another way, to live in public. Such an idea was simply beyond my imagination, or the imagination of anyone I knew.

And yet, for all the nervy thrill of watching a new dimension sparkle into being, what Pseudites and ETBs alike remember about the first year is *parties*.

After a ravey sight-setter at the end of December 1994, the first large-scale event took place in January '95, for which artist-curators Jeff Gompertz and V. Owen Bush filled the space with huge plastic bubbles, tunnels and walkways raked by lights and video projections – all synced to a soundtrack of pulse-pushing jungle music, a kind of clattering electronic jazz fresh from the London underground, but which had been heard by almost no one in New York at that point. The event featured a fashion show and photo shoots and was called 'Jungle File', but what struck most guests was the mix of people: of club kids, techies, fashion models and designers; performers, artists, writers, journalists and businesspeople, the latter including many of the Alley's future millionaire CEOs – the whole downtown demimonde grooving in one place, together. One dumbfounded guest recalls asking Dennis Adamo what Pseudo was about, to receive by way of reply:

'We're breaking the barriers between the virtual world and the real world . . .'

'But how do you make money?' the guest demanded.

'Oh, online stuff,' he heard through the din, wondering whether Adamo was high.

(Adamo *was* high.)

So the inquisitor went away no wiser.

Josh strolled the room in a Rat Pack jacket and tie, almost uniquely drug-free and straight as a die, cigar and jaunty fedora characteristically ill-served by shapeless jeans and tennis shoes, privately astonished at the energy he'd unleashed. A young journalist named Jason Chervokas wasn't alone in glancing around and imagining he saw something new – a near-perfect blending of business and social forces. 'This is what it must have felt like in San Francisco in 1967,' he thought. 'Something big is happening.'

What very few guests noticed was a particular subtextual theme. Alex Arcadia was a street artist and painter whose work referenced fame and mythology – ideas due to conjoin in the concept of celebrity – which may be why the first things he noticed as he entered the Pseudo space were areas covered in white paper and green screens for photo and video shoots, where party-goers would be shot as if they were famous. He noticed that entry was permitted only upon the ritual signing of a release form, granting ownership of all photos, footage, *material*, to Pseudo. 'So this is more than a party,' he thought.

It was 1994: several years before 'celebrity culture' had entered the lexicon or become recognised as the dominant meme of our time. Everything in the room would be the same as everything else: everyone the same as every*one* else. Which is to say public.

Owned.

Known.

By *Josh.*

What most excited guests saw instead was a brash hedonism not seen in the city since the 70s disco heyday of Studio 54. A young rave promoter named Matt E. Silver, brought in to help, wasn't the only one to go home that night thinking, 'I can't believe we got away with that.'

Yet work was getting done. Invited to 600 Broadway by Dennis Adamo, Alex Arcadia knew nothing about the internet but was fascinated to find a scene where geeks owned and defined cool. Almost no one in the place looked like they'd been the hip kids at school, yet by summer '95 their events were pulling art royalty and clamouring crowds, with normally insouciant New Yorkers forcing a velvet rope door policy.

By summer 1995 crowds of three to four thousand excitable Sohonauts were not uncommon in the loft, with a further thousand wrapped around the block outside, spilling into the street and causing traffic jams the length of Broadway. It was incredible. Shut by the police on one occasion, Josh went to the Better Business Bureau and scolded, 'If you want to get the economy going around here and want to get jobs created, then you've got to let me do this – you gotta bend the rules.' And so they did, at a time when clubs like the legendary Sound Factory up the road in 21st Street were en route to being closed. 'A lot of people thought Josh was a bit ostentatious,' one promoter notes. 'But they still had a lot of respect that he could get something like that done in the city at that time.'

The best events followed the Hunter S. Thompson principle that, 'To have a good party all you need is bikers and drag queens,' bringing New York tribes together to clash and fizz, reveille turned to jazz, chord upon chord upon chord ... *beautiful* when it worked. For 'Overstimulation', Marc Scarpa flew ten exotic Virtuality 'virtual reality' machines in from England and rigged multiplayer games to create a ravey, trippy vibe that ran for two days and drew thousands to the loft, including a crew from CBS News. On another occasion, Gompertz and Owen Bush lined the Pseudo loft walls with black plastic for a night sponsored by the newly launched Moonlight cigarette company, who distributed free product samples all night until it was impossible to breathe without crouching in one of the largest timber-framed buildings in New York . . .

Little wonder that company events often ended with police or fire department officials turning up. At one, a guest claims to have watched a group of young policemen arrive with the clear intention of closing the fun down, only to return off duty a couple of hours later and join in.

Less easily explained was the propensity of guests to remove their clothing. And you never knew what you might find in the area to the rear of the space where computers were stored. During parties, Josh's spacious quarters became a proxy VIP area, offering respite from the crush and madness, and lucky initiates would take away stories of everything from beautiful sunrise comedowns to impromptu performances and group sex sessions – though as is the way with these things, no one appears to retain a memory of being *involved* in these, and certainly not of their painfully body-conscious host taking part.

Something about the Pseudo environment caused inhibitions to be shed, just as Josh predicted they would be in the online environment he sought to reflect. He certainly hadn't been the only cyber-evangelist to see the web's potential social impact as more important and interesting than its ability to revolutionise commerce or media (even AOL's Ted Leonsis had talked of 'user experience' being paramount) but the difference between Josh's approach to Pseudo and the 'content is king' consensus on the East Coast was subtle enough that very few people grasped it. Either way, Pseudo's events came to be seen as the essence of the tech district, marker for what could be done. And they made for fabulous marketing.

* * *

A shock came in April, when Josh's Prodigy ally, Scott Kurnit, left to head up a short-lived joint online venture between the cable giant MCI and Rupert Murdoch. For a few tense weeks, the Pseudo head fretted his revenue stream, knowing that without it he couldn't survive. But he needn't have. The fun was about to start in earnest.

Kurnit was replaced by a recruit from the cable music station VH-1 named Ed Bennett, a goatee-wearing, downtown loft dweller who had played in bands in his younger days and could still party with the best of them. Accustomed to working with eccentric entertainers, Bennett 'got' Josh and immediately saw that the only part of the business that worked and produced a profit was the Pseudo area.

Bennett's appointment came as a relief to Josh, who wasn't alone in regarding Prodigy and its joint owner IBM as 'sick' companies whose bureaucratic structures stifled innovation and failed to reward success. For almost a year he'd lived in fear of them cancelling his contract and simply co-opting his work. He also knew that before long all online providers would switch from hourly billing to flat monthly fees, at which point his percentage-based income would dry up. With conglomerates circling, the game could be over in a flash.

In response, Josh persuaded Bennett to invest in a sophisticated new platform, based on a 3D environment similar to the one popularised by *Second Life* a decade later. User 'avatars' would be modelled on the TV-headed figures from *Launder My Head* and, when a close friendship was struck with Bennett's girlfriend, the future interior designer Betty Wasserman, the co-venture became known as Project Betty. 'As long as they're together, I'm in good shape,' Josh joked, and for the next year Pseudo felt safe and there would be money to spend. For Wasserman, meanwhile, finding Josh and his cyberworld was 'like having sugar for the first time ... just seeing what he was putting together, and all these creative people around him, was *exhilarating*.'

To mark Ed Bennett's fortuitous arrival, Josh and Dennis Adamo charged the artist V. Owen Bush with curating Pseudo's largest party yet, to which the whole of the Prodigy organisation – up to a thousand people – would be invited down from White Plains. They also threw him a curveball by insisting on the involvement of a company called Half Baked Ideas, custodians of what was claimed to be the world's largest gravity bong – a showstopping, psychedelicised contraption standing over six feet tall, with eight pipes and a smoke chamber fashioned from an industrial waste bin. Everyone who saw it laughed delightedly: at least one Pseudo fellow traveller recalls thinking, 'This is bigger than my bathroom.'

Bush thought he might get away with hiding the bong in a cupboard, until bang on six o'clock he received a call on his walkie-talkie, saying, 'Uh, Owen, you're not going to believe this, but . . .' The Prodigy staff were arriving at least four hours before SoHo parties normally began, and they were wearing *dinner suits and ballgowns*. The online world had evolved so swiftly that Pseudo and Prodigy might as well have been from different planets: the latter saw the former and thought, 'These people are going to be doing our jobs next week.' And they were right. So after a Prodigy employee wandered into a cupboard later that evening and saw her boss worshipping at the Empire State Octobong, word spread fast and with enough velocity to reach the *New York Post*. Remarkably, Josh and Ed Bennett saw the scandal off and Half Baked Ideas remained premier manufacturers of gigantic smokeware until they moved out of New York and got busted by police in 2002. According to a report in the local *Trentonian* newspaper, 'Investigators expressed amazement at the size of some bongs . . . one pipe was so large it had to be disassembled in order to be moved.'

The apotheosis of the first phase, however, was an extraordinary event called Pseudo Immercion. This grew out of an approach by members of the Merce Cunningham Dance Company (MCDC), whose founder had been in the vanguard of the uptown avant-garde for fifty years and had heard about

Pseudo through the art grapevine. At the centre of the event was a performance of *Suite for Five*, a piece first presented in 1956 to music composed by Cunningham's late partner, the celebrated composer John Cage, with visuals by the MCDC's designer and sometime stage manager, pop art godhead Robert Rauschenberg.

As New York as lox, Cunningham and *Suite for Five* awed the young Pseudites, while the dancer rejoiced in the youngsters' energy and sense of possibility. Adamo and Bush borrowed a sophisticated Silicon Graphics computer animation system which allowed a delighted Cunningham to make a toy monkey dance as if it were alive, with flesh-and-blood members of the Company scattered and projected across the space in a two-hour symphony of sound and movement. The choreographer's sound designer even brought the original equipment Cage used for his 1976 performance of *Branches*, which involved attaching microphones to the quills and flesh of a giant cactus, producing ethereal kalimba-like shudders and pulses when 'played' by guests; there were also outsized theremin poles, which created an electrostatic field dancers could 'play' in the way of a musical instrument with their motion. In return, the Pseudo crew built an orchestra pit filled with experimental instruments, mixed according to Cage's chance-based Fluxus system.

The party lift was broken that night, so there were queues at the front and rear entrances to the building, which met as they snaked around the block: legend holds that Adamo got a walkie-talkie call saying Peter Gabriel was outside, but not on the list – could he come in? Many people were turned away from an event that had been scheduled to run for the early part of the evening, prior to making way for a late-night rave featuring a range of big-name DJs, and for a glorious few hours the two crowds mingled, with the Fire Department turning up but failing to find an offence and the ravers staying till dawn. Owen Bush would feel lucky to have been involved in something like

Immercion at such a young age and Adamo would label the night 'electronic fine art in the highest form'. Immercion had done nothing less than prove the Pseudo model, balancing careful planning with chaos to just the right degree. And everyone had loved it – bar one key person.

That person being *Josh*.

And that night, he says, changed the course of his work.

Josh's problem was a feeling that Merce Cunningham saw right through him and the harder he tried to connect, to impress with fancy conceptualisation, the more distressing the disconnect became. Adamo, ever Josh's harshest critic, would form an opinion that the dancer recognised a fake whose response to art was tainted, and he certainly wouldn't be the only one to remark on his ex-employer's imperviousness to what most of us regard as art. But for Josh the issue was more fundamental. 'The thing is,' he tells me, 'Merce sat there and I saw that he'd seen it before. I thought I did pretty good and then I realised it was nothing new to him, and the more I was explaining how cool the party was, it was like the less cool it was. That was a turning point.'

He spent much of the evening holed up in his quarters, watching TV in Gatsby-like isolation.

Thinking about what to do next . . .

Unaware that down the road at the New York Stock Exchange, something extraordinary was in train – a seismic event which had nothing to do with any of the ETBs, but would change their world in ways even Josh couldn't have dreamed. And as with so much on the internet, it came out of nowhere, like a tracer bullet.

How?

Even before Jerry Levin and Time Warner abandoned dreams of an all-powerful proprietorial Full Service Network, the man charged with realising their vision had decided that it couldn't work and begun to look for the next big thing. Fortunately, the eccentric millionaire computer lord Jim Clark, founder of the ground-breaking Silicon Graphics company, had a knack for surrounding himself with clever people – which by 1994 included the Mosaic web browser's co-author, Marc Andreessen. And this is how, after another fruitless session of brainstorming ideas, Clark came to be asked, as an afterthought, whether he'd noticed the impact of Mosaic on the still tiny but growing web community. The older man hadn't, so Andreessen gave him a demo ... and understanding was instant. *This* was what they were looking for. A 'Mosaic-killer': rarified commercial version of the free browser which had brought the web to life.

Netscape Navigator was released in November 1994, after which it steadily supplanted Mosaic, until within a year it conveyed 90 per cent of the internet's burgeoning traffic – enough for the company to hatch plans to float on the stock market just sixteen months after launch.

9 August 1995. A day which would blow the lid off *everything* and change the Silicon Alley game, and so much else, for good.

8

I'm moving among the Pseudites, trying to build a picture of who Josh was during the dotcom boom and of what he was to them; to understand the relationship between that man and that time and the refugee I found in Awassa. In the back of my mind is the larger question of how much their surreal trip was about them, how much about a set of circumstances which look increasingly fantastical and puzzling to me – and I'm beginning to be aware that I've only scratched the surface.

John Christopher Morton had listened to Pseudo Online Radio's FreQ music show since 1996, when it was the only place you could hear cutting-edge jungle and the darker strains of electronica outside of hip city clubs most people couldn't get into. Eventually he came to New York and hung around the building until someone could be bothered to give him a job, or at least could no longer be bothered *not* to, becoming a popular member of staff as SoHo rocked with dotcom mania at decade's end. Significantly for me, he is also a *de facto* Pseudo archivist and has agreed to show me the empire. It's a bright October morning as we meet outside the husk of 600 Broadway: ten weeks since the death of JudgeCal, with whom I know John worked closely.

'I was sorry to hear about Cal,' I commiserate after initial pleasantries. 'He was one I'd hoped to meet.'

'Oh, but you can,' Morton says with a tilt of his head. 'He's over there.'

My guide points to a grey smattery blob on the glass pane of the building's door while I stare, nonplussed.

A few weeks ago, the actor-poet-turned-Pseudo-producer Robert Galinsky led a small group of Pseudites on a clandestine night-time trek to scatter the presenter's ashes in places of significance to him, contravening an impressive array of New York City health and safety regs on the way. Dodging police patrol cars and beat officers, the coterie stopped at several locations, including here at 600 Broadway and the once achingly fashionable Danceteria nightclub, flinging a spoonful of their friend at each site. Morton is probably right that Cal would have liked the idea of his death leading to an adventure. More even than this, I think he'd have marvelled at his own adhesive properties.

The building is completely empty now and slated for redevelopment, but John nonetheless looks around and beams. 'This crossroads felt like the centre of the world. Every day I'd come to work and I couldn't believe it.' At his tender age, the excitement and attendant temptations were almost too much: like so many others, he's clearly struggled with re-entry to the everyday. When he goes to job interviews these days, he says, 'People either know nothing at all about Pseudo or their eyes light up and they're really impressed.'

We stroll and chat, chat and stroll down the still shabby, formerly industrial lower end of Broadway, past the next-door building into which Pseudo's executive offices spilled; to the enormous first floor loft Josh bought after the sale of some shares in Jupiter Communications made him not just rich, but *cash* rich – the place he rigged with cameras for *We Live in Public* . . . number 519.

And deeper still into TriBeCa, to a tall Italianate former sweatshop at 359, in which a range of events were staged from early 1999, and the ugly concrete box from which crowds spilled during *Quiet*, at 353 – both now boarded and forgotten like decayed ancient temples. The extent of Josh's former reach is astonishing ... I think back to the little house and cratered streets and petit-gangster trouble in Awassa and find it hard to connect the two.

Between 1994 and the time he bought the loft at 519 in 1999, Josh lived in large and beautiful quarters on the rear top floor of 600 Broadway. The place was like a metaphor for the man himself: once used as an office, the walls of the 1800 square foot main room were wood-panelled and the windows ornate but there was no hot running water or fridge or stove. Living with him were a bearded dragon lizard named Maurice (Josh's middle name) and a pair of terrapins, along with two cats named Neuffy and Louie. A frequent woman visitor at the time who still regards herself as a friend chuckles as she describes a small shelf containing books 'all about World War II and stuff like that', adding, 'What amazes me about Josh is that he's *so* old-fashioned.' Three young Pseudo workers squatted in the main space on the other side of a tall and beautiful bookcase one of them had built. Some sleuthed video footage from the time shows a desk groaning with paper and mugs and video cassettes of films like *La Dolce Vita*, an always-on PC and brick walls papered with childlike cartoons and drawings and dizzy grids of ideas.

'He'd walk through his door in the morning and everything would be going on,' John Christopher Morton says, going on to amuse me by applying the term 'forcing factor' to his former boss – an evolutionary concept normally reserved for the likes of ice ages and comet strikes.

Later in the week, I'll visit Morton at the rented Brooklyn garage he's living in, where he shows me various documents, business cards, artefacts gleaned from the office or Cal's apartment. For the first time he notices a tape in his old friend's VCR, presumably the last video Cal watched, so we plug it in and find a chaotic scene from the days of Pseudo Online Radio, early 1996 at a guess and featuring Cal, Robert Galinsky and various people milling about laughing and looking like they're having fun. And in the middle Josh, grinning in a blue check shirt that's not so much antifashion as *a*fashion; sheeny-eyed and fit and unexpectedly handsome in the boyish way of businessmen, with luxuriant black hair and no sign of the physical or psychological load he would be carrying just a few years later, talking in complete sentences and clearly having the time of his life ... looking and sounding the one thing I could never have envisaged – that thing being *normal*. To my further bafflement, he turns out to have been a decent interviewer.

Again, there's no way *not* to ask: what happened to him between then and *We Live in Public*. I get back to my Williamsburg digs and am pleased to find an email which runs:

a.

latest ... from the awassa ...

big week here ... everything works perfectly, net, water, power, etc ... why? The prime minister is here ...

fekerte my neighbor has been ripping me off (at least $150) ...

my newest tortoise is a male and is humping the other two females daily ... boardering on embarrassing

graza (monkey) is back ... fed him three bananas and he basically got drunk ... didn't move for an hour ...

j.

* * *

The only way to approach the tangle of narratives and names I brought back from Ethiopia was to trust intuition and chance as guides; to lose myself in the story and try to plot a way out, much as you might lose yourself in an unfamiliar city as a means of finding it. Thus, through a fortnight's Indian summer I track and meet people from different phases of Pseudo and the Alley explosion almost at random and I've seldom been more consistently entertained, nor more entertainingly confused.

Like city lights, receding . . .

Nancy Smith, an artist and quilt-maker who came to Pseudo late and went on to found the lively artloversnewyork blog site, takes me to the vibrant New York Art Book Fair opening party and a couple of streetsy downtown galleries, describing current trends as we go. She makes me smile by asking whether I was intimidated by Josh (the way she was), and then smiles back when I describe his current circumstances, saying, 'But he likes that, it makes him feel alive: otherwise everything's too slow for him.' Somewhere amid the sea of Campari cocktails at the Fair, we bump into an ex-boss of hers, a publisher who, when told what I'm doing, spits, 'Who cares about Josh Harris?' – followed by an artist named Michael Portnoy, who ran an absurdist gaming table installation at *Quiet* and confesses to having been 'critical' of the event at the time, 'because I think art needs to have boundaries and there weren't any', before furrowing his brow and grinning, 'Looking back now, though, I think it was amazing!' At the end of the night I feel guilty because, having dragged Smith back into Josh's cosmos, she finds it painful to pull away again and doesn't want me to leave.

The next evening I go to meet David 'the Impact Addict' Leslie at Veselka, a twenty-four-hour Ukranian joint beloved of the East Village art crowd, only to find the place closed while a large film crew packs up. Admitted a little later, we learn that the production is for *Bored to Death*, an HBO series starring the *Cheers* actor Ted Danson and scripted by local novelist Jonathan Ames, who read at Josh's *Quiet* spectacular and had his nose broken by Leslie during another event. 'And Ames is still upset about that,' a passing friend chuckles. 'He *still* carries that wound.'

A growing sense of *Quiet*'s ubiquity and the work I have yet to do in assembling a credible account of it – in trying to sift myth from 'reality'. Leslie calls the event 'the marker for an era's end', almost as if it carried presentiment.

Leslie was on the *Tuna Heaven* boat, which he says 'was like going to the Moon'. He tells the story of how a group of firemen were hurling homemade bombs overboard on a prior trip, when one of the men was fooled by a fuse which appeared to have gone out, but hadn't. 'So it explodes and blows off his hand and disembowels him. He asks if his cock is still intact and they tell him "yes", so he tries to hang on, but they're too far out to make it to shore or be reached by helicopter, so he dies. *That's* how far out you are . . . it's almost spooky.'

Another place where the normal rules and imperatives of life don't apply, where personalities and proclivities can seep into the open.

As I travel, small surprises: that Alex Arcadia's description of his violent, bullying father is beginning to sound familiar among Pseudites; that the company's final CEO David Bohrman thinks it could have succeeded, suggesting as he sits in CNN's uptown operations room that 'It was a very interesting group of people and there was something *really* there, and I thought Josh was fascinating. . .'

Against which an ex-business partner of Josh states gruffly: 'I think he is probably in need of psychological help, and I think things like the book you're writing are just enabling him to avoid facing up to things, so I wish people would stop talking about him.'

Yet the most surprising feature of my first post-Awassa trip is the dearth of sentiment such as the last. Indeed, most interviews follow a pattern, with a list of infuriating character traits and unfathomable behaviours being followed by insistence that, 'Oh, I love Josh!' when a subject is asked directly whether they like him or not. Moreover, almost everyone seems to see him differently.

Most emphatic is Spyro Poulos, who I meet in a noisy bar round the corner from where I'm staying, and he lives, in Williamsburg. Now working as a journalist and editor, Poulos readily admits to having been a drug-addled mess by the time he was forced out after only eighteen months. If anyone was going to be bitter, I thought it might be him. But he's not.

At the end of another catalogue of mortification and mystification and tales of irregular behaviour, I ask The Question – did Poulos *like* Josh – and am flabbergasted to hear an ardent: 'I *still* love Josh. I love him to death. There were times I wanted to see him hit by a truck and taste his own blood. He would get to this boiling point. And you could see it coming, it wouldn't happen all at once . . . but he would end up threatening to fire everybody. And in fact he fired us a couple of times and rehired us a couple of times.'

'He did this regularly?'

'He did it when the money was getting low. And then once the money was back he got real happy again – ha-ha-ha! And at that point where there was no money, we'd be going, "All right, we'll have to throw another party."'

He talks humorously about the mania and unpredictability of the place.

> But generally it was a much more positive than negative experience. I don't blame Josh for anything that happened. A lot of us probably didn't think that at the time, but we were young, *very* immature. We were all kind of free-spirited and free-willed and felt a bad boy sense of entitlement – that we were cooler than the rest of New York. I mean, I had people coming up to me and going,

'You work at *Pseudo*?' I'd be getting into clubs that wouldn't let me in before, because somehow they knew about this. I was getting swag all the time, from all these companies who just thought it would be good to be associated with us.

There were other companies trying to do stuff similar to what we were doing, who were working with the internet. But the heads of those companies were *standard business guys* and the head of our company was a raving lunatic cyber-pirate. Seriously! I mean, Josh would show up to meetings with people that were going to give us millions of dollars in a wrinkled suit with his hair looking like a scarecrow's ... and I'm like, 'Dude, you can't do this!' And he would power through the meeting. I've done a lot of sales jobs since then, and everything I know, I learned from Josh. I took so much from that job and I took a lot of it for granted.

Once Josh almost fired him for getting the wrong cat food, he says. 'And you could do a whole chapter entitled "Josh's Foot in Mouth". He found ways to alienate on a regular basis, really not meaning to.'

'He lacks social skills, you mean?'

'No – not at all! His social skills are insidiously sharp. You can't create a community like that without having some level of social skills. Being able to *choreograph* a group of people to interact in a way that will produce something creative is a real, serious skill. So he had social skills.'

'Like the Pied Piper had social skills, you mean?'

'Exactly! That's the perfect analogy. He had no manners though. I mean, Josh could meet someone's mother and go, "Wow, she's kind of fat." He would say things to you that were really just *way out there*. And you could look at him and tell that he wasn't trying to be malicious. What's weird is that he was also a lot more charming than anyone ever seems to let on. Because for the person he just offended, he also made nineteen people crack the fuck up. The guy has a great sense of humour.'

The thing is, this is true, and you somehow feel it shouldn't be; that the playfulness and sense of humour are out of step with the framework you need to make sense of Josh: are incongruous. Poulos also lets slip that when his drug intake became a problem, Josh was generous in providing help – as he was with a number of friends and ex-employees. 'Everyone thinks Josh has no conscience or morals,' he concludes. 'But I've seen him be incredibly kind and caring towards people.'

As we prepare to part, the former Pseudo producer heading for a gig down the road, me for another meeting, he points out that as a youngest sibling, he feels a particular affinity with Josh because he too was babysat by the screen. And as I trade the bar for night and the hoard of young hipsters talking or texting or staring into their smartphones, I find myself thinking: 'Weren't we all?'

9

'Here comes everybody!'
– James Joyce, *Finnegans Wake*

So.
9 August 1995, morning. Jim Clark and his Netscape staff wait for shares in their company to start trading on the New York Stock Exchange. The hour approaches and tension mounts. The feel is of Mission Control during a moon landing.

In the past, 'going public' has been a drawn-out business, preceded by a stepped series of hurdles. That a company had reached the market implied – in and of itself – that it had a track record and a tail of investors who had already shown faith in it. 'Going public' was a way of raising money with which to expand and in its ideal form, the process ran something like this:

1. While tinkering in my shed, I stumble across the technique for a device which will cleanly and humanely *vaporise* any person shouting into a mobile phone within a ten-metre radius. I use my own money and/or contributions from friends, family, acquaintances to build a prototype, apply for patents and so on. There is

no business yet, so these investors are taking the highest possible risk and this initial funding can be referred to as the 'angel' or 'friends and family' round of investment, with the money sometimes called 'seed capital'.

2. Investors see commercial advantage in adapting my device to vaporise phones rather than users and reluctantly I agree to make this change. We now consider the idea to be worth a million pounds and manage to find an investor to buy our valuation. The new investor thus supplies £1 million for the hire of premises and staff and owns half of a business valued at £2 million, with the remaining half in the hands of myself and my 'seed round' angels.
3. My investors and I consider the Cellulator™ to be worth £10 million at its present stage of development. We persuade a third investment party, likely to be a venture capitalist (VC) firm, to match our valuation with £10 million of further funding as we move toward production. As a condition of their investment, VCs demand that my Cellulator *silence* rather than vaporise offending mobile phones and, heartbroken but feeling suddenly quite rich, I accede. The company is now 'worth' £20 million, with the VCs owning 50 per cent, the second-round investor 25 per cent, myself and my angels 25 per cent.
4. As we prepare for the marketplace, with demand assured, we value our work so far at £50 million. So we find another investor or group of investors to pony up £50 million in return for a 50 per cent stake . . .

And so it went, on up the scale, with risk and reward diluting equally as the business matured. The individuals and institutions who owned the business would be called 'shareholders' because they owned 'shares' of 'stock' in the company (though these terms were and are often used interchangeably, along with 'equity'). Eventually a decision might have been taken to offer a proportion of the company's value, in the form of shares, to the general public via a 'public offering' – a process often referred to as floating a company on the stock market. The first such offering of shares was called an Initial Public Offering, or IPO.

'So classically, you needed a long story,' one expert tells me. 'All these theoretical values are only meaningful if someone else wants to buy a new share.'

Then a warning.

'It's not spurious, it's real,' my expert said, 'but on each "round" the value of the company had to go up and you had to find a bigger investment.'

And if you couldn't, the story drifted away like steam from a New York manhole cover.

The process of going public is typically 'underwritten' by a merchant or investment bank, who take responsibility for any unsold shares. In the past, these bankers expected to see something like three years' worth of accounts and four consecutive quarters of profit before agreeing to underwrite an IPO. They would set the offer price – the price at which shares would be released to the market – in the expectation of seeing a small rise by the end of the first day, so providing a modest profit for those who'd bought stock at the offer price: a reward for their faith.

Now. By these or any known criteria, a Netscape IPO in August '95 is wacky. The company has traded for sixteen months and posted a loss of $4.31 million for the first half of the year, on revenues of just *$16.6 million* ... chump change to Wall Street. But far (far) worse, there is no clear path to profit. Q: how do you make money from a web browser? A: no one knows! There's been some unpleasant-sounding talk of 'monetising eyeballs', which means advertising to people who ignore you while they surf the cyber-tide to somewhere more interesting, but no one has seen this done yet.

About the only thing Netscape has on its side in received business terms is the Morgan Stanley research analyst Mary Meeker, who has a messianic zeal for the net and will be the model for a new rock star-styled market analyst, for whom the job of 'transmitting the vision' of tech companies overshadows the fusty business of getting down and actually, y'know, *researching* them. There again, how would you even do that? Last night Meeker and Marc Andreessen calculated that there were no more than 400 people *on the planet* who 'really get' the net . . . the *Net*, incidentally, of which *Barron's* magazine will presently crown Meeker 'Queen'.

The oddity of the situation boils down to this: no profitless company has ever offered shares to the public before, the rub being that it's happening now only because the yachting enthusiast Netscape founder Jim Clark saw a really big boat sail into San Francisco Bay and decided that he wanted one too, but bigger, and *computer-controlled*, which meant he needed cash. Just five years ago, in 1990, Clark took part in a PC conference panel discussion entitled, 'Will Personal Computing and Personal Communications be Combined, or Will it Just Remain as Science Fiction?' Now here he is, ready to supply an answer to a question no one outside of his orbit has even heard.

The prospectus mooted an offer price of around $14 per share, but yesterday the underwriters – yes, Mary Meeker's employers Morgan Stanley – doubled it to $28. A venture capitalist who happens to be visiting Morgan's offices walks in to find phones ringing off the hook with clients wanting a piece of the IPO . . . he looks at his partner and says, 'Holy shit, what's happening?!' The moment in which he knows this is not just another technological shift, but something much, much bigger.

In addition to upping the price, Morgan Stanley have

increased the number of shares available from 3.5 million to 5.75 million, a figure representing 13 per cent of the 'outstanding' (total number of issued) shares, with the rest retained by Clark, Andreessen, company staff and early investors. All of whom now watch astonished as shares hit the trading floor like fireworks and before anyone can even express surprise are trading at $71, rising soon to *$75*. *The New York Times* will note breathlessly that, by noon, 'money managers at big mutual funds and other institutional investors fortunate enough to be on the ground floor' – i.e. pre-allocated shares at the offer price – can 'cash them in for a near-200% profit'. Not bad for a morning's donut-munching while the numbers fly. More astounding still is the volume of trading, as a manic afternoon sees Netscape shares change hands 13.88 million times; an average of almost two and a half times each, with some racqueted back and forth like tennis balls . . . a curious pattern which will become familiar to dotcom stock-watchers.

The closing price is $58.25, making Netscape the most dramatic issue of its size in Wall Street history, with the company now theoretically worth $2.2 *billion* in total. But imagine this: Clark began the day a 50-year-old millionaire and ends it on the way to his first billion, with his 9.7 million shares valued at $566 million, while the 24-year-old Andreessen leaves with a paper fortune of $58 million after less than eighteen months in the game. Come to that, an engineer who joined the company in July will be worth $10 million by September. And what this says is: the normal rules of work, life, business, *everything*, are suspended until further notice. This notwithstanding the fact that five days hence *The New York Times* will offer readers a piece headed 'So What's a Web Browser, Anyway?' – with an op-ed explaining that 'The personal computer is already an old story. The next revolution to sweep computing, goes the conventional wisdom, will be the Internet, which links millions of formerly isolated computers into a global information and entertainment bazaar.'

The genie is out of the bottle. The web is nobody's secret any more.

Jim Clark later told the writer Michael Lewis that: 'People started drinking my Kool-Aid. Netscape obviously didn't create the Internet. But if Netscape had not forced the issue on the Internet, it would have just burbled in the background. It would have remained this counterintuitive kind of thing. The criticism of it was that it was anarchy. What the IPO did was give anarchy credibility.'

Investors scrambled in search of the 'next Netscape'. At a stroke, profit was subordinated to rapid growth as a signifier of potential, the aim being to grab a patch of this shiny new terrain – which, *still*, almost no one understood – and then decide what to do once you got there. In every sense a trip into the unknown. As Lewis, himself a former bond salesman, notes, from this point onward having a past counted *against* a company, because 'a past was a record and a record was a sign of a company's limitations'. The most attractive companies were those in a state of 'pure possibility'. And what was true for companies would also become true for people.

Jim Clark went on to found a company called Healtheon, which aimed to revolutionise the American health care system. Like his Time Warner Full Service Network project, Healtheon would end in fiasco (following another lucrative IPO, natch), but not before one of its engineers had caught the mood perfectly by giving a new twist to an old ETB mantra. 'There was a feeling that we were about to change the world,' he said. 'And we all now knew that was how you made money, by changing the world.'

A message from the 60s, remade for the 90s. Indeed, to the business establishment, Netscape must have been terrifying in the way acid had been to middle America thirty years before. At a stroke the enemy was unknown to you – something you could neither see, understand nor anticipate. Your nemesis might be an anarcho-capitalist like Clark, but could just as easily be three nerdy teens in a garage. Suddenly, balance sheets and management theories were useless. Doing business was like tip-toeing past a hive of invisible bees.

The old ways were dead. Or as Clark put it, 'It's not about business plans. You can't plan chaos.'

* * *

Not everyone dug chaos.

Take Alan Greenspan. The Fed Chairman had been concerned about the disproportionate strength of the stock market even before the Netscape IPO, as had Clinton's co-ordinator of economic policy, Robert Rubin. Rubin convened a meeting of advisers to interrogate the seemingly anomalous rise in prices, but none of what Greenspan heard from the assembled experts rang true.

As Chairman of the Federal Reserve, Greenspan's hope through the first half of the decade had been to keep inflation down, while preventing the US economy from tumbling into recession – a delicate dance indeed. His chief weapon was the Fed's ability to set interest rates, classical theory holding that if the economy grew too fast, prices would rise and inflation would occur – in which case the Fed could raise interest rates, making money dearer to borrow and so decreasing demand; prices; inflation. But if the mandarins overdid it, especially with the economy still fragile after its late-80s jolt, the US could easily slip back into recession. And no one would thank them for that, least of all the president in whose gift Greenspan's job was. No one had ever managed to steer a painless 'soft landing' for the economy in comparable circumstances, but by 1995 the Chairman had begun to believe it possible. The only discordant note was that weirdness on Wall Street.

Both a consummate diplomat and ruthless backstage player

when threatened, Greenspan had started out as a musician, studying clarinet and piano at an early iteration of the Juilliard School. A year spent touring with a 1940s-style bebop jazz band confirmed what he already knew and we might have guessed, however: that he was a terrible improviser, but virtuosic at keeping the band's books. In musical parlance, Greenspan liked to play 'by the sheets'.

A mark of the Fed Chairman's skill is that he was a strict free-market Republican and acolyte of the radical libertarian philosopher Ayn Rand who nonetheless kept his job through two terms of Clinton presidency, even establishing a bond of trust with White House staff. In turn, he found Clinton refreshingly versed in economics and far more capable of grasping difficult concepts quickly than were his predecessors Ronald Reagan and George Bush. The economist had expected a tussle when he advised the freshly elected president to make budget deficit reduction a priority, but in the event he didn't get one. Ironically, one of Greenspan's selling points for debt reduction had been that the stock market would rise, but now the question was: 'Why this much?' And why *right now*, with the Dow index at a record 4000 points and climbing?

Greenspan's deep rate-cutting had been designed to get the economy moving again. In 1992 he'd delivered the lowest overnight interest rate since the 1960s – 3 per cent, down from 8 per cent in 1989 – an approach designed to stimulate consumer demand and drive the economy forward. At the same time, the Fed's purchase of Treasury Bonds resulted in a pool of cheap (to borrow) money sloshing about the economy, as the country's immediate cash supply grew by 12 per cent in a single year, the fastest increase ever. What neither Greenspan nor most economists anticipated was the psycho-social impact of these actions, as capital came to be treated as just another commodity, with debt coming to be seen as a *medium* in its own right. Cash, debt and equity became things to buy, sell, borrow, trade, leverage without fear, liberated from the solemnity with which previous generations had approached them. One of the key rules of capitalism had always been that in order to borrow money, you needed already to have money, but the pyrotechnic 'leveraged buyouts' of the 1980s made this idea seem antediluvian.

For many on the right of the political spectrum, this freeing of access to money represented nothing less than the *democratisation* of capital; as significant a social evolution as universal suffrage or the abolition of slavery. The *New York Times* columnist Thomas Friedman would capture this ecstatic view in the phrase 'one dollar, one vote', as for the rest of the decade we would all be treated as capitalists. Meanwhile, the so-called efficient-market hypothesis, which held that markets always, by their nature, reflect all information relevant to them at all times, had become orthodoxy in the minds of economists. On this basis, outside interference with financial markets was deemed counter-productive and 'deregulation' became not just an idea but a creed, predicated on the belief that markets were by definition rational, honest and, according to some, *moral*.

So there was money to be spent, but why was it spent on stocks? From February '95, Greenspan and the Fed raised interest rates steadily in a bid to stop the economy 'overheating' and causing inflation. Clinton was furious (the problem was too much economic success and too many people working!?) and commentators were beginning to complain that the Fed Chairman hadn't understood the changes wrought by new technology, in particular the efficiency gains ushered in by computers. High growth and low inflation were no longer incompatible, they claimed, because the game had changed. Greenspan should take his thumb out of his ass, relax and enjoy the ride.

He didn't. The hike in rates appeared to impact the 'Old Economy' to an almost alarming degree – but not the stock market. And again the question was, 'Why?' The mechanistic 'efficient market' theories of the time, which denied the influence of what John Maynard Keynes had called 'animal spirits', offered no clear answers, but this is not to say there weren't any. As with so many things, you just weren't likely to see them if you were playing by the sheets.

Here's one view of the mystery.

By the late 1970s, with corporate profits sluggish and the population ageing and companies looking ahead with disquiet to a time when Baby Boomers would be retiring *en masse*, Congress passed legislation allowing individual workers to manage their own pensions. Through the 1980s, companies gradually shifted their workforces on to these '401(k)' schemes, to which they would make contributions without shouldering responsibility for the outcome. This simple change gradually turned millions of people into investors: in 1991, a third of workers were managing their own funds; by decade's end this had risen to two-thirds. A tidal wave of cash had to find a home – much of it directed not by professionals, but by non-specialist working people with day jobs and limited time.

Pension fund managers of the past had tended toward safe investment in bonds, which provide low rates of interest over a pre-agreed period, but the army of new investors had plenty of reason to feel nervous of this approach. Continually told that they weren't saving enough, that social security was running out and many of the remaining company pension schemes were underfunded, they'd also watched house values collapse during the 1990–1 recession and job security weaken as a result of globalisation. According to a 1993 survey, the typical Boomer believed themselves to need a nest egg of $1 million to be safe in retirement, but saved only $6,300 per annum – maths which suggests that when ex-flower children claim the dope was better back in their day, they're probably right.

With the prospect of comfortable retirement slipping away, the 401(k) investors were inclined to think they needed greater returns than bonds could offer. And especially with interest rates low, the obvious solution was to gamble on stocks. By 1993, individual savers were betting more than half of their savings on stocks and stock funds – many of which were marketed specifically to their anxiety. In 1995, almost 90 per cent of monies flowing into the giant Fidelity Magellan Fund were thought by managers to derive from retirement savings. And this money couldn't just sit there – it had to find investment. From the Netscape IPO onwards, the loudest, sexiest investments would be tech stocks. Bonds seldom made headlines, but as of August '95, the web surely did.

The stage was set. There were now two economies: a real one, where stuff was made and value added, and a speculative one, where value was traded, leveraged, staked. In the past – in relation to stocks at least – these two economies maintained a connection in the form of a relationship between a traded company's stock market valuation and its earnings. Through the twentieth century, the average 'price-to-earnings ratio' was roughly fourteen to one, meaning that for a business to be valued at $14 million, you would expect to see annual profits of $1 million. During the bull market of the 60s, valuations (particularly of any company whose name ended in 'onics') rose substantially above this ratio. And that ended in the crash of 1973–4. Now Netscape blew this measure so far out of the water you could all but see it from space. If the previous decade had seen a shift from the real economy to the speculative one, Netscape's IPO suggested a next-generation *virtual* economy, where stuff got speculated, value *conjured*.

The medium was the message and money was the medium. And as businesses became progressively more focused on short-term stock market performance, so relationships between players in the economy grew looser, more ephemeral, less grounded: precisely equivalent to the social fears many had for the internet. Interestingly, a similar shift seemed to be taking place in popular culture, where fame was already mutating into free-floating celebrity, a form of equity whose Wall Street would be the electronic media. More intriguing still is the possibility that the success of both was being propelled by the same parallelogram of forces; was part of a collective drift into the imagination.

BOOK II

The Wired Piper

10

Unreality. Reality. Virtuality.

Where am I?

A diner on 14th Street, sharing a sandwich with Jess Zaino, who walked into a Pseudo party-cum-FreQ music show webcast and fell instantly in love. A Queens-born daughter of Italian immigrants, she knew from the age of nine that she wanted to be famous and saw in Josh's creation a space where everyone was, or could be, or *felt* they could be part of the looming celebrity continuum. And she was consumed by the creative energy of the place, the beautiful hardwood floors and screens and computers and art on the walls and people doing things she didn't understand in every corner.

It was JC, JudgeCal, who'd invited her after their meeting in a record store and within the hour she ended up in the web booth, co-hosting the show with its usual host, a DJ named Uzi. Afterwards, Uzi invited her back to co-host at a big Levi's-sponsored party, and at the end of that second night she found herself in drunken conversation with someone she didn't know, saying, 'I would literally lick the floors to work here,' only for the other person to reply, 'Well, you know what? I'm the janitor, so you're in luck!' Josh gave her his card and said, 'Call me in the morning.'

She started as a receptionist, but like almost everyone, soon had her own show on Pseudo Online Radio and went on to become one of Pseudo TV's star presenters, with a mainstream presenting career afterwards. She found Josh scary and intimidating when they worked together, but by the time he tried to recruit her to Operator 11 in LA in 2007, the fear had mellowed to what she describes as 'a very sweet fondness'. She gets up and shows me the Pseudo tattoo on the back of her leg.

Zaino wears her intelligence lightly, but has a talent for capturing the essence of things in an offbeat phrase or image. So Josh is 'the strangest *juxtaposition* of a person' and Pseudo 'like a watercolour', with everything bleeding into everything else, 'this artistic circus full of caricatures from French paintings' – the French paintings in mind being the Toulouse-Lautrec ones she knows from the side of Roaring 90s champagne bottles. To her, Pseudo was like a modern reality-TV show, 'a very competitive, high-stress environment in which you were designed to crack and they were gonna push your buttons and abrade you to the point where your real personality was going to bleed through'. She should know, she adds, because she's just starred in one.

Synapses spark.

Just three days earlier, I went to an afternoon-long workshop at the New York Reality TV School, which is run by Josh's old friend and Pseudo *compadre* Robert Galinsky. Among the fifty-odd people present were a trio of casting directors which included a goateed, shade-wearing Robert Russell of *The Apprentice* and Risa Tanania of *Wife Swap*, along with a handful of former or present reality-show stars. Galinsky, bearded with dark curly hair and an easy charisma, introduced the class by announcing that, 'The three things we deal with here are confidence, authenticity and how to tell your story. Those are the three things that will make you a standout on any reality TV show. A standout in any situation actually.'

To my amusement, it quickly became clear that close to half

the class consisted of media interlopers, with reporters and photographers covering the school's story for outlets including the *Washington Post*, French *Elle* and Swedish *Vogue*, not to mention British *GQ* (the *Daily Telegraph* and *News of the World* having already been). There were camera crews too, from Canada and Oklahoma, and the English documentary-maker Chris Atkins was filming for a Louis Theroux-style exposé of celebrity, which is how I come to be an accidental extra in the feature film *Starsuckers*.

The proceeding hours were spent sharing secrets ('OK, I paid for these,' waving hand over breasts the size of Spain), devising our dream shows, watching peers burst into renditions of 'The Star-Spangled Banner' or, alternatively, tears; acclimatising to the ardour of eviction-night fans – and, if we happened to be an attractive woman, being called to the front of class and finding a casting director's tongue in our ear. But, most of all, taking advice on how to succeed as simulacra. Among my favourite pieces of wisdom were:

> Speak in complete sentences and always include the question in the answer, because it helps for editing and is more likely to make the cut.
>
> If you don't argue enough they'll definitely throw more drama at you.
>
> For me it's about going to a casting with a new story.

And:

> Just be yourself – but not too much!

A former *Beauty and the Geek* star said: 'I've been completely disrespected all my life, but after doing *Beauty and the Geek* all these girls who would've blown me off before were calling up and saying, 'Jason, Jason, will you go out with me?' And the most satisfying thing is putting them in their place …' While a classmate said: 'I want to be on *The Hill* because, er. I don't know.'

During a break Robert Russell told me that his job is a lot easier than when he began, because people know what TV directors want from reality these days. Asked whether women come on to him at castings, he admitted that at the beginning of the reality dating craze 'all these hot girls would just do anything to get on the dating shows … seriously, *anything*', before adding that no one wanted to know about these shows when they started and he often cast people he saw in the street. He then chuckled, as though recalling a quaint and distant past. 'But now, people don't just want to *be* on reality TV, they have their own reality show going on *in their head*.'

A smile …

I didn't hear anything to prepare Jess Zaino for the trials of *Glam God with Vivica A. Fox*, a VH-1 reality show which dumped twelve stylists in one house. She'd been presenting on the Style Network for the previous few years, but the ten-grand gigs hosting parties or product launches had gone the way of the economy, so when VH-1 came to her with *Glam God*, she saw 'a chance to get back in the mouths of the people who make the decisions'. And so she took it.

Regret hit her like a Siberian wind. Contestants were placed in a hotel without magazines, books, music, phones, computers or *televisions*, with 'Personal Assistants' stationed outside their doors to keep them isolated, and food strictly rationed. All you could do was lie on your bed, churning, until the show was ready to start and 'you came out of the box like an effing tiger, ready to *kill* someone'.

In the house there was one small rubbish bin and nobody to clean: there was one bathroom with no door and stage lights programmed to stay on until the last person went to sleep . . . and there was always at least one of the drama queen stylist contestants up causing havoc or grating nerves. The producers would wake you at 4 a.m. to do an interview and make sure there wasn't enough food so you had to fight for it, with cigarettes and alcohol plentiful and nowhere to excercise – all in the company of people chosen to rub you up the wrong way, with whom you had nothing in common except that they were desperate to be on telly too. In effect, contestants had been dumped into the life of Liam Gallagher, a tough gig even for him.

Zaino reached episode six of the stylist wars, having made a point of involving herself in conversations that would get camera time and be sympathetic, but the job made her 'so sick that when I got out I was like, "I need my mom" . . . to literally go into the foetal position and re-evaluate my entire life. It was retarded. I felt like I needed rehab afterwards.'

'Which would be a great idea for another show,' I say. 'Reality Rehab. Perfectly circular.'

'God, that's a great idea. No seriously – that's a great idea!'

And I'm already on the phone to Robert Russell. But here's the thing. We're talking about Jess's post-Pseudo career, with me asking whether she still enjoys the TV work and her replying: 'I don't know what I enjoy any more. I went right from Pseudo on to television, right from television out to LA, to big television, and created a sort of pseudo-celebrity for myself. But after the reality show and seeing all these people being so ugly for the sake of fame, I just felt, "I don't want that any more." So who am I, then? What does that make me? I mean, I'm like, a "style expert"? But I've never styled anybody in my life . . .'

And her voice trails off. I follow her eyes to the door.

'Speaking of reality television,' she breathes. 'Such a familiar, familiar scene for me . . .'

A man with a video camera; another with a boom microphone and headphones. Three young women and a fourth, slightly older. Sashaying into the diner and back towards the kitchen.

'These girls are doing some type of reality show.'

'What? How can you tell?' I ask.

'Because they don't look like superstars, they just look like regular people? And that "on the fly" crew? See how they're hanging back like they're not involved, and yet they're following the three girls.'

She goes over and comes back nodding, then sits down and laughs wildly, her brown eyes widening. She looks away into the distance and shakes her head.

Reality. Unreality. Virtureality.

Where am I again?

Oh yeah.

... Across town, asking the affable V. Owen Bush to explain the immersive pull of Josh's parties, with him saying: 'It wasn't just the events, it was Josh's world in general – it was like an alternative reality, there was a kind of "reality distortion field" around him and everything he was doing ... and people would get kind of addicted to that and want to stay in it all the time.'

... Asking Bush whether he thinks Josh believes the narrative theosophy he's woven around Gilligan and the DMT-inspired Ticklers, expecting a laugh and indulgent shake of the head, but getting: 'Oh, I think he believes it.' A pause. '*Yeah*, he believes it.'

And from Jeff Gompertz, a stark: 'The answer is ... yes.'

... In an East Village café, being entertained by Robert Galinsky's ticklishly accurate Josh impersonation, with him admitting after a few beers, *entre nous*, that most of the students in our Reality TV School class had been 'cast' by him; that the only 'real' thing was the media, if that counts as real. And of course *the story*.

Huh?

... Noticing that the woman in my local Brooklyn corner shop has a habit of repeating my questions before answering them.

... Or back in London, bumping into Peter Gabriel at a memorial service for a dear mutual friend, and him claiming no memory of Pseudo Immercion at all, or of ever having been to the place. His raised eyebrow and 'and I think I would remember that' as he turns to go.

And of course I believe him. Why wouldn't I?

11

> 'If personality is an unbroken series of successful gestures, then there was something gorgeous about him, some heightened sensitivity to the promises of life, as if he were related to one of those intricate machines that register earthquakes ten thousand miles away.'
>
> – F. Scott Fitzgerald, *The Great Gatsby*

Netscape's IPO had a galvanic effect on the Early True Believers. Big tech companies like Microsoft and AOL, Prodigy and Intel had been sending scouts into the area during 1995, but they were usually given short shrift, often invited to cyberslacker meetings and roasted like chestnuts. That such meetings produced 'culture clash, big time', is no surprise: at Microsoft, the word 'random' was used as an insult, but these people rejoiced in it, seemed to *wear* it the way Batman wore his cape. Even so, some ETBs developed lucrative niches in web consulting and design, and most remember the pre-gold rush time as something akin to 'magical'.

Now ETB dreams of running their own businesses seemed not just realistic – it was a no-brainer, *obvious*. Startup energy surged through SoHo like a mains spike as cash poured in and media followed, eager for a route into this sexy new story. Up to this point, no one in the Alley crowd had imagined wealth as part of the web deal, but suddenly it was, and the most satisfying thing it brought was *vindication*. Who wouldn't be a technobohemian now? Perhaps for the first time since the Victorian era, tech was socially hip. Wired-kid hangouts like the Blue Diner and Eureka Joe's coffee shop in the Flatiron District buzzed with anticipation of what was to come, because this revolution decidedly *would* be televised. Or, more accurately, 'streamed'.

The New York Times and *Wall Street Journal* had first employed the term 'Silicon Alley' the previous February, the same month *Newsweek* conferred cyber-celebrity on the young web designer Jaime Levy by including her in a big '50 for the Future' feature. The internet had been a niche story back then, but in November *New York* magazine ran a cover feature headed 'High Tech Boom Town', illustrated by an image of the landmark Flatiron Building ploughing uptown like an ocean liner. According to the journalist Jason Chervokas, the initial dearth of journalists versed in science or technology or business rendered the mainstream media vulnerable to hype, and interviews with the new Alley players would often end with writers asking after jobs.

One of the first companies to appear was Razorfish, in 1995, a year after Pseudo. Former schoolfriends and founders Craig Kanarick and Jeffrey Dachis had already made names for themselves by creating one of the web's earliest animations, which they called 'The Blue Dot' for the simple reason that it consisted of – yes! – a bouncing blue dot, at a time when there was almost no colour or movement online. With the dot as calling card, Dachis and Kanarick now promised to help Old Economy businesses adapt to this opaque new cyber-sphere, with its unseen threats and impenetrable language and pierced-nosed kids round every corner declaring yesterday dead.

Razorfish became the exemplar of the Silicon Alley startup.

Kanarick took to wearing bright Ozwald Boateng and Paul Smith suits and dying his hair different colours by the month, and the honeysuckle yellow office contained sleek steel tables and desks and expensive Aeron chairs, a velvet-covered coffin with inset DJ decks and works of art which would have appeared on the 'random' side to Microsoft folk, like a giant painting of a penis penetrating a vagina (Ed Bennett's Prodigy people would have fainted). In the company Kanarick and Dachis created, you could bring your pets to work: staff were called 'Fish' and the internal computer system 'Mom'. Jorge the receptionist owned the first floor in black jeans and tank top and army boots and one Halloween spent the entire day dressed as Lara Croft from *Tomb Raider*.

Like Pseudo, Razorfish became known for extravagant parties. You would work hard, but it would be fun and even secretaries could become paper millionaires courtesy of stock options. And to cap it all, this was a proper, profitable business. After little more than a year, the media company Omnicom paid $7 million for a 20 per cent stake in the firm and revenues stood at $32 million. Dachis became the cocky deal-hound rocking SoHo on his 900cc Ducati Monster bike, Kanarick the creative brains and reason everyone wanted to work there. The unreal rush of wealth and celebrity felt like a drug high, according to Dachis, who said, 'To be conscious of that when it's occurring ... it's like when you get stoned or something, you know? "Are you feeling what I'm feeling? Is it coming on?"'

Even so, when I ask Kanarick over coffee in a Canal Street café whether he'd ever imagined what was to come, he shakes his head vigorously. 'Never! Not in my wildest dreams. We started in a living room with three people and I fantasised about maybe sixty people in New York, twenty in London and twenty in LA ... excuses to travel to places I really like.' He pauses, looks out the window. 'Then, when it started to go beyond that, I thought, "Wow, I got on the wrong train, but it's an amazing train – I'm just going to ride it!" What I wanted more than anything was to create a place where we and our people could all work for the rest of our lives.' The kind of company X-ers thought they would never see, but now had a chance to make.

With an irony Kanarick and Dachis could never have understood at the time (even Alan Greenspan didn't), an early gig was to build schwab.com, one of the first online stock trading sites. Early on, they asked Jaime Levy to join them, but she refused, insisting that, 'I don't want to spend my life designing tampax.com.'

Other Alley startups followed thick and fast. In terms of online media and entertainment, there was @NY, Word.com, FEED and the erotica site Nerve.com; AlleyCatNews, TotalNY.com, the music site SonicNet and the Latin portal StarMedia. In terms of raw business, two of the highest profile startups were the networking site TheGlobe.com (started April '95) and the online marketing outfit DoubleClick (class of '96). Others were the women's site iVillage, web designers EarthWeb and SiteSpecific, the alternative news service disinfo.com and an accelerating stream of others. Newly formed local venture capital firms like Flatiron Partners and the Giuliani-backed Prospect Street Ventures distributed finance, with pension funds and the public piling in too. In early '95, the mayor's Lower Manhattan revitalisation task force reported its vision for a tech district to rival Silicon Valley, and work began on a 'wired space' at 55 Broad Street, two blocks south of Wall Street. The World Trade Center, still 30 per cent unoccupied in 1995, would ultimately be marketed as part of the Alley.

The culture clashes proliferated as Big Business and Old Media reluctantly tried to adapt. Tales of a fist-fight between John F. Kennedy, Jr. and the head of online activities at his *George* magazine were typical. When the conservative head of the conservative cable company TCI saw the politically left-leaning contents of disinfo.com, into which his company had shuffled more than $1 million, he hit the roof. 'What is this anarchist bullshit? – get rid of it!' he reportedly demanded. And of course, disinfo left with TCI's money and became one of the most successful sites on the web, after which TCI abandoned the internet and disappeared as a business in 1999. General Electric, NEC and News Corp all left the web too, unclear as to how they were going to make money. At the same time, AOL moved to flat-rate pricing in '96 and *soared*, Vice Chairman Ted Leonsis boasting that, 'It took *The New York Times* one hundred years to get to $1 billion in revenue . . . it took us *three*.'

Yet, the more you look at Silicon Alley in 1995–6, the less the story looks like being about the businesses themselves. Risk-seeking venture capital rained into the city. According to the National Venture Capital Association, in the 1980s and early 90s VCs invested roughly $2 billion a year, but for 1995 the figure rises to $9 billion; for '98, $29 billion; for 2000, *$103 billion* – 40 per cent of which is estimated to have gone into technology. Jerry Colonna and Fred Wilson of the newly formed Flatiron Partners raised a relatively modest $150 million and invested in twelve companies over the next two years, all but one of which were sold on for a vast profit. Fred Wilson won't tell me what he was worth at his peak, but he does glance bashfully at the floor as he laughs, 'It was a *gigantic* figure.'

The gathering investor frenzy was stoked by an entirely new phenomenon, in the form of the cable business channel CNBC, whose morning show *Squawk Box* treated the stock market like a sporting event. With global interest rates still falling and the Dow rising from 4000 to 5000 points in a mere nine months, the TV reporting was breathless, 'like a bull market frat-house party' in the words of one analyst, reflecting what a more cautious peer warned was 'a market that's been feeding on itself: the whole situation is turning into the party of the century.' One of the show's presenters, Maria Bartiromo, became the first journalist to report from the New York Stock Exchange floor as trading opened, and also the first to have access to Wall Street investment house 'morning calls', in which investment teams, analysts, managers and brokers discussed strategy for the day. No one thought to ask why the houses would want to share such valuable and privileged information with the public.

The result? According to figures published by *Fortune* magazine in April 1996, individuals poured an average of $25 billion per month into stocks that year, or roughly $100 per person – either directly or via mutual funds and retirement plans. Wealthy Americans had always held stocks, but from 1990 to '95 the middle class weighed in, followed by less affluent households through the second half of the decade. Companies started to report financial results on a quarterly basis, focusing attention ever more squarely on the short term, and anyone going to the barber's was as like to find CNBC presenters sweating and shouting stats from the shop TV as they were a baseball game. Encouraged by headlines hailing 'The Triumph of the New Economy' (*Business Week*) or declaring 'US Sails on Tranquil Economic Seas, Recession No Longer Seems Inevitable' (*Washington Post*), something very, very strange was happening: Wall Street was joining the pop culture. Over the next few years, Lehman Brothers would be bigger than the Spice Girls.

Intriguingly, when I relate these thoughts to Jerry Colonna, one of the voices I've grown to trust, he cautions me to keep in mind that, 'This is a complex story: it's not just white hats and black hats.' Then he adds, commenting on the suggestion that CNBC treated finance like sport in the 1990s: 'Yeah, it did. It does. And I would argue that, even more intensely than sporting events, what it does is serve a primal need, a primal sense of, not *greed*, but a feeling that, "If I make enough money, I will never be anxious again."'

He stops to let this sink in.

'And in a capitalist society, that feeling – that if you're

watching CNBC enough, you'll never be worried again – is *powerful.* Just like if you wear the right deodorant, you won't smell bad. It was an anti-fear mechanism. You know, *get rich.* Well, why should I get rich? So you're not afraid.'

The final Cyberslacker party in November '96 was a bittersweet affair. So much had changed in the few years since Jaime Levy invited her first handful of friends to pool knowledge and support. The business plan had become not a dream, but a route to fast money and now all her friends could talk about was stock options and IPOs. The Cybersuds gatherings she'd disdained had latterly evolved into SuperCybersuds events, drawing hundreds, soon to be *thousands* of eager young things, all looking for a piece of the action.

Even those who embraced the arrival of investors with more enthusiasm than Levy recognised that this was the end of one thing and the start of something else. Nicholas Butterworth, who'd begun the decade as bassist in a punk band and now fronted the promising startup SonicNet, delivered a fifteen-minute rap-come-rant to a backdrop of jungle music, which lurched from lament to battlecry. Around a riff of 'Baby needs new shoes, and I'm a baby!' he yelled: 'It's the death of the web as we knew it. It's over! And wasn't it good while it lasted? The dream was to be a media assassin, to be a guerilla – and to be paid! Well, let me tell you something. Now you have a choice. You can be a guerilla, *or you can get paid*. You cannot do both!'

SonicNet would ultimately be bought by MTV's parent company, Viacom, with Butterworth heading up the web-based MTVi, so he got paid. Levy would work as a designer for Word.com, before finding a rich angel investor for her own company, Electronic Hollywood. Of the hundred or so people in the room that night, perhaps half would become millionaires on paper.

'That last party, I just remember there being a shift in consciousness with everyone,' says Marc Scarpa, who went on to start a company called JumpCut. 'It was like, "OK, the dream is over but it's not gone – it's a new dream now." And some people rejected that. Jaime *really* rejected it. But folks like me just thought, "Great, we can finally make some money with this." It was very exciting. We were all working fourteen and fifteen-hour days at that time, seven days a week. It wasn't a job, it was our *lives*. And all we wanted to do was show that our ideas and instincts were right. That this secret we shared *would* change the world.'

* * *

Josh didn't go to the final Cyberslacker gathering. He was on his own trip and didn't need anyone else.

In fact, not much changed at Pseudo over the first year of the web-rush. There were more VCs and investors and journalists at parties, but still nothing to prevent Josh flying from his lair a few weeks after the Netscape IPO with instructions for everyone to drop what they were doing and prepare for a Madonna party, to feature 'Material Girl' drag queens and impressionists and Japanese karaoke singers and Bible readings and specially commissioned art works. Coincidentally or not, the event was one of the tamest yet staged at Pseudo HQ and also the first to be covered at length by *The New York Times*, in a piece headed 'Where Silicon Alley Artists Go to Download'. Pegging Josh a 'multimedia pioneer', the article began, 'Welcome to what some consider the Warhol Factory of 1995,' and went on to suggest that, 'All Silicon Alley has lacked to become a fully-fledged arts scene is its own after-hours hangout, in the same way that the Abstract Expressionists of the 50's had the Cedar Tavern and the pop artists of the 60's had Max's Kansas City ...' – until now. The reporter noted the curious ascendancy of 'techies in thick black glasses' in the downtown scene, but politely waited until the end of his piece to point out that Madonna was a curious card for a firm of super-wired futurephreakers to be playing in the mid-1990s. What the reporter didn't know, because almost no one did, was that Josh's grounds for choosing her were not entirely 'cultural'. 'No, he wanted to date her,' insists Robert Galinsky, by then a close confidante. 'That was *it* – there was no other reason!'

The queen of pop let this moment pass, but the coming year would still be Josh's favourite, with Prodigy chat and software work continuing and a well-equipped studio installed at 600 Broadway, ready for the launch of Pseudo Online Radio in January. Astutely, Josh played down the 'Warhol of the Web' angle, telling the *Times*: 'The difference here is there's no real Andy. It's this thing called Pseudo, sort of its own entity.' Programmers and producers had been experimenting with various ideas, including auction software and viral video, but now, thanks to the recent release of the RealAudio Player, radio took centre stage as the dash to New Media hotted up.

There were eighteen members of staff, with the size and makeup of the group growing and changing by the day. Shortly after the vibrant launch party for Pseudo Online Radio at the end of January '96, a burned-out Dennis Adamo left to go corporate, victim of the manic pace he'd helped set. Not only was the Executive Producer exhausted, he was losing control of his drug consumption and becoming unpredictable, to the point where colleagues felt it necessary to stage an 'intervention'. Even then, while riled co-workers were ready to cut Adamo loose, Josh surprised many by stoutly defending the troubled exec, paying for an expensive course of rehab and insisting on holding a place open for him should he want to come back. Surprising to some, the boss had a conscience.

But Adamo didn't want to come back. The business was changing and he was frustrated. On one hand, the product – and specifically the online radio portal – was becoming more professional, but on the other he considered much of the content to be 'sub-par', hostage to Josh's inability to discriminate between artists and entertainers of different value. As no one knew what the web would become, choosing a direction was like cupping mist in your hands and Josh's vision was being constantly reconfigured. Pure possibility: no one embodied this better than he. All the same, as Adamo saw it, his mentor's startling original vision was slipping away, and some promising technology was fading with it. He still sounds frustrated as he tells me:

> Josh had had this idea of the virtual world and communications under one platform, and it was brilliant. The simple philosophy was, 'We have this room – whether it's a virtual room or a physical room – and it's empty ... so let's fill it up with things, and people, and see what happens.' But then he couldn't stay focused.
>
> Look, for me, I ended up leaving the company and going into rehab, basically, from all that. But Josh is Josh: he kicked it up a notch and kept going, sometimes in directions that had no bearing on what the original idea was, which was to grow these virtual worlds and create communications around them.

And I'm thinking: the story of this diffusion is the story I have to find; is the story of Josh and Silicon Alley and the first dotcom boom.

From January there was a steady stream of newcomers, too, most of whom describe the same scene upon entering the loft for the first time. There would be: a) a pack of dogs pounding down the hall to the lift, scattering cats to the wind and often led by JudgeCal's Rottweiler, Memphis; b) young people distributed through the space, working intently alone or in knots, virtually living there, in; c) an environment where job titles were meaningless and dress discretionary (at times *optional*) as outsiders wandered up from the street to gawp at; d) the Betty project, this avatar-driven 3D world designed to be Prodigy's secret weapon in the battle with AOL. Also notable was the fact that almost everybody in the house seemed to have their own show.

In the back, Josh might be found reclining, feet on desk and cigar in mouth like some Gap-garbed Churchill – 'arrogant prick!' laughs one ex-staffer – or gazing into a huge aquarium left over from a party, which he spent a fortune stocking with exotic tropical fish, most of which would quickly expire for no apparent reason and much to their owner's vexation.

One newcomer, who'd turned down a job at Microsoft for Pseudo, describes being alarmed by the lack of boundaries at first, but growing to love this early phase, which was built on 'a really organic – yet *digital* – environment, nothing such as you'd get in a place like Microsoft'.

No: Pseudo wasn't just *random*, it was the Manhattan Project of randomness and the only sin in Josh's world was to bore him. And if money was still tight, it always seemed to arrive when necessary.

Best of all, outside the loft, Silicon Alley was coming alive, as other companies arrived and started throwing extravagant parties of their own, to the point where you never had to buy either drink or dinner and could survive on free sushi for weeks on end if so minded. Incomers had heard about the hedonism of the 1980s, but as one points out, 'That was mostly on Wall Street and now *kids* were getting money! . . . Has that ever really happened before? In the 60s they got laid, but apart from the rock stars they didn't get money . . .' Or, as another entreats: 'Imagine being in your twenties and all of a sudden everyone's able to take control of their fucking lives in terms of what they do – *complete freedom*, because all of this software is coming out. *And*, there's this thing where we can *publicise it* ourselves, and not be completely a slave to the *Village Voice* or *New York Times* or the PR industry, which was starting to control everything else. It was amazing!'

Pseudo stood at the gateway to SoHo, was pre-established and with a production facility ready to be used by other start-ups: energy blew in from the street like air from the lift shaft. New arrivals typically earned 25–30K in 1996 dollars ('pretty good compared to the previous five years!') and understood the remit as being 'to make a media network for the web'. As with everyone else in the Alley, the mantra became 'build it and they will come' – the phrase taken from the movie *Field of Dreams*, in which farmer Kevin Costner hears voices instructing him to raze his corn and build a baseball field for ghosts to play on.

But the dotcommers wanted to build something different from the corporate America that had rejected them. In this respect, these hopeful first dotcoms *were* equivalent to the communes of the 1970s, the big difference being that this time the establishment bought into what they were doing. Police raids stopped. Greenback tendrils crept over from Wall Street. A more exciting place than SoHo was hard to imagine that year.

Of course, working for Josh Harris was still its own thing, with its own unique aggravation. Jim Hall joined in January on an eccentric remit that included oversight of the art department and tidying the boss's chambers, until he downed tools on the latter ('it was a *pigsty*!') – in response to which Josh, being Josh, simply re-assigned Hall and hired some other poor soul to tame his mess. Hall, who lives and works in London now, was highly computer-literate, so had seen through the 'buzzword spew' Dennis Adamo deployed to recruit him, but was surprised at how bright and hard-working the people in the building were. All the same, he quickly saw the downside when one Friday Josh called him in and blurted, 'You have to fire all my designers – I want to clear 'em out.' Needless to say, after a miserable weekend of fretting, taking advice, steeling himself for the task,

Hall arrived at Pseudo on Monday to a casual announcement that the boss had changed his mind. Josh was forever trying to make his artists more productive, Hall says.

> And it was tough for me, because these guys were dyed-in-the-wool artists, who thought differently, spoke differently and lived life differently than 99 per cent of the population. Owen, Jeff Gompertz, Jacques Tege … these were in my opinion the real talent, and when they did their thing, when they created a space, did their installations, their stuff was *incredible*. It was art of a quality that not many other people associated with Pseudo can lay claim to. But the problem was reconciling them to a business, getting them to do something that was appealing to the *other side*. Cos in 1996 the audience was on Prodigy, not the web, which was still like the Wild West.

In June Josh's worst nightmare came true. As part of a general retreat from the internet on the part of US big business, who saw no means of profiting from this anarchic new medium, IBM and Sears sold Prodigy to a Mexican telecoms firm for a fraction of what they'd invested (with the Mexicans paying $78 million according to a subsequent IPO filing). In the shake-up, the party-loving, bong-worshipping, Josh-getting Ed Bennett left, making the switch to flat-rate billing even more inevitable at a time when free chat forums were springing up all over the web. On 16 October, Prodigy duly became the second online service provider to dump the hourly billing model, and Pseudo's life-giving royalty income with it.

Josh had known this was coming – the question had only ever been *when* – and had long harboured fears that Prodigy management, more resentful of the money he was making than grateful for the far larger sums he brought *them*, would simply co-opt his work and cancel the contract anyway: a classic case of what he colourfully termed 'the corporate drive-by'. But again he'd been one step ahead. By insisting that the original contract be signed 'in perpetuity', he had ensured that Prodigy's only means of escape was via a payoff.

To help with exit negotiations, Josh enlisted Anthony Asnes, a well-regarded businessman he'd been courting, and a deal was struck whereby Prodigy acquired Pseudo's existing chat business and share of the Betty Project for $2.1 million, paid in installments. From the jaws of defeat, *victory*: the Broadway and Houston upstart now had a substantial income from something which would ultimately have withered to nothing; their first guaranteed long range funding. Better still, the well-heeled Asnes now felt safe to sign on as President and Chief Operating Officer (COO) for no salary but a 25 per cent share of equity in the company. In the blink of an eye, Pseudo looked like a business. Josh could move to the web without fear.

* * *

Asnes is an intriguing one. Dashing and charismatic, with something of the *Blade Runner* actor Rutger Hauer about him, he exudes ease and entitlement, simply couldn't be less like the greater rump of Pseudites. All the same, before being allowed to activate my recorder in the upscale midtown eaterie he chose for our meeting, I'm amused and a little alarmed to be subjected to a stern interrogation.

Why? Because the 'Pseudo: a Fake Company' letter I found Josh writing in Awassa, in which he claims the dotcom always to have been an art project, never a business, has recently been published and Asnes is not alone in being both offended and wary of legal action by angry former investors. He wants to know whether I believe the 'fake company' line, so I tell him truthfully that I don't; that I think something more interesting is going on in Josh's head as he constructs this grand narrative of self, but that his ambitions for Pseudo were genuine – in the beginning, at least. What I don't tell him is that the harder I stare at Pseudo's flash rise and fall, the more extraordinary it looks and the less it seems to be about Josh.

Eventually satisfied as to my intentions, Asnes describes a career which began with a computer science degree from Yale and Masters in Management from MIT; which took him to the Stock Exchange floor ('much less chaotic than it looked and kind of fun') and into management consultancy ('exciting, I loved the strategic element'). By the mid-90s he felt ready 'to roll up my sleeves and build something', saw what was happening in the 'internet space' and 'realised this was going to be an interesting place to have an adventure'. He put out feelers, spoke to some people, soon heard about Josh Harris and the scene at Broadway and Houston. For several months the pair met once every week or two, for hours over coffee in SoHo, with Asnes 'trying to get comfortable with the ideas, asking, "What are you doing, what are you seeing?" . . . It wasn't that we had an interview,' he says. 'I was intrigued by Josh and this crazy place.'

Asnes explains the intuitive appeal this 'space' held for businesspeople – something Jim Clark of Netscape had been among the first to see. Thanks to its cybernetic structure and ethos, the special property of the internet is that if you have twenty users and add one, you create not one, but *twenty* new relationships. Add two and you have forty-one new relationships.

And so if you add a million . . .

Numbers become vast in the blink of an eye: growth is exponential. Business can 'scale' in ways that had never been dreamed of before the web and in the early days you didn't need much capital or a factory or to worry about the lead times associated with manufacture. The essential tools were intellect and imagination, two imponderables New York held in abundance. The only problem was how to make it pay, but no one doubted that this would be solved sooner rather than later.

Most of the other web New Media startups carried conceptual baggage from the Old Economy, their philosophy being to create 'content' which drew 'eyeballs', an *audience* which could then be 'monetised' through advertising in the way of real world newspapers, magazines and TV. Yet the former Pseudo COO insists matter-of-factly that Josh *always* had the idea that Pseudo users would generate the content one day; that the experience would be about interaction.

> The theory was that, in order to get users to start doing this, we needed to show them how interesting it is, by making our own stuff. And then once they were with us, we would set up facilities to help them participate. This made for a rich creative environment – ten channel teams all within one building ultimately, each working on their own subculture and creating this programming. But actually, the original thing, the thing we were working at that ended up working *at scale* ten years later, was the simple software that would allow you just to upload your own video.

I listen quietly as Asnes speaks, still as wary of this line as I am of Josh's claims about *Launder My Head* and the fake girlfriend. How many people out there retrospectively think they dreamed up YouTube, I wonder? Roiling waves of anamorphic memory . . .

I also wonder what persuaded someone like Asnes to buy into a wild card like Josh. He smiles at the question. 'Well one of the things that happens when you have these conversations over a protracted period of time is that you get to know people well. And one of the things I liked about Josh is that I felt he had a high degree of integrity. That he was trustworthy. Because effectively we were venturing into a partnership. He'll do what he needs to do to be successful, but I don't think that he would do anything dishonest. In fact, I *know* he won't.'

I'm dumbfounded. Really?

'Yeah. And you see, that's why this "performance art" stuff doesn't fit. Josh is smart like a fox, and I think he really cared about his investment. It wasn't *just* performance art.'

Asnes goes on to say that one of Josh's strengths as a businessman was in being able 'to argue and still keep communications open – at least that's what I found, and I think he was the same with everybody.' The only consistent bone of contention between the two men was over the value of press. Josh thought all publicity was good publicity: Asnes didn't.

* * *

In the midst of Prodigy negotiations, an event of even greater moment for Josh took place. Round about September 1996, he met Tanya Corrin.

When Josh talks about women he's had relationships with, his head waggles like a nodding dog's and his eyes laser panic. He'd been a virgin when he arrived at UCSD and remained so until his junior year. A first girlfriend, with whom he didn't have sex, left him pining for months; a second had sex with him twice before they split, leaving him alone until his final term. Read any of his private musings on the subject and confusion eddies across the page, a mix of anguish and hurt and powerful longing for something he wants but can't seem to have. A suspicion that women are perpetually on the lookout for something better or which he can't provide.

In an unpublished memoir he began while holed up in Malta one winter, he refers drily to 'the only time I can say for sure that I made a woman come,' adding that 'I've still never received a great blowjob' (frankness, as ever, employed as a form of concealment, because how could he know – they might *all* have been great). Most of us are capable of detaching sex from emotion to one degree or another, but there's a special kind of detachment to the way Josh speaks of 'getting the deed done' or writes, 'As per my occasional habit, I used the bathroom as a means of escaping a mild case of post-orgasmic disgust.' The moment of truth: an instant following orgasm, in which a man is compelled to see himself with a clarity available at no other time; in which he knows why he's there, what lies or truths he may have told on the way and whether he wants to be there still ... in which, stripped of carnality, vulnerable in those moments, he sees *who he actually is*. Josh isn't the first male to find this alarming. For all his embroidery and self-mythologising, he can be heartbreakingly sensitive to his own truth, in a way that most more 'normal' people are not.

Against this, he speaks with real feeling about a couple of encounters he had in Paris while working on a report for the EU during his time at Jupiter, one with an Irish woman he couldn't bring himself to declare his desire for, another with a married stewardess he knew he couldn't have. Most of his pre-Pseudo sexual experiences with women seem to have involved either a) them wanting him, he not them or b) him wanting them, but backing away from sex or c) having sex and the relationship ending soon after. There's a touching poignancy to his later declaration that, 'I am asexual. I do not believe it is a permanent condition but rather a rational lifestyle choice, a *modus operandi* if you will ... my strategy (to date unproven) is to have one great love in my life instead of a string of lesser amours.' All suggesting either rationalisation or an antiseptic, *screen-fed* view of love, romance, relationships, sex. When Jess Zaino, who has a 'ridiculous affection' for Josh, says, 'He's a weirdo with women,' she's not wrong, even if most of the men find him weird too. The twist is that women tend to be bafflingly fond of him.

At Pseudo, Josh's relationship to women changed. Now he was leader of the team, the quarterback, and women previously unavailable to him by the cruel algebra of attraction suddenly *were*. If he didn't know what to do with his new nerd-jock status, it's hardly surprising – which is not to say that he gorged himself, as might have been expected. And you have to wonder what man other than Josh would not only count the total number of lays during his four-year stay in the back of Pseudo HQ (thirty-five, with eight different women), but classify them as either 'one-nighters', 'taste-testers' or 'business', and then admit that, 'I can't recall one really good session over the duration.' He tells me with a laugh that 'statistically-speaking, Tanya accounts for 20 per cent of my overall masturbation fantasies . . .' Information you don't necessarily covet when sleeping in the next room in the depths of Africa, but then Josh is Josh.

The Pseudo games started with Kim, who came to one of the first parties and captivated Josh by singing a version of the Velvet Underground's 'Femme Fatale', which he'd never heard previously. Before he knew it, she'd moved into his chambers at 600 Broadway, nominally working as a Pseudo PR, introducing him to Nico's wonderful *Chelsea Girl* album and encouraging a brief flirtation with hedonism. Alex Arcadia recalls seeing Josh come out of the back in a kind of trance one night, with white stuff on his nose.

> And I don't know if he was doing coke or what – she did a lot of it, but I didn't think he was that type . . . and he just started like, almost convulsing to the music on the floor. That's when I first realised that he wasn't the stuffed-shirt, corporate fucker that you could perceive him as. He was always dressed pretty preppy, with the tie and everything. But when I saw him do that, with everybody else there, I thought, 'OK. . .' The thing is, Josh never did anything to excess. What he did, he did in moderation, and always as a part of something else. As a *prop*, basically.

In truth, Josh had never forgotten the night he stayed up snorting coke with a drug-dealing USC room-mate, only to find 'some psycho-centre urge' calling for more a fortnight later, promoting a resolution never to surrender his self-will so completely again.

The relationship with Kim lasted six weeks and, despite the sharing of his bed, was largely asexual, partly at least because her overindulgence in alcohol reminded Josh of his mother. When he told the singer to move out, at least three staff arrived for work the next morning to see a limo pull up and dump her on the pavement, near-naked in panties and open shirt in the middle of a New York cold snap, then pull away as she ran unshod, mascara streaming, feet bleeding down the snowy street – carrying a boa and flinging herself on to the car's bonnet, screaming, 'Madonna stole my purse!' by one account, 'Madonna needs towels!' by another. When the *Launder* animator Jacques Tege persuaded her away from the limo, she ran into a car wash on the north side of Houston, where she stayed until police carted her off to Bellevue. Afterwards, Josh expressed guilt that he hadn't seen the signs and arranged help sooner. The socially conservative Tege, meanwhile, began to worry that his friend had slipped out of his depth. 'The beast is out of the cage,' he thought.

I've changed Kim's name in deference to her current life, but Josh claims to have remembered this earlier drama when he met Tanya Corrin at a Pseudo party. His version is that Corrin turned up with a boyfriend, was beautiful and vivacious and subtly signalling interest, but when she went off to the bathroom he stayed talking to the consort and found a man whose spirit had been crushed, who was '*hollow*, just dead like a zombie – like she'd taken him and scooped him out piece by piece'. And he was fascinated by this power, remembered the sour-sweet breeze of Nico singing Lou Reed's 'Femme Fatale' . . .

Here she comes, you'd better watch your step . . .

And the next time Tanya came to a party she was on her own. Available. And in a flash he had the germ of his *We Live in Public* project . . . thought about it repeatedly over the coming months and decided to make it happen. Tanya had shown him the way to his own unique art form.

I haven't met a single person who buys Tanya as 'fake girlfriend' or believes Josh's version of their relationship as an art project, though opinion as to the relationship's true dynamic is strikingly divergent. I look for patterns of view according to gender, age, vocation, but can't find any. Nancy Smith the quilt-maker thinks Tanya loved him, he pushed her away, while Jess Zaino considers the opposite, saying with a sad smile: 'Did Tanya love Josh? *Honestly?* No. Tanya was really ambitious. She was so beautiful and doe-eyed, almost breathtaking, and so *smart* – but almost, like, smart but *dumb*. It always seemed like she knew what she was doing.'

Asked why *any* woman would try to have a romantic relationship with Josh, she all but shudders. 'Well I was so intimidated by him, but as a woman, he always has this aura of, like, "Stop". There is a very clear shield around him, so you just sort of step back. He's one of the funniest, most fascinating men ev-ver – in the history of men! But you never want to be close.'

Betty Wasserman knew Josh as well as anyone back then. Now a successful interior designer, she treats me with caution at first, perhaps because her current life is so different to the wild ride of her mid-twenties – a contrast I see clearly when she invites me to an expensively catered *Interiors Magazine* party in an apartment which looks, as is the way in New York high society, not so much as though it's been designed by Ivana Trump, but by Ivana Trump's *hair*. Over thimblefuls of cold soup and increasingly fantastical cocktails, she's soon laughing as she tries to explain Josh, whom she hasn't seen or spoken to in years and thinks of as 'like an idiot savant'.

'He's socially ri*di*culous. I mean he has *terrible* social skills. And I think he was actually quite shy, despite what he was inventing and hosting.'

She tells me about the time he was sick and didn't have anybody ('or wouldn't *let* anybody') look after him, so she made a motherly matzah-ball soup and took it in to Pseudo. Everyone warned her against bothering him while he was ill, but she knocked on his door anyway. He told her he was sick and she explained that she knew as much, so had brought food, at which point he asked what it was and she told him matzah-ball soup. 'And he said ... I will *never* forget this. He said, "Are they hard? Because I don't like 'em soft."'

A gleeful laugh.

As though he could see the soup, but not the meaning of the soup – the gesture.

'Exactly. His social skills were horrendous! And I said, "They're the way that I make them, and it's the way you're going to *have* them. *Open the door.*" And he opened the door and he took them, and he looked me in the eye, and he was like, "Thanks." And then he closed the door and that was it, he never brought it up again, and he never talked about it again.'

Wasserman's take on the relationship with Corrin, whom she became close enough to that Josh imagined yet another affair, is more nuanced than most. 'I believe that he didn't love her,' she says after a pause when I raise the subject. 'I think that he wanted to and tried to, and there were things about her – I mean she was beautiful and kind, and she was madly in love with him. But I don't think he liked him*self* enough to love anyone. I *don't*.'

She posits a situation in which he was trying to keep her satisfied while getting nothing back for himself. 'That's how I always viewed him in relationships, anyway,' she says, exhaling deeply as though tense at the memory. 'I think he liked the idea of having someone there and interested in looking after him. But with Tanya it was almost more the eye candy than anything else. I don't think he ever really believed in her or felt that she was his equal. And I'm not sure that she was, quite frankly.'

I suggest that Josh must have had people coming on to him for the first time in his life: that one of the only regrets he will admit to is that he didn't make more use of his opportunities. Again, she laughs.

'*Yeah!* Because he really was quite a nerd actually. And because he was a little socially awkward, a *misfit* in a way, and was difficult to understand and to reach and to read, I think that made him *more* attractive. I think people were confused by him, and didn't know how to react to him or talk to him. And I think all those things made him kind of sexier. More mysterious.'

Does Betty think he might have sensed and played on this appeal?

'Yes, absolutely. Abso*lute*ly. He is a really smart guy – nothing gets past him.'

Again that apparent contradiction, between social skills that are at once clumsy and (to quote Spyro Poulos) 'insidiously sharp'.

Wasserman smiles.

'I *know*. So he really is an interesting guy. A *complete* observer. That's why he was so quiet all the time: he was always listening and watching and noticing and studying. I do believe, though, despite what anyone else might say, that he has a good heart. He's sweet underneath it all. And he's trustworthy. If you confide in him, he'll keep it to himself. He can keep a secret.'

So we come back to the idea of Josh as what Malcolm Gladwell would call an 'outlier'. Someone who, thanks to an unusual set of circumstances, is in advance of the rest of us. Betty notes that her 7-year-old daughter's idea of a 'play-date' is to sit on her bed with a friend, each playing on their own Nintendo DS; that 'The idea of emailing or texting is far more appealing than just getting on the phone and talking to grandma.' And I feel a little pang, because my two children have just asked me to text rather than phone when we're apart. Is Josh, for all his oddness, simply *ahead of the game*? In fact, is that what his oddness consists in? Are we, in some unconscious way, *him*?

There was another reason I wanted to talk to Betty Wasserman, though. As part of Josh's inner circle during the mad boom years, she was present for many of the wilder private excursions, such as the small, private DMT drug party Josh spoke about in Awassa, where she watched a handful of New York hipsters flip as they tripped with 'Brian the Evil Shaman' in Josh's bedroom. 'It was huge,' she says when reminded of that night. 'I mean, personally, I wasn't really that interested ... I think I was more frightened than I was curious.'

She claims not to remember the details of her trip and doesn't recall Josh being one of the most deeply affected. More significantly, she doesn't think he changed or became more erratic afterwards, so agreeing with Owen Bush ('no, he's always been the way he is') and Jupiter Communications' CEO Gene De Rose ('one of the most unorthodox people I'd ever met, right from the outset'), and with Jess Zaino, who says simply that, 'Josh has always remained completely consistent to me. I mean from then til now, *completely consistent*. It's like he threw himself into the spotlight and then withdrew as much as a human can withdraw.'

Again the question is *why?* What did he see?

12

The next meeting with Josh is comically different to the first. Shortly before I went to stay in Awassa, I'd been unsettled to learn that a filmmaker was making a documentary about him. My discomfiture lessened upon hearing that the filmmaker was Ondi Timoner, whose rockumentary *Dig!*, about the relationship between two musician friends whose career paths diverge wildly, is a favourite of mine. I also learned that the Californian director had found the same early incomprehension among producers as I had publishers – until suddenly in early 2008 and for no easily discernible reason, a few began to get it. Something, clearly, had changed.

When I called, Timoner told me that her connection to Josh went all the way back to the Millennium happening *Quiet*, which she had been hired to record for a movie he planned to make. Afterwards, she'd taken a rough edit to the Sundance Film Festival in the Rocky peaks of Utah, only for her employer to show up and snatch the footage back, apparently possessed of a fear that he looked fat in it. She took this to be the end of her place in the crazed Harris story, until she won the Best Documentary award for *Dig!* at Sundance in 2004 and he reappeared, imploring her to finish the *Quiet* job. Understandably reluctant at first, she changed her mind as the first decade of the new century progressed and the online world began to take hold, and it became clear that society was being dramatically changed, *evolved* in ways which few of us could have foreseen, some of which concerned her. And the more she listened to inquiet debates about the social implications of this parallel domain, the more she began to see Josh Harris mirrored in them, just as I had; to recognise things he'd been saying and ideas he'd been testing – often with destructive abandon – for years, but which almost no one, not even she, had properly understood.

I was amazed to learn later in the year that Timoner had rushed to finish a cut of the film, now called *We Live in Public*, and that it had been accepted for competition at the next Sundance Festival in January '09. Josh had been keeping me up to speed via email, so I knew that while he and the director clashed prodigiously on every aspect of the production, he also harboured a hope that it would offer him some sort of creative lifeline. When he suggested I fly out for the first screening, I readily agreed, astonished and a little awed at the anomalous arc he traced.

The intervening months had seen the social implications of the web inch to the front of media debate. Interesting to me was the way most commentators fit the mould of either evangelist or Cassandra, with a strong sense of *kismet*, fatalism, as if the technology had robbed us of agency or choice, was good or bad in and of itself. The fact that young people ran and roamed these spaces at will, free from the controlling hand of grown-up economics, was disconcerting to elders. Suddenly cyberspace was looking more like the Wild West of old – 'old' in this compressed reality being circa 1994.

All of which seemed to miss the point, because tools gain power only from the uses we put them to, the needs they meet, and what made the web special was its extraordinary reflexivity – the speed and accuracy with which it could reflect us back to ourselves, free of routine social constraint. That people were using it to play with identity, to reconfigure them*selves* and their relationships to the world, suggested that the old identities/selves/relationships were no longer satisfying. It was as though our environment had changed, *we were changing*, but no one had noticed until the web thrust a mirror to us. On the plane to Utah, I couldn't stop listening to a tune called 'Aidy's Girl's a Computer' by an electronic duo called Darkstar, which caught my attention after someone likened it to 'the sound of circuitry crying'.

'The sense you get from "Aidy's Girl" is that the human, physical world has revolved ever so slightly out of reach,' wrote one reviewer. 'It's heartbreakingly beautiful.' For some reason it makes my spine shiver.

To people in most parts of the world, the Sundance Film Festival would look freakier than anything the citizens of Awassa could perpetrate. Hosted annually by the actor Robert Redford in the Rocky Mountain prospector's-town-turned-ski-resort of Park City, the jamboree began as a forum for independent filmmakers, but in recent years has been hijacked by the major studios. Among those who regret this tinseltown invasion is Redford himself but, as he points out, there's nothing he or the committee can do to stop it. 'We're just going to have to wait out this trend,' he says.

Picture. A tiny ski resort suddenly overrun with thousands of AmEx-waving producers and execs and actors and celebs – and trailing army of TV camera crews, all spinning from *this* 'gifting suite', where rich famous people are invited to help themselves to designer goods by brands eager to be associated with them, to *that* private reception, to one of the ski slopes which empties right on to Main Street. But working hard, too, if by work you mean the work of avoiding any contact with actual independent filmmakers, or indeed *films* ... Sundance is a Robert Altman movie waiting to happen, from the Groundhog Day bus system, which could have been modelled on an Escher sketch and turns even the shortest journey into a forty-five-minute Homerian odyssey, to the mirror-shaded, headset-wedded playas barking into iPhones, oblivious to the people giggling around them. Favourite overheard ejaculations are:

'Bob is VERY angry, Bob.'

'No, she has her breast reduction surgery that week.'

'Yes, he cuts pieces off of his body. He's looking for a woman who can appreciate him.'

And:

'Yes ... yes ... yes. Just make sure Jake doesn't kick the llama, OK?'

I also love the way 'historic' – the word Americans use to describe anything older than Britney Spears – is attached to absolutely everything in Park City, and suspect the film people's constant motion owes something to a fear that if you stand in one place for too long you might actually qualify as 'historic' and have a sign slapped on you. Park City is 8000 feet above sea level, an altitude at which air thins and money dissolves in your pocket; the spiritual (and actual) home of the twenty-dollar tuna sandwich. There is nowhere else quite like it.

For all that, everyone agrees that the star of this year's show is the recession, with numbers down and celebs harder to spot. The length and breadth of Main Street, tanned TV presenters march toward cameras trying to sound excited as they gush, 'And unconfirmed reports that CHRIS ROCK! hit town last night are as yet, uh, unconfirmed,' or interviewing members of the public who say, 'Oh yeah, I saw ... what's his name? The one from *Twin Peaks* . . . you know? And *Dune*? Gosh, it'll come to me in a minute! Oh, and Weird Al Yankovich, I think . . .' More importantly, by the time I arrive for the second of the festival's two weeks, only two distribution deals have been done for the hundreds of independently produced films on show. The word is that the middle ground, the space for films made on budgets of $2–30 million, is collapsing, and that the environment is most hostile to documentaries hoping for a theatrical release – ironically, one of the creative success stories of recent years.

The other big story is the internet, which is changing the economics of the business in ways which still aren't clear. As a result, the place to which I find myself drawn is the parallel Slamdance festival, run from a hotel at the top of the main drag by the British producer Peter Baxter, for films made on budgets of less than a million dollars. Baxter likens the present situation in film to the first wave of dotcoms, in that new distribution models are laying waste the old ones, but no one's worked out how to organise or make money yet. It's exciting and frightening in equal measure – and precisely what Josh and his peers were grappling with at the end of the twentieth century. At a seminar on web distribution, someone even says, 'All of this comes down to real estate; planting your flag.'

Josh and I have been in constant touch about his Ethiopian gangster friends and the graza monkey; about another tortoise and a baby baboon he took as a pet but was forced to return when it proved needy and unpredictable. He's enthused about his idea for turning the traditional Ethiopian tea ceremony – a friendship ritual performed over four or five hours by women – into a league which could be televised like darts, wanting me to approach Channel 4 with the idea, and has wished me Happy New Year on Ethiopian New Year's Day, which, remarkably, falls on our September 11. I also know, though not from him, that a Brooklyn filmmaker has been interviewing former Pseudites for another film, this one merging his story with that of the scandalous 1920s poet Harry Crosby, 'recontextualising' the filmed testimony to fit a fictionalised character called Cardero. Fantasy and fiction melding again ... I try to picture how the movie might work, but can't.

In the months since I last saw Josh, an account of his early life has started to take shape. As an interviewer, you never know how much store to set by specific childhood memory, but emotional memory does have force for me, as though it gets locked inside the body, becomes part of a person's fabric and *has truth* – whether what it relates to is 'true' or not. So when I ask Josh about his early life and he tells me about his family sitting down to meals together maybe five times a year; or the memory of burning himself as he reached into a deep-fat fryer to grab a burrito before they were all gone on one of these occasions, and no one seeming much concerned; or of his father preening in the bathroom as he readied himself for work, offhandedly telling him to get his cough seen to by the doctor after school, a cough which turned out to be pneumonia; or of his mother moving the seven Harris children to a tiny apartment in Ventura after her husband lost everything on pork belly futures and simply *left* ('The markets are a crap-shoot,' Ted Harris later warned his son); or of sharing two cheap metal-framed bunk beds with his three brothers and a neighbour's kids not being allowed to play with him because he didn't come from a 'good family' ... I believe the psychological truth of what he's saying.

By Josh's account, Ted Harris had fought as a Marine during World War II, then bounced from job to job afterwards, emulating the experience of his own father. The boy's happiest time was after 1970, when Ted swooped back from a five-year estrangement and took the family away to Geneva, to live in a seventeenth-century villa fronting the lake. Stable though this time was for the clan as a whole, Josh still settles on his struggles at the private Collège du Léman after his father misguidedly insisted he skip a grade, and on his maternal grandmother crying over her sixtieth-birthday cake, because her birthday had never been celebrated before.

The Harrises stayed in Geneva for nine months before transferring to Ethiopia, where in Josh's pre-teen eyes the old man became a dashing, dangerous figure who mixed with leaders and diplomats and introduced the awestruck boy to Emperor Selassie; who cheated at cards and let Josh carry his gun on payroll runs and whose friends had either the 'I have killed people' or 'I am soon to be brutally murdered' veneer to them. Whose occasional war stories – of holding a friend whose legs had been blown away while he died, and of coming home with a Purple Heart – suddenly made sense. Even as an adult, Josh likes to cast his father as a spy, the undercover dad whose attention and approval he craved but could never rely upon: interestingly also the most common complaint against *him*.

After living in Addis and Awassa, the Harrises returned to LA then split, Ted taking an apartment on upscale Wilshire with his long-time mistress. Josh resented his father's remarriage to a woman he claims to have looked 'just like Tanya Corrin', and the new regime did nothing to curb the trademark paternal vanishings. To say that Harris senior had a weak heart sounds like a metaphor, but the truth is that he *did* have a weak heart and had come home in part to have it treated. In the middle of a third operation, however, at about the age Josh was when I found him, Ted Harris died, removing even the semblance of a father figure from the 15-year-old son's life.

Thereafter, Josh's best times came on fishing trips to Santa Monica pier in the company of similarly nerdy friends. He coasted through school; won his place at UCSD; set about rebuilding the world on his own terms.

*

The next morning is pure Josh. Having arrived last night and warned me that, 'I'm on the meathook here,' he suggests that I come along to some of the interviews he's doing, but thanks to a combination of garbled information and the fact that almost no one knows where anything is, I manage to reach each venue just after he's been dragged away to the next, harbouring an ever-so-slight suspicion that this is what he'd intended. 'You missed a good one there,' he teases by text, sounding upbeat and as though he's enjoying the attention and chance to tell his story, so re-affirming its value. Story is pretty much all he has now, it occurs to me, followed by a disquieting thought: that perhaps it's all he *is* now.

We give up and agree to meet at dinnertime, leaving me to enjoy the incongruities of the festival. Barack Obama is to be inaugurated as President tomorrow and the movie people will throw their gifting bags in the air and cry for joy in the street, but today's *New York Times* carries a piece on his favourite books. 'Like [Obama's autobiography] *Dreams of My Father*, many of the novels Mr Obama reportedly admires deal with the question of identity,' the paper notes, adding that the President-elect had recently been spied carrying a collection of poetry by Derek Walcott, whose verse 'explores what it means to be a "divided child", caught on the margins of different cultures, dislocated and rootless perhaps, but free to invent a new self . . .' It adds that 'This notion of self-creation is a deeply American one – a founding principle of the country and a trope addressed by such classic works as *The Great Gatsby* – and it seems to exert a strong hold on Mr Obama's imagination.'

The paper also quotes from a 2005 *Time* magazine essay in which Obama compared his humble beginnings to those of Abraham Lincoln, a man he admires and who reminds him of 'a larger, fundamental element of American life – the enduring belief that we can constantly remake ourselves to fit our larger dreams'.

The afternoon passes brightly. Marching up Main Street en route to meeting a friend who (not uncoincidentally) ended up co-producing *We Live in Public*, I find a large crowd gazing expectantly at the door of a restaurant, like a colony of penguins waiting to be fed at the zoo. I stop and watch and when nothing appears to be happening, whisper a query to the ski-jacketed cameraman next to me.

'Oh, they think Jim Carrey's in there,' he blurts without breaking his own gaze at the door.

'Right. So is he?' I ask.

'No,' he replies.

I think I'm getting the measure of the place. Over coffee, the producer John Battsek and his partner Andrew Ruhemann fill me in on the battleground that has been *We Live in Public* post-production. I myself had a minor run-in with Ondi Timoner when she wanted a piece of footage I brought back from Awassa on a hard drive, and I was taken aback by how quickly a disagreement over how to get it to her escalated. What I didn't know was that post-production money had all but run out and Timoner, heavily invested emotionally and financially, was at her wit's end – until an 'angel' investor turned up at the eleventh hour.

Now I learn that there have been serious clashes over content, too. Timoner's decision to open the film with a video Josh sent to his mother as she was dying, a cool goodbye that, being without context, was felt to instantly set him up as unsympathetic. Most everyone but Timoner thought this an audience-alienating disaster, but she stuck to her guns and relationships remain strained all round.

When I see the freshly minted screen star in a café at six, it's all I can do to stop from laughing out loud. The last time I saw him was in Africa, playing spy in the streets of Awassa eight thousand miles away, with servants and a compound and gangsters at the gate – and now six months later here he is, sat alone at a round, white, *empty* Formica-topped table, wearing the khaki trousers I took to Awassa and a thin beige jacket, chomping a cigar and gazing in apparent amusement at the hypergroomed movie spods swishing past in expensive ski gear, looking so definitively out of place and time and lacking in style code or dress sense that the monastic lack of 'look' could be mistaken for a look. I'm imagining what a fabulous painting he would make when he cracks into a grin and I'm surprised at how happy I am to see him. Unlikely as it sounds, his aura is changed from the last time I saw him: here in the mountains, he radiates a sense of *peace*.

I tell him he looks well and he instantly relates this to his weight, in the heartbreaking way that dieting women sometimes do. He recounts an eventful night in the steam room at the Addis Hilton prior to his long journey here and laughs as I describe my bus trip from Awassa to Addis in detail for the first time, before unfurling a trademark yarn about the shady character who ghosted on to his US-bound flight at the last minute and sat next to him, whom he imagines to have been an IRS tax spy. 'And I realised I took care of that side of things pretty well . . . it made me feel safe,' he says before accepting an offer of coffee and something to eat, with an 'OK, I'll let you. I only brought forty dollars to America. And I feel so comfortable about that.'

They poisoned the dogs in Awassa just before he left and for a couple of days the neighbourhood was edgy and silent, its natural warning system gone. Tensions have increased since I was there, he adds, with the government stepping up verbal attacks on NGO relief agencies and two *faranji* having been murdered in the past couple of months. He describes a recent trip to court, which consisted of a couple of large women behind desks, with one prospective convict having made a little bonfire on the courtroom floor to facilitate the lighting of his roll-up cigarettes. 'It was pretty relaxed,' he concludes, expressing horror at the doughy culture he finds himself re-immersed in here. 'You should hear all the people in the house I'm staying in . . . they're so obsessed with selling themselves,' he says. And seeing my amusement at this statement, he beams and adds: 'Yeah, I guess I was like that once.'

As if from a sense of duty, he hints at still being watched by sinister State agencies, which I should beware of lest they target me by association, then talks excitedly about a big new plan he's got for the web and a hoped-for meeting at Microsoft to discuss it. He doesn't say as much, but I can see that *We Live in Public* represents both vindication and a potential new source of 'leverage' for him, after going so long without. No one remembers any of the other early forays into cyberspace and despite the fact that the British Library is now desperately trying to collect as many Web 1.0 websites as it can find, it's too late, because most are gone. And now here's Josh, who documented and kept everything.

We arrive twenty minutes into the prèmiere, with the large foyer and café almost to ourselves as a few staff linger and the occasional gasp or peal of laughter escapes the main hall. On the bus ride I saw that he was more nervous than I first thought, probably about the audience Q & A session which follows the screening. 'I hope you're in control of this, because I can't be,' he'd chuckled, worrying that we might be on the wrong bus, which in fact we were. I've assumed he'll catch a screening later in the week, but now he tells me he doesn't want to see it at all, 'because it's Ondi's view of me and I'm not sure I want to see that.' Consistent with the production in general, relations between him and the director have been fraught. He wants me to see it and tell him honestly what I think.

I get myself a coffee and Josh a sugary juice-water drink and some breadless tuna mayo and we perch on a podium in the centre of the space, and gradually a kind of twilight descends, as though the next hour is suspended, floating free of the people and the place and the unforgiving business of making movies –

as though the building has transmogrified into a great ocean liner heading to a place of sanity and safety, where everything will be looked after; will turn out all right for Josh as he spins through America on his still story sea. We sit and chat, enjoying the sensation as the film runs in the next room, which might as well be the next century, because it feels a universe away. Various acquaintances come and go and Josh enjoys a cheeky chance to sell his *Tuna Heaven* idea to a movie exec, laughing delightedly at the exec's puzzlement. I laugh too, because the sell could be so simple: it's like a version of *I'm a Celebrity ... Get Me Out of Here!*, but with real blood and sex and relationships, and fish instead of celebs, and 200 miles out to sea so no one can leave and the drama *has* to play out – and a real question behind it: 'Is it all right to kill the fish?'

When the exec leaves, it's my turn to be puzzled as Josh tries to tell me about his big new idea, but I grasp little beyond the fact that it anticipates a further fragmentation of the human self, which he holds to be inevitable as the facets of our inner and outer lives collapse into each other – as we blur together, with time and place and physical space becoming progressively more incidental to who we are and what we do, and with whom. A prognosis that still sounds outlandish in 2009.

I haven't mentioned it to Josh, but this morning when I left my motel I found the check-in guy engrossed in a tortuous-sounding mobile phone conversation in the back room, and when he eventually came out, he said: 'Sorry about that. I'm having ... relationship problems.'

I expressed sympathy and he continued.

'Unfortunately, I've been getting too involved in meeting on the internet. And I've been saying, "No, it doesn't mean anything, it's not unfaithful if we don't meet in the real world," but she doesn't agree ... I mean, it's virtual. It's not real, is it?'

And I told him honestly that I didn't know.

*

The film ends and Josh is called into the theatre, grumbling as he hears Timoner announce the presence of Tom, the slate-eyed brother he hasn't seen since the *Tuna Heaven* voyage eight and a half years ago. The audience is young and excited, Timoner professional and Josh unexpectedly winning, expert at offering glimpses of his glass-bottomed inner life, without any real sense of revelation. 'The thousand-and-one nights of Josh,' I find myself thinking, struck again by his rare amorphousness, the propensity to distort and change shape with the slightest alteration of viewpoint – wondering also whether this lack of clear resolution is the source of his charisma; whether the ability is conscious or involuntary; whether we will follow as our world progressively evolves to resemble his? Or whether he merely exploits a talent we already possess, and which at least partly explains our attraction to cyberspace? Are any of these drifts inevitable?

We Live in Public clearly leans heavily on the pre-Millennial, month-long *Quiet* event, which I'm still struggling to piece together in terms of myth and substance, and to which many of the audience questions relate. When someone marvells that Josh got away with it, he draws a laugh by shrugging, 'Well, it was New York' – as if this was explanation and absolution enough. When someone else mentions the proximity of 9/11, he claims that 'We could feel the whole thing coming ... we were just surfing the vibe,' leaving Timoner to add that: '*Quiet* couldn't happen after 9/11. I mean, you could really hear the gunfire from the firing range out in the street. I was thinking, "Why aren't they coming to arrest us?"'

Asked why he didn't watch the film, Josh confidently repeats what he told me. Only when the issue of the fake girlfriend is raised in a way implying scepticism does the head start to waggle and sentences begin to fray.

Josh's old friend Jason Calacanis is one of several former cohorts to fly in for the screening, others being the crazy-haired performance artist Missy Galore and Adeo Ressi, founder of one of the first dotcoms, TotalNY, and another rare winner in the dotcom game thanks to a series of well-timed sales. All are now based on the West Coast and all were on a high at the aftershow party, while Josh drank seltzer and chatted with the casual awkwardness you stop noticing after a while, and was still there, enjoying himself I think, when I had to leave for the long drive to my motel.

The first thing I did at the party was arrange to meet Calacanis, which is why we're sitting on a sunlit terrace outside a restaurant at the lower end of Main Street. Driven, direct, fearsomely bright and confident to the point of cockiness, someone has already described him to me as 'like a functional version of Josh'. With none of his friend's wry self-deprecation, it would be easy to take against the former *Silicon Alley Reporter* man, but he talks so fast and is such good value, and the sight of his thumbs *flying* across his BlackBerry is so awesomely diverting, that somehow the question of whether you *like* him never gets a chance to form. So you surrender and assume that you do.

'Josh talks in five-word fragments of sentences,' he begins. 'When I first knew him he spoke in full sentences. It was only over time that the sentence structure got lost. I think he likes to challenge people with the way he talks, to see if they can keep up. Almost like a jazz artist. You know, it's a Miles Davis thing or something.'

He laughs and goes on a riff about the decline of New York and how you can tell the currency of a city by the way you get into clubs: that in the 90s the way you got past doormen was 'to look interesting or be with an interesting group of people', whereas now it's 'by agreeing to pay 400 bucks for a bottle of vodka'.

Calacanis himself is a classic New York story. Of mixed Irish, Greek and Swedish heritage, he grew up in Brooklyn with the dream of making it to Manhattan, 'the island'; a couple of miles and seeming world away back then. In constant trouble at school, he found discipline through martial arts and computers, and rather than follow his brother into the NYPD (and thence fire brigade), he worked hard to inch his way into jobs where his net savvy mattered. When the downtown scene blew up, he was first off the mark to start a magazine, despite knowing nothing about how to run one – first as a photocopied freesheet with artistic spelling and zero fact-checking, then as a more serious organ, hand-delivered on a shopping trolley or hidden inside copies of the *Village Voice*, before its swan-like emergence as a slick, strutting glossy, the definitive voice of the Alley, with its editor able to walk into any room or party and know that he was the most important person in it.

Often likened to the Studio 54 proprietor Steve Rubell, disco-running gatekeeper to hip New York in the late 1970s, Calacanis quickly grasped 'how you play the press game and how you get the press to write about you' and one of his most controversial acts was to institute an annual 'Silicon Alley 100' issue, in which he listed the 100 'most important people' in the sector. This wasn't popular with many ETBs, but as the cyberslacker-turned-academic Clay Shirky pointed out, 'As so often, Jason understood what was happening.' Among his unlikely achievements is an appearance (as himself) in the dotcom date movie *August*, which starred Josh Hartnett and David Bowie.

If Calacanis disdains the 400-dollar-vodka-bottle door policies of Manhattan clubs as much as I do it's on principle, because after he left he started a blog network called Weblogs, Inc. which was quickly sold to AOL for $30 million, making him rich in a way he hadn't been in the 90s when he'd stubbornly refused to cash in. Yet he recently called an end to his own blogging and now tells me about a piece he's writing for his opt-in email list, in which he declares that he no longer believes in the vaunted freedoms of the web. 'Anonymity is probably the worst thing we have on the internet,' he says. 'It's only the hippy, 60s,

Electronic Frontier Foundation [EFF] contingent who still want that. Anonymity is great for a mature person; for an immature person or a damaged person, it's not. Empathy filters get turned off.'

He invokes 'Godwin's Law', named after a humorously intended observation by EFF co-founder Mike Godwin that, given enough time, any online debate will end with one party likening another's views to those of Hitler or the Nazis – at which point all hope of dialogue ends. Calacanis now extends this to something he will end up calling 'Harris's Law': that at some point, 'all humanity in an online community is lost, and the goal becomes to inflict as much psychological suffering as possible on another person.' He cites a spate of recent cases where people have committed suicide or 'real life' murder after online persecution and talks about most committed bloggers burning out after a few years, worn down by the bitter anonymous comments posted namelessly below their work.

I'm startled to find someone who owes everything to the web saying this and to me it sounds a little like turning against houses because burglars can burgle them. I point out that many TV reality shows and picture-bylined newspaper columns in the UK run on similar cruelty, but he counters that the people behind these are *known*. And burglars are committing a crime. Columnists and criminals may be aloof from the community, but they still have to move through it in physical space.

He meets my eyes and calls me an asshole.

Leaves a scratchy gap.

'Now I look at you and I see a "blush reaction", he says. 'And my own skin prickles because I feel I shouldn't have said it. These reactions protect us in society. The net draws socially unstable or disturbed people because you can say these things without having to look anybody in the eye, but it has the same impact on the person on the receiving end. Trust me.'

And cruelty gets attention.

'Everybody wants to have the ability to impact the world. That's part of Warhol's fifteen-minute theory.'

I wonder how Josh struck him when they first met.

'He wasn't that eccentric at the time. He would talk in full sentences and had a strategy, a very coherent strategy: he was not crazy, like he seems to people now.'

I ask whether Jason thinks Josh is crazy and there's a long, long pause. He looks away into the distance, at the mountains winking sun, and when he speaks, he speaks slowly. I wouldn't previously have thought this possible.

'*Josh*. He's had a lot of life experience, you know? And he's got his version of reality. Just like other people have their version. It's sort of like Kurosawa: three versions of the truth – yours, mine and the actual. *Rashomon*. I don't see him as that different from everybody else. His story just happens to be more interesting than most of ours. He-he.'

Since handing over Weblogs, Inc., Calacanis has started another company, a lively social networking-come-aggregator site called Mahalo. Given his own success, I wonder what he thought of Josh's quixotic Operator 11 comeback venture of 2007–8? Another surprise.

> I think he was operating in a Web 1.0 way, in a Web 2.0 environment. He expected that someone would see it being advanced and interesting, and that would be enough. And it was *both* those things, but the second phase of the web wasn't about making the blue dot move across the screen any more, it was about making the cash registers ring. You make the blue dot move, it doesn't matter. Unless you can find a way to make it pay. But he was blowing $30,000 a month on a space he was renting. I think he thought, 'You go big, you attract the investors.' And the investors have changed: now they look for something small, that shows growth, that *they* can make big. Not something that is

going big and they can give money to, to make go *bigger*. But Operator 11 is more advanced than YouTube or any of the other video sites out there.

Really? Could it have worked?

Yes. The idea of mixing up multiple video streams into some coherent video show is a great idea, and other people are experimenting with it. But even then, they *still* don't understand what he was doing. He was taking multiple streams and letting one person be the live editor at the switch. He's letting the nominated video master *be* the live switch, who makes the live show by choosing from among the individual feeds, anointing people for their fifteen minutes, or five minutes – until they get boring or something else gets more interesting. So everyone's their own video master, making and mixing their own show. In some ways, Josh needs a business guy to say, 'That's a great idea – let me make it happen for you!' He can't be the business guy.

Calacanis stops, cocks his head to one side.

Actually, I take that back. I think he *does* have business acumen, because he did show it in the first two companies, Jupiter and Pseudo. I think he has no *interest* in that phase of a business. He just wants to explore the ideas and investors don't want to back the interesting artist guy these days. In meetings I play the rabid business guy with fire in his belly and never-says-die attitude, who has too much pride to fail. And they're always going to back me over Josh as a result. You want the guy who will die rather than fail, who'll fight till the last dying breath, the last nickels in the bank. And Josh ain't that guy. Nor will he *play* that guy. The guy he's playing is different.

The bill comes and I plop a card on the tray. Calacanis looks at me and furrows his brow.

'Are you expensing this?' he asks.

I tell him there's no one to expense it *to*, but that's fine.

'OK,' he smiles. 'Let me give you a piece of advice. Let the millionaire pay. That's what I always tell my family, who are always trying to pay for things – let the *rich guy* pay . . .'

So I do.

The next night, my last, we go for dinner at a Mexican restaurant: me, Jason, Josh, Adeo Ressi and Philip 'Pud' Kaplan, who charted the slow death of the dotcom 1.0 sector on his Fucked Company website, channelling the anger of former dotcom workers along the way. Riding the Sundance tide, we've been to a couple of bars and are in good cheer, enjoying the festival, the film, the chance to revisit what for everyone here was an extraordinary time. There is heated discussion as to whether JudgeCal, who was found kneeling, naked, with a rope around his neck and a couple-dozen girlfriends confirming his enthusiasm for auto-erotic asphyxiation, died by accident or committed suicide, and Calacanis demonstrates the power of Mahalo and the web by posting a message asking for info on this guy (me) who's just interviewed him, to find data flowing back within a couple of minutes, most of it perfectly accurate. I feel a prick of unease, but also an unexpected and embarrassing little glow of affirmation.

Josh and I snacked earlier at a reception for documentary filmmakers, so don't eat much. But it's nice to see him jousting with people who know him and accept him for whoever he is. When the bill comes, Calacanis pays his friend's portion and I wonder whether Josh has any feelings about the fact that the last time he was in this company, the rich man picking up the tab was *him*. Yet for all that, there's a deference towards him, an implicit supposition of him as something precious and important, whose loss would be cause for sadness. A twist to this impression is my inkling that the same would not be true in reverse: that if everyone here disappeared overnight, the emotional content of Josh's tomorrow would be little changed.

We wander down the street toward the bus station, the rest en route to another bar, me to catch a midnight screening of *We Live in Public* before driving back to my motel in Salt Lake City, ready to fly tomorrow. As the others move off, Josh and I smile at each other and I experience a genuine swell of affection for this strangest of men. I tell him that I'd give him a hug if I didn't know from our conversation in Awassa that he hates being touched.

'Aw that's ok, we can do an Ethiopian hug,' he grins, leaning forward to bang shoulders in the prescribed way.

Here's the thing, though: in this moment I'm sure I feel warmth from him. He *is* an enigma, Josh Harris, and I find myself wondering when I'll see him next and what the coming year will hold for him. At this moment anything seems possible.

I promised I'd give Josh an honest assessment of the film when I got back to London, which I don't quite do. I tell him that I think it's fascinating and stylishly made and that Timoner has approached both him and the subject matter with integrity. The first third, which provides some personal background, is riveting to me, and Timoner's thesis – that our wholesale move online will stunt our development as individuals – is clever and cogent. What I don't tell him is the degree to which I share the producers' doubts about the way the film starts, and more generally about Josh as a subject. In portraying him as a manipulative Svengali, an example of what our children could become, he is made to seem not just unsympathetic, but *unlikeable*. And the curious thing about Josh is that he's *not*. When I ask Timoner on a visit to London whether she likes Josh, she admits that, despite all their spats, she does. Jason Calacanis shares this caveat, saying: 'Josh comes across as sadistic, which I don't think he is – I don't think that's his true personality. In fact, he has a really sweet side. Josh curated his events, but where the artists and participants took them is not his responsibility. Which was the point: to see what people would do with their freedom. In the film it looks like he had a master plan to break people – he didn't.'

A few weeks later, I'm not surprised to see that by the time Calacanis's Sundance article reaches his email list, it's called 'The End of Empathy'. I'm absolutely *floored*, however, to find the original internet maven saying:

> We're all canaries in the coal mine now, like Josh was back in the 90s. We're harvesting our lives and putting them online. We're addicted to gaining followers and friends (or email subscribers, as the case may be), and reading comments we get in return. As we look for validation and our daily 15 minutes of fame, we do so at the cost of our humanity. What a shame, because there is so much to be gained from sharing.
>
> In summary, how we treat each other does matter. It matters because, without empathy, our lives are shallow, self-centered and meaningless. The Internet and technology are turning on us, just like the story in *We Live in Public*.

13

> 'People like you are in what we call the reality-based community. You believe that solutions emerge from judicious study of the discernible reality. That's not the way the world really works anymore ...'
>
> – unidentified aide to President G. W. Bush, later revealed to be Karl Rove, to *The New York Times*, 2004

Blame Greenspan's bath – or more specifically his status as the last American to *take* baths in 1996.

'Irrational exuberance.' It popped into the Fed Chairman's head while he soaked and worked, as was his habit, early one December morning. How exotic that a term coined to describe incaution on the stock market should become to the 1990s what 'one small step for a man' was to the 60s – a phrase tracing the motion of a whole decade. As usual, Greenspan framed it with a question, in one of those brain-implodingly dull speeches he seemed to take special pride in.

'How do we know when irrational exuberance has unduly inflated asset values, which then become subject to unexpected and protracted contractions as they have in Japan over the last decade?' he asked on page fourteen of an eighteen-page address to a conservative think tank. He then returned to his table and asked his long-term girlfriend, 'So what was the most important thing I said?' only to receive a glazed head-shake in return: safe to assume he didn't get any that night. But his news journalist partner wasn't the only one in the room who failed to hear a warning in the words – in fact, almost no one did. The 'irrational exuberance' speech was a near-perfect expression of Greenspan's approach to public utterance. 'Constructive ambiguity,' he called it.

The previous month, November '96, Bill Clinton had been re-elected with a healthy 49 per cent of the vote. His coordinator of economic policy, Robert E. Rubin, should have been overjoyed – as should Greenspan, the right-wing Republican Clinton had re-appointed Fed Chairman earlier in the year. But these two men were vexed. Since they'd last fretted the surging stock market, it had risen another 26 per cent, with the Dow now standing at 6000 points-plus. Neither man had seen anything like it before, and both were lost for an explanation. Another puzzling feature of the prevailing data was that unemployment stood at its lowest level since 1973 (4.9 per cent), with the economy growing strongly, and yet there was no sign of rising inflation. Everyone from Marx to the Chairman himself agreed that capitalism requires a pool of unemployed labour to keep wages – and therefore inflation – down. According to classical theory, the present situation was impossible.

For Greenspan, the question was whether it would be appropriate to intervene. Just as Josh was Josh, the Market was the Market, and the White House was basking in its glow. More than once President Clinton's advisers had suggested he accept an invitation to ring the closing bell at the New York Stock Exchange, which through the 1990s was met with giddy applause from traders, but Rubin had counselled against, on the grounds that markets can go down as well as up . . . much like presidents . . .

Greenspan had decided to intervene, flashing the blade of that phrase. 'Irrational exuberance.' Not quite Henry V and yet enough wonks heard 'rate rise!' for the Chairman to take flack and markets to stutter, then ... carry on regardless. Two months later, he received scathing criticism when, with the market having risen an extraordinary 80 per cent since the beginning of 1995, he voiced the same concerns before the Senate Banking Committee. But no one wanted to hear: he was accused of being a relic who failed to understand the 'New Economy', as indeed was anyone who expressed doubts. On his Federal Open Market Committee (FOMC, the group responsible for setting interest rates), there were inflation 'hawks' and 'doves' and it was Greenspan's job to steer a path between them, to manage a bubble he could never acknowledge, because acknowledging a bubble would cause it to burst, leaving a ruined economy with his name on it. He was in a no-win position.

What happened next is fascinating. During 1997, even as the FOMC took the unpopular decision to raise interest rates, consensus began to form around the idea of a game-changing New Economy. Not least among the theory's proponents was Bill Clinton – but who could know? And if new technology was increasing productivity, the only variable that could explain the situation, why didn't the Fed's data reflect this? In May the Dow hit 7000 points. An answer to the conundrum had to be found, and fast.

No one suggested the influence of cheap money, retirement fears, market manipulation or media frenzy as stock investment became the 'national pastime'. For economists like Greenspan, what counted was the maths, and as things stood the maths didn't tally. So he did something very brilliant and beautiful in strictly economic terms: through a series of clever deductions based on existing models of the economy, he came to the conclusion that the Fed figures were *wrong*. The re-tooling of the economy had indeed increased productivity, he decided, while data compiled to serve the needs of the Old Economy had failed to keep pace. Meaning that the idea of high growth, low unemployment and negligible inflation wasn't absurd: we *could* have it all. The New Economy was real. In July, after Greenspan revealed his epiphany to the House Committee on Financial Services (presenting it in the form of a question, obviously), the Dow raced past 8000 points.

Often forgotten is the fact that Greenspan continued to issue warnings from under the bubble bath. He noted that information technology advances which allowed capital to flow freely in a global economy had a 'punishing downside', in that shocks in one market could flash through others, and in October he declared the economy to have been 'on an unstable track'. As if to prove the Chairman's point, his remarks presaged the largest single-day Dow index fall ever, of 554 points, when a serious crisis in the Asian markets belatedly spread to the US. In the long run the Chairman's description of events in the stock market and wider economy as 'breathtaking' made for better headlines. Like it or not, Greenspan was the New Economy poster boy.

The parent had left the party and the kids were free to play.

* * *

With the headspin of cash came exhilaration, vindication, *excitement* in the Alley. Even the word being applied to these new companies – 'dotcom' – sounded like the name of a Japanese manga hero. No less fantastical was the July '97 issue of *Wired*, whose cover pledge that 'We're facing 25 years of prosperity, freedom and a better environment for the whole world' reflected a new reality for the internet talisman: that with the departure of its eccentric founder Louis Rossetto following two failed IPO attempts, the magazine was stealthily evolving into a business organ, its intellectual Kool-Aid replaced by Wall Street blow.

For a time in the 1980s the pop cultural route to quick riches had been the screenplay; now, amazingly, it became the business plan, which evolved into a stream-of-semiconscious *genre*, Carroll abridged by Trump, capable of running to dozens of pages without resort to a single specific ... 'we want to be a new medium, an entertainment force to come ... we don't want to be compared to other entertainment sites ... we've been underground for a purpose ...' etceteraetceteraetcetera. Unlike traditional business, the internet presented few barriers to involvement and six months' experience was equivalent to ten years anywhere else, simply because so few people understood it. As one dotcommer notes, 'You were a genius if you knew how to set up a modem at that point. Even a *browser* at first.'

The face of the city had changed dramatically in the space of a few years, too. Mayor Giuliani had reduced crime and cleaned up Times Square and New Yorkers no longer discussed mugging the way Brits do the weather – though at the expense of black and Hispanic resentment over strongarm police tactics. More importantly for Silicon Alley, the local economy was beginning to join the national boom, with unemployment falling and the trickle of venture capital becoming a flood. Gary Baddeley of alternative news site disinfo.com arrived in 1997 and remembers that, 'There were so many parties and it seemed like everybody had so much money to spend. It definitely felt like something new was happening.'

Idealism remained in the burgeoning field of online magazines and 'e-zines', with the likes of Rufus Griscom of Nerve.com still insisting that, 'To me, it's less about the internet as a religion than as a process of breaking up and complicating the power that controls the media.' At the same time, the FEED co-founder Stefanie Syman joked, 'It used to be that I'd go to parties and meet my friends' friends and we'd start sleeping together: now my friends introduce their friends to each other and we all go into business together.' The turnaround in fortunes for the gilded few had been so rapid that there'd barely been time to wonder at the process by which it happened, or to consider where it might lead. Or in the words of Jason Calacanis: 'Young people began to believe they could do anything, because they were trying things and they were working. And then something radical happened: you could try things, have them work, and *become a millionaire*! And money was available to you to do this.'

Starting a business became to 90s New York what joining a band was to 60s San Francisco. Why wouldn't you? As the journalist Michael Wolff put it in *Burn Rate*, his account of leaving Old Media for New: 'It was start-up time. If all else failed, you could still have the satisfaction of knowing you'd been there; it was like Hollywood in the teens or Detroit in the twenties. A new American industry was being born . . .'

Pseudo was like a jetliner emerging from cloud to see a bright-lit runway. *Suddenly the path was clear*. Josh knew that Progressive Networks were ready to replace their industry-leading RealAudio Player with the video-streaming RealPlayer, signalling time for the big move from radio to netcast. With cash-rich latecomers dancing around him and broadband rumoured to be around the corner, Pseudo needed to grow and the Prodigy money was being smoked fast: to build a studio, he was going to need more, was going to need investment. An investor-focused business plan from June '97 begins, 'Pseudo Programs, Inc. is a leading Internet entertainment production studio which is well positioned to leverage its existing management expertise, marketing presence and brand name into a significant worldwide Net-TV operation.'

And the advantages of netcasting over broadcasting were persuasive.

'Lower per-show production costs; lower cost of distribution (enabling deeper vertical niche programming); on-demand archival capability; virtual distribution footprint (instead of geographic); and the integration of real-time (chat) and non real-time (bulletin boards and e-mail) communications with audio, video and text . . .'

Pseudo could – and *would* – run a show that made three-minute movies at the request of viewers. The Empire State Building at dusk? On the site for you tomorrow. 'TV you won't see on TV,' they called it.

But Josh, normally so secure in this new world of virtuality, had misjudged the trajectory. While he'd been waiting for the technology to appear, for netcasting to be *technically feasible* before moving into it, others had dispensed with these Old Economy niceties. Most notably, over in LA, a pair named Marc Collins-Rector and Chad Shackley had founded Digital Entertainment Network (DEN) with $50 million votes from the likes of Microsoft, Dell and Chase Manhattan-backed VCs, with Ford and PepsiCo signed on as 'charter sponsors'. The company was a sham, but it was in Hollywood, a pleasant few hours' drive from Silicon Valley and, as Josh now realised with a start, *they got my money!* By the time Pseudo came calling, investors easily attracted to the idea of webcasting were already committed.

He'd thought he could play it long. But the ground had shifted too fast even for him and suddenly any cheese-eating MBA who'd just discovered *Wired* could turn up and compete. And in many respects be at an advantage.

So while Pseudo staff fought and played and slept together and prepared for the next culture-crunching leap, Josh spent a year on the phone and in meetings, and the parties changed from arty excuses for marketing to *actual* marketing; to ever more naked means of forming relationships and gaming the press. Few Pseudo workers noticed, but instructions to clear the space and do something fabulous were now often followed by rejoinders like, 'There's some guys coming in from Seattle who I need to impress.' By 1997, 'There was always some ulterior motive, in terms of climbing the social ladder or the fiscal ladder,' says one manager, without having understood why at the time. In October, with one month's cash left in the bank,

Josh took over the fifth floor of 600 Broadway and started buying equipment, in a show of bravado which still causes friends to guffaw. And that same month, when the Gartner Group invested $6 million in Jupiter Communications, Josh went back to some of his original Jupiter investors – who'd just made a handsome return on their money – and persuaded them to back him on Pseudo.

At the eleventh hour, $2 million arrived. Enough for another year. But it had been a miserable, nerve-jangling experience for Pseudo's founder, and it took a toll.

Not that Josh's life lacked colour. He still had the radio, including his own neo-*Gilligan* show, for which he steered some lively interviews with people like the Factory face Taylor Mead (star of the Warhol film *Taylor Mead's Ass*, conceived after a reviewer complained of an earlier work that 'people don't want to see an hour and a half of Taylor Mead's ass'). On another show he interviewed characters from the East Village sex scene, asking questions like 'What proportion of fetishers are foot fetishers?' and 'How does the backroom operation in a brothel work?' His ongoing courtship of Tanya involved making her an employee and giving her a show too.

The parties could still be extraordinary. The French champagne industry sponsored a show called 'The End is Near', which gathered together paintings on the theme of the apocalypse. At the other end of the scale, several hundred gamers descended on 600 Broadway over three days in May '96 for the launch of QuakeWorld, with action projected on to the walls and up to a hundred enthusiasts and members of the public playing simultaneously. Computer gaming was now a billion-dollar industry, still unacknowledged by the mainstream, and John Young of the online ad agency Tribal DDB, described 'such a visual overload ... there were all these nooks and crannies, and someone pulled me down the stairway saying, "Hey, look, here's an Avid [video editing] Studio!" I thought, "Whose trust fund paid for this?"'

But there was no trust fund.

Bigger and better still was the 'Coma' event at the Roseland Ballroom, a beautiful 3500-capacity hall nestling in the mid-town theatre district and mentioned in stories by Fitzgerald, John O'Hara and Ring Lardner, whose history is the history of twentieth century New York itself. For this one, the now Creative Director Jeff Gompertz and his 'Fakeshop' team returned to their bubble technology, using acres of plastic to fill the entire main space and create a ten-thousand-cubic-foot silver womb, with semi-naked male and female dancers suspended on hydraulic lifts above the ecstasy and acid-tripping crowd. Elsewhere in the building was a folk-rock room and chill-out space filled with beanbags and spoken word poetry. A $60,000 projector, hired with sponsorship money, wasn't even used.

Natalia Tsarkova, a Latvian who became one of the first members of an Eastern Bloc country to win a scholarship to Harvard and thence MIT post-perestroika, was newly arrived in New York when a date invited her to Roseland. After refined Boston, she couldn't believe her eyes – the starry crowd and floating naked dancers and sense of *fin de siècle* abandon. The night had begun badly when she found that her date was also seeing someone else in the room and she was sitting alone at the bar, depressed, when none other than Jason Calacanis arrived to chat her up.

'And after a while he said, "Let me introduce you to my friend Josh,"' says Tsarkova. 'I thought this was so cool, so he took me up to Josh's VIP room and there he was sitting in the middle, like some kind of mystic, with all these very hip and glamorous people swarming around him, this "visionary" that I'd heard about before I even knew who he was ... and with even Jason deferring to him. It was incredible.'

She chuckles as she recalls realising that Calacanis was using the Pseudo man 'as this trump card to score the chick', and for a few months afterwards they all hung out at clubs like the uber-chic Pravda in SoHo – she and Jason and Josh and Tanya, wearing fedoras and playing poker and drinking watermelon martinis, sometimes with Calacanis's bulldog Toro in tow, until she finally tired of the manic dotcom scene and moved on, while remaining friends with Josh, who she still considers 'a kind of soulmate'. Josh claims to have considered her for the role of 'fake girlfriend', but Natalia laughs the idea off. When she fell out badly with Calacanis, the Pseudo man was 'the only one who proved himself to be a real friend'.

In truth, Tsarkova didn't much care for the dotcom scene, whose denizens struck her as self-important and avaricious; as making poor use of their abundant freedoms. Her own love of maths, she says, stems from the fact that under the Soviet communism she grew up with 'the only thing you can be sure of is that two plus two equals four'. The irony being that over the next couple of years, such simple certainty would evaporate in her new home.

* * *

Pseudo TV began in 1998, struggling with the same bandwidth problems and revenue quandaries as everyone else. Before Google revolutionised the advertising market by tying revenue to search, most online media business plans assumed a system similar to print, the goal being to deliver an audience and make advertisers pay to reach it. Silicon Alley's DoubleClick pioneered systems for gathering information on surfers' behaviour, data with potentially vast commercial value, and while civil rights groups objected, citizens quickly grew used to trading privacy for the consumer Utopia of what they wanted, when they wanted it, and *cheap* – just as Josh had predicted they would. DoubleClick's CEO Kevin Ryan declared that 'personal information is the oil of the twenty-first century' and the covert surveillance he spoke of came to be known as 'data mining'.

Making shows was a gas. Now Pseudo had a clear purpose, with winking, flashing machinery to match. Josh commissioned a special desk with screens allowing his presenters – Tanya among them – to engage with studio guests and online users at the same time, and above the studio door was a light which flashed 'ON THE WEB' when programmes were in train. All of a sudden commercial TV looked like what it was: a corporate sham in which viewers were forced to watch ads they didn't want to see, then pay for the intrusion through increased consumer prices – and all on the flimsiest of evidence that such advertising worked.

As far back as the 60s, Andy Warhol, in an interview with *Vogue*, defined his filmmaking against TV by saying 'They're not-real people trying to say something and we're real people not trying to say anything,' and so was the feeling at Pseudo. Work began on a proprietary 'player' and software which would enable viewers to upload their own material and interact with each other come the rise of broadband (which, given that the technology already existed, was surely *close*). The usual investor response to this latter goal was, 'Why would you want to do that?' so the company played it down. All the same, before long anyone at Pseudo who wanted a show had one, each their own star with their own 'fifteen minutes'. Jess Zaino, who started as a receptionist in January '98, remembers Josh coming up to her after a few months, saying, 'You know, you kinda suck as a receptionist. What do you want to do here?'

If Old Media was intimidated by Pseudo's emergence as a netcaster, it was because few execs were online and fewer still had seen any of the shows, the earliest of which looked like Howard Stern, *high*, trapped in a postage stamp. Slowly, shows on the All Games Network and 88HipHop and StreetSound channels built modest online followings, eventually dividing like cells into other channels with themes running to art, space, women and sex, street culture and celebrity, even sport. It was still the case that any passerby could board what was by common consent the slowest lift in New York (graffiti-tagged nightly by the same infernal artist) and step into Pseudo's website a minute or so later. For the ETB Clay Shirky, Pseudo was 'the tree fort of the internet', a place no one could quite believe existed, but which came to be seen as keeper of the questing original spirit other companies surrendered to VCs and investors and demands for discipline and order, or at least something which might make sense on PowerPoint. Before long, established media figures like Jeffrey Katzenberg of DreamWorks were dropping by to see what was up and it's probably no coincidence that the junction of Broadway and Houston stars in a key scene from the 1996 Ron Howard thriller, *Ransom*.

Josh still thought he was doing more than bringing the real world online: in his mind he was birthing a medium that would become 'exponentially, the most powerful ever invented; a mind-blow of massive proportions'. The early web theorist Mark Stahlman has said that in his very first close conversation with Josh in 1994, the Pseudo CEO insisted that, 'We're *all* brainwashed. My job is to allow people to brainwash themselves.'

Or, according to a later formulation: 'We are being programmed, for better or for worse. So if you can put a layer of programming on there that says, "Let's at least program ourselves with more consciousness, and manage the electronic calories we consume. Then it's better ... or maybe it's not. We'll see. But at least it should be something we look at. I think the business is programming people's lives. I *direct reality*.'

Not that this reality was always straightforward to direct. At one point someone hired a worker we shall call 'Gawain', who looked and spoke like an Arthurian knight on his way to a joust – shortly after which, Josh noticed staff behaving erratically; smiling a lot and staring at walls. Investigation led to Pseudo's latest arrival, who had been hired by ... actually, no one seemed to know who'd hired him, but the *why* became clear as tales emerged of staff dropping to one knee and being 'knighted' with a drop of liquid acid to the tongue.

The problem of Gawain was easily resolved. More bothersome was renewed interest from Mayor Giuliani's Stasi-like Social Club Task Force, the 'Five-O', so-named after a TV police drama which ran on US TV from 1968. With SoHo now hip, Pottery Barn had moved their flagship store into 600 Broadway's ground floor retail space and events like 88HipHop's weekly webcast party, which featured guests such as Eminem, 50 Cent, Public Enemy and the Boo-Yaa T.R.I.B.E., invariably spilled into the street and drew complaint. In response, promoters developed a walkie-talkie early warning system to keep them one step ahead of the law. Show-themed webcast parties were now almost nightly.

Josh no longer graced all of the events, would stay in his chambers watching TV or movies, sometimes entertaining guests of his own – which is where he was one night when word came that the Five-O were on their way, ETA twenty minutes. Multiple witnesses describe the same sequence of events as two hundred guests crowded into the patron's quarters behind the only door in the space, where they remained sniggering like kids in a closet as Josh answered the door, all Hugh Hefner with his bath robe and flourished cigar, breezing, 'Oh hi, officer, what's the matter?'

'So he goes out and walks them through the space,' explains one guest, 'going, "No, really, there was nothing, we had a little private soiree, that's all." And they're asking why all the chairs are there, and the drinks – and why the turntables are *still spinning* and stuff, and Josh goes into one of these moods he gets into, where he gets all indignant, and he's saying, "There's nothing you can say that can keep me from having a little private gathering – give me your name, I wanna know who you are now!" And he *takes their numbers*.'

The officers left and the party restarted: just one of many frustrating nights for the Five-oh at the junction of Broadway and Houston. Pseudites started to believe they could get away with anything.

The proprietor had problems, too, mostly still attached to money. Caught on the get-big-fast tide, Pseudo was burning cash fast and would need more soon, but with stocks flying and startups proliferating and big business blinking awake to the web, Josh struggled to attract investment on the scale now required. For months he feared that the edifice he'd built would collapse at the end of the year, right in the middle of the revolution and with so many people depending on him, simply because he couldn't get the job done. The problem was exacerbated by his refusal to allow his design, production and programming departments to do outside 'real world' work, as some within the company suggested and other Alley design shops were doing. 'We're not a rental house,' he would say, according to one producer. 'Stay pure. Stay online. Know your audience. Know your product. Keep burning it in, making those mistakes, correcting those mistakes. We're ahead of everybody else.'

A stance some staff thought courageous, others crazy.

Redemption came from an unexpected source, and it was a curious kind of redemption. The cousin of an angel investor in both Jupiter and Pseudo was in the process of raising $10 million for his own business. The angel – a wealthy investment banker named Joshua Weinreich of Deutsche Bank – set up a meeting, at which the cousin told Josh, '*Look*, I haven't closed the deal yet, but I will have in ten days' time. Come back then and I'll give you the keys. I'll tell you how to do it.'

Josh waited his ten days and came back, like Arthur visiting Merlin, to news that it took nine months to raise capital and anything arriving before that was lucky. The only way to get what he needed was to find a list of VCs – Merlin gave him one – and then call each one *every single day* until the money came. 'Sit at your desk from early in the morning until the last possible call can come in,' ran the instructions. 'Just call and say "hi" and tell them what you're doing. Then do it again. And again. That's *it*. In nine months you'll have your money.'

Josh took the advice, setting himself a target of *three* months, but at eight he had no firm commitments and was worried sick. The matzah-ball soup incident happened at this time. Pseudo had by now taken over the third floor of 600 Broadway and was operating as a fully-fledged production house with over sixty staff, all of whom relied on Josh to come through with fresh investment – but he wasn't coming through. Tony Asnes had lent the company money and Josh had staked everything he had on it. Exhausted and demoralised, the CEO hadn't felt so wretched since he was a child in Ventura.

Then came what he thinks of as his 'New York epiphany', a moment such as the city must have seen a million times. Standing at the junction of Bowery and Great Jones Street, he was feeling angry and unsettled, scared out of his wits. And at this lowest of points, a calm spread through him. 'Why am I pissed off?' he recalls asking himself as he waited for 'WALK' to flash green on the other side of the street. 'This is why I'm here. It's why I came to New York, and I can either raise the money or I can't, there's no one else to blame. And if I fuck up, at least I know it was *me*. This is pure *situation* ...'

Josh relaxed and stopped pressing so hard and with his desperation gone, the money came a couple of weeks later: $19 million from Prospect Street Ventures, Sycamore Ventures, Intel, Tribune Company, the European fashion empire LVMH and others. But Josh was about to learn that – as he explained to me in Awassa – 'money doesn't show up with nothing attached to it . . . the freedom of money is illusory.' Because, as a condition of investment, the VCs leading the deal demanded a trebling of staff, the hire of a sales team and *a new CEO*, to be appointed from outside the company. Josh would become 'Chairman', corporate equivalent of 'Queen'.

The backers wanted a grown-up in charge.

There were 400,000 websites in the US by 1998, up from 2000 only three years before, and the tech sector had moved from a philosophy of 'survival of the fittest' to 'survival of the *fastest*'. One magazine servicing the sector was actually called *Fast Company* and media ads for a new city-sponsored network of Silicon Alley 'plug 'n' go' office buildings ('It's workplace and lifestyle joined at the Hip') were illustrated with a shade-wearing, business-suited yuppie surfing his keyboard over the Hudson River, tie lashing past one shoulder as the World Trade Center loomed across the other – business as extreme sport.

Yet understandable. The first big IPO of the year involved the online marketing and advertising firm DoubleClick, whose shares had been offered at $17, but opened the first day of trading at $29 and valued the company at roughly half a billion dollars by close, making its founders Kevin O'Connor and Dwight Merriman notionally very, very rich. In the words of one ETB, DoubleClick's float was 'the day Silicon Alley became real' and for the next six months IPOs were big news. In August, a small California-based company called GeoCities saw its own shares, again offered at $17, climb to $37 through the first afternoon of trading – and this on a day when the market in general was jittery. The company had been operating for only thirty-six months and, significantly, was fronted by a recruit from New York Old Media, who was now 'worth' millions in shares. As eBay and others floated too, the message was clear: this was the way to quick riches. What did GeoCities do? The question seemed anachronistic. At root, it hosted websites.

There was a flurry of deal-making, as established real-world media companies and punky upstarts like Razorfish hoovered up potential competitors and useful ideas, with the aim of growing fast. Razorfish expanded abroad through the purchase of companies in London, San Francisco and Stockholm, ending the year with a workforce of 1100, while Pseudo bought a company across the street simply to acquire the lease on its premises. Often, these deals would be financed with stock, which had become a form of currency in its own right. Pseudo paid for the third floor of 600 Broadway with stock and options to buy stock, and many Silicon Alley workers were primarily remunerated in this way. In the words of Candice Carpenter, founder of the women's site iVillage, 'Initially, a lot of the people we hired were hung up on salary . . . and we were like, "*Hello? Excuse me?* Your salary is to pay your rent, that's all!'

As tales of instant wealth stacked up, more interlopers joined the web-rush. Three college students sold a tiny stock discussion site called Raging Bull to the search engine giant AltaVista for $167 million, once more mostly in shares, and a 26-year-old named Bo Peabody did likewise with his tiny website building outfit, Tripod, which another search engine snapped up for $58 million. The *Village Voice* journalist James Ledbetter recalls his introduction to the downtown net scene at a celebration party for Tripod in February, where, invited by a colleague, he walked in to find that at thirty-three he was conceivably the oldest person in the room; that despite the familiarity of the setting, he didn't recognise a single face and couldn't understand a word of the techie creole his fellow guests were speaking; that the cowlicked blond *boy* at the centre of proceedings was being treated like Kurt Cobain. Later, as he tried to describe the evening to his girlfriend, he claims to have found himself 'practically in tears', hardly able to articulate why he was so upset –

before finally admitting that, 'It boiled down to fear.' Within the year, like so many of his peers, he had left Old Media for the online financial news service the Industry Standard.

Almost no one commented on the curious way in which firms were being sold as *stories*. Ernst Malmsten of the London-based fashion startup Boo.com reports being told by one enthusiastic banker that, 'The market appetite for big internet stories like this is enormous.' And by a more cautious one from Goldman Sachs, 'Don't get me wrong, we *like the story*.' Similarly, a visitor to the web department of the cable giant MCI relates a meeting in which someone praised an idea for a new business venture with the words 'This sounds like a good press release' and when an interviewer labelled Jason Calacanis 'the Mayor of New York City', he replied '*No*, I'm not the mayor, I'm the press secretary – it's more important than the mayor.'

Meanwhile the market was getting harder to read. In the autumn of 1997, a Western-led bubble in Asian stocks had burst when investors lost confidence and abruptly withdrew, threatening a global crisis on the scale of 1987. Ultimately, confidence returned, with both the Dow and the NASDAQ Composite index (which better reflected technology stocks) continuing their priapic flights. Yet throughout 1998 the plot seemed lost: even the sweatiest, shoutiest, most pop-eyed CNBC pundit, the hedge fund manager and journalist James Cramer, confesses that, 'We just couldn't get the rhythm of the market that year ... bizarre things were happening, things no one had ever seen before.' Things which came to a head in the autumn, when markets succumbed to another panic, this time over rumours that Russia was ready to default on its foreign debt.

Why?

Anyone who had been to Russia knew that by 1998 it was a mess in civil, political and economic terms. But this hadn't stopped the world's largest hedge fund, Long-Term Capital

Management (LTCM), from selling it as a nouveau capitalist wonderland. LTCM had grown fat through the skilful sale not just of investments, but of its own story, which incorporated pseudo-scientific 'models' claimed to have been devised by academics and 'Nobel laureates' and sold by Harvard-educated barkers – conceits which a seasoned pro like Cramer knew instantly to be eyewash. But other fund managers had bought the story and followed LTCM into Russia. Like the hedge fund itself, many were also highly leveraged, having borrowed money to invest more heavily.

What happened? Rumours of a default caused the default: Long-Term Capital collapsed in September; the market slid and hit freefall. On the first day of October the Dow shed 200 points, then carried on in a similar vein for a week, prompting anguished calls for rate cuts before too many other funds, brokerages and banks went under. Despite a cut by the Bank of England in Britain – a measure which failed to stem a sell-off in London – Greenspan held out while the market continued to crumble, bringing colossal losses and a looming spectre of recession in the final year of the century. With the underlying economy considered strong, the Chairman's instinct was to avoid an interest rate cut and its inflationary risk.

Yet there was no telling where the fall would stop.

So on 8 October he capitulated to the markets. First, word emerged that Greenspan had been working the phones to his interest rate-setting FOMC colleagues; then that a highly unusual half-point reduction was likely. And before an official announcement had even been made, the Dow and NASDAQ began to turn and then levitate. The latter had halved in value in the space of a week, from 2900 to 1450, but it wouldn't stay where it was for long.

The finance sector breathed a sigh of relief.

Then carried on as if nothing had happened, like a boy sauntering away from a broken window.

Both the Asian and the Long-Term Capital crises came close to producing intractable credit crunches. Greenspan and others did just enough to postpone such a fate, but he wasn't alone in starting to wonder whether consumers and investors had an exaggerated confidence in the Fed's ability to protect them from themselves. The Chairman thought Wall Street's quick recovery from the crash of 1987, when the Dow plunged a heart-stopping 22 per cent in a single day but the finance world didn't collapse, was inflating the index by several thousand points now. Neither was the Chairman alone in noticing that he had become a cult personality, a celebrity, revered even more abroad than at home, where headlines such as 'In Greenspan We Trust' (*Fortune*), 'Alan Greenspan's Brave New World' (*Business Week*) and 'Who Needs Gold When We Have Greenspan?' (*The New York Times*) had become commonplace.

Opportunities to share the limelight were nonetheless spurned: just as Razorfish's 'Fish' were invited to 'be the brand', so Greenspan accepted his invitation to *be* the economy. Rates would be cut a further half point by the end of the year, encouraging yet more investment in stocks.

The market shocks in Asia and Russia should have seared themselves into the public consciousness, but by a bizarre coincidence, both had cover. More interesting than the Russian default to most people was a salacious debate as to whether oral sex counts as sex for presidents: more momentous than the Asian meltdown was the death on 31 August 1997 of Diana, Princess of Wales, accompanied by TV images of mourners throwing themselves on to mountains of flowers outside Kensington Palace and weeping in a way which seemed out of kilter, unrealistic, *too much* for the loss of someone so remote from their own lives, whom they neither knew nor knew much about. But which also appeared genuine . . .

* * *

Dotcom nerves had special reason to fray by the time of the Long-Term Capital Management farce. Back at the end of 1997, the authoritative *Crain's New York Business* had broken ranks with the rest of the media to report a cooling towards Silicon Alley on the part of merchant banks, even if the banks promptly made fools of *Crain's* by leading the IPO charge through the first half of 1998. Over the summer, however, offerings seized up amid the general uncertainty and many were cancelled or shelved.

Now, on 16 November, *Crain's* ran a piece by Judith Messina and Jon Birger which, in the starkest language, questioned the fundamentals of the dotcom boom. The pair accused VCs and Wall Street bankers of peddling 'cyberschlock' to 'suckers' and described Silicon Alley as a 'late-90s Ponzi [or pyramid-selling] scheme'. The piece was called 'Up in Smoke' and opened by describing the rise of a Silicon Alley firm called EarthWeb, which moved from designing websites, to chat, to 'online community' for techies, all without profit or anything which might foretell success.

'What's most astounding isn't that EarthWeb raised $20 million in private equity without generating a dime of profit,' the line ran. 'Rather, it's that EarthWeb's story echoes throughout New York's Silicon Alley. Since 1994, local software and Internet-related companies have raised more than $1 billion from angel investors, venture capitalists and public markets. Yet after four years of hyperactive fund-raising, virtually all of these new media companies are still losing enormous sums of money, and most have yet to find a profitable business strategy.'

Unsurprisingly, the piece got a hostile response in the dotcom community ('Inevitably they just said we didn't "get it",' laughs Birger), but the two writers felt they were on to something big. Judith Messina had been on the tech beat for three years and had watched 'all these little startups sprouting up downtown'.

'For New York it seemed very important,' she explains. 'The city had lost manufacturing and most of its traditional industries, so this was our future – everyone wanted it to be true. By 1998 we were seeing a lot of boy wonders straight out of school and now their companies were going public. It became more clear to us that there was something here that hadn't been reported.'

She points out that although *Crain's* had been supportive of Silicon Alley up to that point, it was the only publication interrogating the dotcoms as *businesses*. Even the *Wall Street Journal* and *The New York Times* wrote mostly about ideas and personalities. 'I remember going to interview one young kid CEO and he was forty minutes late! Suddenly these kids were big celebrities and they were acting very egotistically, but also *casually*. Yet they had investment bankers knocking on their door. The business was sucking up a lot of capital, with not a lot to show for it.'

The picture was chilling. 'Up in Smoke' revealed that while the Silicon Alley tech sector was on its way to creating 80,000 new jobs in 1998, the first three-quarters of the year had seen DoubleClick lose $14 million on sales of $51 million; the online music store N2K Inc. $54 million on sales of $28 million; EarthWeb $5 million on earnings of just $2 million, while the women's site iVillage had burned through almost $70 million since its launch, never approaching profitability. At the very least, Messina and Birger's piece should have introduced a note of caution.

Yet …

Yet …

– Again! –

The most extraordinary thing happened: the week before publication, the puny site-hosting firm EarthWeb went public. Almost two hundred IPOs had been shelved through the summer, but the underwriters J. P. Morgan & Co. had kept this one on the table and despite accumulated losses of $14 million, investors found a taste for it. The offering raised almost $29 million and at one point on the first day valued the company at close to half a billion dollars. *Outrageous.*

And yet still just a rehearsal for the main event, because the very day 'Up in Smoke' hit newsstands, the investment bank Bear Stearns hustled another small Alley outfit called TheGlobe.com to market. Run by two 24-year-old Cornell University grads and regarded by Alley insiders as a wannabe GeoCities, a genuine 'fake company' with no substance or vision or real understanding of the web, Bear Stearns had kept the Globe.com 'dog and pony' investor roadshow going while others bailed and went home. At the end of a ten-day, thirty-city, hundred-meeting slog, the hoped-for IPO had been first discounted, then delayed, then iced through lack of interest. But on the evening of EarthWeb's float, TheGlobe's founders Stephan Paternot and Todd Krizelman got an unexpected call from Bear Stearns, saying, 'Guys, you're never going to believe this. The phones have been ringing off the hook. Everyone wants into the deal.' And the two men couldn't believe it. By midnight there were orders for 45 million shares, with only 3 million on offer.

This is interesting. Each company could experience an IPO only once, so almost no one other than underwriters and VCs understood the IPO process to any level of detail. Even Josh admits that he didn't know how it worked and had to watch others do it before he could feel able to commit, which he never did. In a case such as TheGlobe.com, where demand was high, the underwriters set an 'offer price', then sold all 3 million new shares in advance to whomever they liked – typically favoured clients, staff, friends, Wall Street insiders – at that price. Money thus raised went to the dotcom being floated (minus multimillion dollar fees and commissions, of course). The important thing to note, though, is that if the share price rose after trading opened, some staff might become rich on paper as the value of their own allocation rose, but the company as a whole wouldn't benefit: a situation analogous to an artist who sells a painting, but doesn't profit from subsequent sales at higher prices. Also worth noting is that in most cases, the dotcom's own staff were barred from reselling their shares for a 'lock-in' period of twelve to eighteen months, while 'friends and family'; underwriters' favourite clients; Wall Street insiders, *weren't*.

With TheGlobe.com began a perplexing pattern. Against logic, Bear Stearns kept the offer price at the discounted rate to which it had fallen through the summer – $8, pushed to $9 the day before trading – and this is what the company would receive per share, whether values rose or fell upon hitting the open market. Tellingly, even at this low price Paternot and Krizelman struggled to disburse their 'friends and family' allocations, simply because most people in their orbit didn't know what an IPO was. The pair barely did themselves.

On the morning of the launch they were limoed to Bear Stearns, kept in a separate room then marched to the main trading floor to be distracted with card tricks and muffins. They were told that, owing to demand, trading was likely to start at between $20 and $30, meaning that anyone who'd been allocated shares at the offer price of $9 could immediately 'flip' them – sell them fast – to double or triple their money in seconds. This was the market's 'vote of confidence', they heard the 40 and 50-year-olds around them enthuse, and as they both owned significant numbers of shares, they would be rich beyond their wildest imaginings. Except that, unlike Bear Stearn's own lucky staff … clients … friends, Paternot and Krizelman couldn't sell their holdings for at least a year. There was also a slow dawning that TheGlobe.com would see none of the premium: at $9 per share, they would be raising very much less cash than they had initially hoped for and would probably need more investment capital down the line. 'The market' seemed to be valuing the 3 million shares before it at up to three times what the company was to receive from their sale. The start of trading was delayed while offers flooded in, driving the price upwards.

Someone came in and said, 'No, that was a mistake,' and the pair breathed a sigh of relief, thinking, 'Ah, of course, we knew it,' waiting to be told that the opening price would be in the historically consistent range of $12 to $15, maybe $18 if they caught a flier. Instead, the Bear Stearns man said, 'It's going to open at fifty to sixty.' Again that queasy mess of excitement as the NASA-style countdown to trading began, and a gloaming unease, masked by utter, abject *impotence*. They were kids at a grown-up party, drunk on alcopop while their minders sipped Cristal; helpless, stupid and though they hadn't yet grasped it . . . doomed. A kind of reality distortion field had opened up. And still it was a fantastic day – thrilling to be the smart, sexy creatures 'the market' said they were that day, to be in receipt of such faith. During the afternoon, TheGlobe.com shares would reach a peak of *$91*, amid furious trading, before falling back to close at $63.50.

In theory the Globe IPO was the most successful in Wall Street history. Though not for long, because the Netscape factor had reached New York. A Danish banker friend who worked on Wall Street for Goldman Sachs at this time tells me: 'We were like gods that year. We were basically *handing out money . . .'*

The immediate downsides took Paternot and Krizelman by surprise. Suddenly staff thought the company richer than it was and grew bitter at not being paid more, with new arrivals lacking the infectious evangelism of the early web workers and disappointed if they hadn't become millionaires within a year, as plenty of their colleagues (again in theory, on paper) had. Meanwhile everyone in Silicon Alley hated them: in the *Reporter*, Calacanis dismissed them as 'posers' and predicted a share price collapse, while Clay Shirky accused them of 'money-chasing in the most shockingly egregious way'. More general among ETBs and latecomers alike, however, was the line taken by Seth Goldstein, a 27-year-old who'd left Condé Nast to found the interactive marketing firm SiteSpecific. 'You kind of looked at that and were offended by it,' he says. 'But at the same time, felt like, "I can play that game." And that's what led to the internet mania. The blind following the blind.'

The Globe.com IPO had raised $30 million for the company, but some estimates have up to $200 million 'left on the table' – which is to say snarfed by Bear Stearns and friends who'd bought shares at the offer price.

How could the market behave with such apparent irrationality?

Birger and Messina wouldn't win any awards for 'Up in Smoke'. By the time votes were cast, scepticism was back out of favour and even *Crain's* was cheerleading again, as waves of IPOs hit the market, nearly always exhibiting the same characteristics as EarthWeb and TheGlobe.com – the modest offer price; delayed start; dizzy rise chased by internet 'day-traders' and late-afternoon sell-off. And at the end, a company which was valued beyond conventional reason or sense, *but which would see none of the money exchanged on the day*.

Not to mention:

Managers and staff who felt rich, but in real-world terms, *weren't*.

Complaints that the company founders were con men as the stock fell back over coming weeks and months.

Kids squinting into the glare of a reality they were utterly unprepared for.

Now VC cash showered the city like golden spring rain, reaching a peak of $6 billion per annum – money used to fatten companies for market, much as Long Island farmers once fattened livestock for sale in the Meatpacking District up the road. Since 1994, 342 new venture funds had been started. The Alley

Latin site StarMedia scored an $80 million investment, eight times the $10 million injections that made headlines two years previously, and in December, a nothing site called booksamillion.com climbed almost 1000 per cent in a few days at IPO, before shedding two-thirds of its 'value' within months. Then, as if to prove that things can always get stranger, an online version of the creaking TV-advertised music company K-tel hit the trading floor and instantly tripled in value, with a queue of others set to follow.

The K-tel deal rattled even some insiders. VC Jerry Colonna was estimated by *The New York Times* to be worth $300 million as his company Flatiron Partners liquidated their first fund to set up a new, bigger one – but the successful float of a dog like K-tel told him something was wrong. He penned an op-ed for the *Times*, warning that a lot of powerful and important ideas were going to be lost or damaged if IPOs continued as they had been. But to no avail. The networking organisation Cybersuds, kicked out of its original venue for producing insufficient bar takings, was now SuperCybersuds, drawing 3000 dotcom hopefuls to Chelsea Pier, with ETBs pinned to walls by brash young things pressing half-baked ideas and business cards, occasionally bumping into each other and exchanging wild-eyed looks that said, 'Oh my God, *what happened*?!'

For *The New York Times*, the New Media scene had become the '*Bright Lights, Big City* of the late 1990s . . . a social outlet that for another generation might have been discos or clubbing.' Business equivalent to clubbing? Was this possible? For ETBs the change had been impossibly sudden. One day Rufus Griscom of Nerve.com woke to the realisation that a night in his bed could be seen as a career move, while Syl Tang, President of HipGuide.com, found herself stalked by a wannabe dotcommer who went so far as to seduce her boyfriend. Bright-eyed hopefuls were now coming from all over the world; from Britain, Japan, Europe, Latin America – everywhere.

Prime movers like Josh stopped going to parties and public events at all. Silicon Alley had its own gossip columnist now, the socialite Courtney Pulitzer, and a daily list of parties and events called Bernardo's List. Confidence flooded through the downtown district and New York in general. The city's big media companies like Time Warner were busy buying startups and establishing online divisions of their own, to the extent that it was still possible to imagine the net as sown up and owned within a few years, helping to reclaim New York's place at the head of world cities. Mayor Giuliani marked the start of his second term that year by declaiming, 'Four years ago, when I stood here and said, "New York City is the capital of the world," there was doubt. There was fear. There was a feeling that New York City's best days were behind us . . .' Not any more, he told them, prompting *New York* magazine to run bus-side ads saying 'Possibly the Only Good Thing in New York Rudy Hasn't Taken Credit For'.

The city was crazed and electric in equal measure: New York again. And of course no one knew where it would end. Or even *if* it would end. Dotcom believer or not, there was nowhere you'd rather have been as the final year of the Millennium approached.

14

'If you don't know who the fool in the room is, it's you.'

– old Wall Street maxim

Paranoid thought . . .

'What if this is always true, everywhere?'

One night in November 1998, Josh spent from 7 p.m. to 2 a.m. phoning the automated line at Chase Manhattan bank at steadily decreasing intervals. Each time he asked for his cheque account balance and each time the robotic female voice repeated the same figure. 'Five . . . dollars . . . and for-ty . . . three . . . cents.' He went to bed in a state of anxiety, fidgeting as he tried to sleep, mind refusing to settle, then rose at eight and called again, heard the same flat voice intoning figures.

Now his head swam as he realised the figures were different.

'. . . two . . . million . . . one hun-dred and se-ven-ty-three dollars. . .nine-ty three cents.'

He put the phone down and redialled, heard the same voice, same number. Tried to breathe. The deal had gone through. A year on, the Jupiter shares he'd just sold would be worth substantially more than now, but he still had plenty left. For the first time, Josh was cash-rich, with a confirmed paper fortune still in his back pocket.

That night he took Tanya and Natalia to dinner at Mr Chow's on the Upper East Side, where the trio were given a high-visibility berth at the front of the room. A few feet away, the world champion boxer Mike Tyson couldn't keep his eyes off them, no doubt wondering how the nerd at the next table had scored these two beautiful women. Almost immediately, though, Josh was overcome by a sense of suffocation. He began to sweat until his clothes felt sticky and tight, like they belonged to someone else, and his stomach was both bloated and empty. He reached for the cheque book in his pocket and ... found it – *relief!* – but then remembered there was another one in his chambers at 600 Broadway and that stuff had been disappearing from the building. In the glaze on the plate in front of him he saw the thief creeping into his loft and writing $2 million worth of cheques. He went to a payphone, transferred the money into his savings account and felt a little better. But still like he'd changed into someone else.

Back in Awassa, Josh described this to me as 'the worst day of my life'. What came with the wealth was 'depression' he said, and when I asked if this was due to unmet expectations, a moment which had failed to perform, he grew impatient, saying: 'No, it's not ... doing *Quiet* on New Year's night and having it go well and sitting with my nephew and hanging out – *that's* a big moment. Sitting on the back of my boat, alone, hooked into a fifty-pound yellowtail kicking my ass – that's a good moment. Getting money, it was sort of like *weight*. It was like I went into the heavy-weight position. I moved up from light heavyweight to the heavyweight position.'

Registering my confusion, he stopped and chuckled, while birds sang outside in the dark. We were a long way from Mr Chow's.

'I guess it was the dawning that money doesn't show up with nothing attached to it. The freedom of money is illusory. And the other thing is sudden wealth syndrome: you don't change, the people around you do, and you don't really like it any more. You've moved up in the thing and once you've moved up, you're somebody else to them.'

The conversation had begun with me asking when he'd first felt rich and him replying, 'Never!'

'There was a moment in time when I felt a little free,' he'd elucidated, 'but I never felt rich.' And when asked why: 'Because I always knew I'd end up this way. My current situation, I knew it was going to happen.

Really?

'Really.'

Opaque and rapacious and with a tenebrous logic that dissolves the moment you touch it, the Money Culture was mysterious to me when I set out, and learning its tics and tropes has been electrifying. Now I walk into the world and what I see starts to make sense (if only through an appreciation of how profoundly it makes no sense), while a young person's choice of Wall Street for their kicks or a British style magazine's description of finance journalism as 'the new rock 'n' roll' no longer seem perverse. Rock and roll, which so excited me as a youth, holds nothing to the boundless id of Wall Street.

The ETB turned writer-academic Douglas Rushkoff has embarked on a similar journey. We started out in the same field, me writing for the pop culture magazine *The Face* in the UK and him for its New York equivalents, and I think it's interesting that we've both ended up trying to penetrate business and finance; tells you something about the way the world has moved.

It's sparkly Manhattan spring and we're in an old family diner a few blocks from Central Park on East 60th – he en route to a dental appointment, me in town trying to get my head around the cash and what *really* happened to the original dot-coms. A kind of hipster Woody Allen, Rushkoff fizzes intellectual energy, enthusing, 'It's great, isn't it!' when I tell him who I've been talking to and how much I've enjoyed trying to chase down the money.

Rushkoff has just finished a book called *Life Inc.*, in which he, a media theorist, decided to study money 'as a medium, with its own embedded biases'. The Silicon Alley people, even at companies like Flatiron Partners, he maintains, understood IPOs, but *didn't* grasp the nuances of investment capital. He points out something that had never occurred to me, but which is obvious as soon as it's said: that we're misleading ourselves when we speak of 'money being wiped off the market' or say, 'Oh no, DoubleClick's stock has fallen to five dollars – the money's gone!' Because the money hasn't 'gone' in the sense of disappeared: the last person who sold at five dollars, all the people who sold on the way down ... *they* have it. And now they have to find something else to do with it. 'We didn't realise – and what I've been writing about *to this day* – is that cash is a medium as well and that if you infuse the network with *cash*, you end up changing the quality of the whole thing. You change the nature of the experience.'

Rushkoff spent much of the period from 1995 to 2000 telling people, much more directly than Josh ever did, that the primary web revolution was going to be social rather than commercial. He opened one conference address with the words, 'I smell your fear; I talk to you in the lobbies and I know that none of you know what you're talking about, you're all faking it and hoping the others won't realise.' A charge which was both true and mightily convenient for Rushkoff, who would be paid $5–10K just to go and tell businesspeople how the internet worked, taking home a cool $200K one year – a fortune for someone like him. He describes one golden night when, after rocking a

Razorfish party held in a bank vault, he and a *Wired* writer friend hooked up with a couple of women and went to Pravda, where they blew $200 on vodka and blinis.

'I mean,' he smiles, 'I know that wouldn't be considered outrageous by a lot of people . . . Jason Calacanis was worth 40 million on paper and I was 200 *grand*, but all the same, I remember my friend looked across at me and said, "Doug, this is as wealthy as we will ever be. This is New York at the wealthiest it's ever going to be. We're going to look back on this as the Gay Nineties of New York. So even then, those of us who wrote about it, who *thought* about it rather than did it, we knew.'

So flush was Rushkoff that he decided to make his only dotcom investment, ploughing a $25K book advance into Pseudo after Josh invited him to join the 'family and friends' investment round. Like Tony Asnes, he resents the suggestion that Pseudo was a 'fake company' and I've seen a testy email he sent Josh on the subject. He shakes his head when I raise this. 'To me, streaming media and web TV was obvious: I thought Pseudo would be YouTube,' he says. 'Better streaming was being developed at Cornell University and people had little webcams by this time, so it seemed a natural evolution for Pseudo. These were people I cared about and believed in, with a bottom-up approach to the net that I thought could stand in the face of Big Media incursions, like Rupert Murdoch's Delphi effort. I felt that this was *our* net. So I resent him pretending now that the whole investment thing was a scam on rich people, because I saw it as putting my money where my mouth was.'

Does he still think Pseudo was a viable business?

'Yeah,' he says. 'And it was weighed down by sex and drugs and insanity.'

'Really?' I ask. Because I'm starting to think the depth of intemperance was exaggerated – even though I know Rushkoff was at the notorious DMT party. The truth is that drugs, particularly cocaine and ecstasy, were everywhere in the 1990s. I remember being *awed* by a forty-metre queue for the men's toilets at the 1998 Brit Awards, with government minister John Prescott chattering away in the middle of it, oblivious to the reason for its length. Better yet, the Oasis guitarist Noel Gallagher insists that when he asked Tony Blair how he'd managed to stay up through the night of his election in 1997, the new Prime Minister's smiling reply was, 'Probably not the same way you did.' At police insistence, pubs and clubs in the UK *and* New York removed toilet seats and hid the tops of cisterns so they couldn't be used for chopping out lines – that's how routine drugs were in the 1990s.

Rushkoff smiles as he considers this. There's a pause, then: 'Yes, you're right. It's exaggerated. Every month or so there'd be a crazy thing. But people talk about it as though it was the Heaven's Gate cult or something, which is a good story. But it wasn't that. It really *wasn't*. There were people working really hard and seriously there. I think Josh was living two lives. I think he was pretending he was outside the whole thing when actually he was more inside it than anybody.'

There's an old tech adage that, 'Intelligence moves to the edge of the network.' What the internet did was allow for *value creation* to come from the edge, without the need for large-scale borrowings or permissions from corporate gatekeepers. Yet the borrowing and permission imposed themselves anyway. Curious. 'The VCs turned up and gave money to companies that did not need it and did not have a chance to pay it back,' Rushkoff says. 'I mean, who needs venture capital, *except to be rich?* If Craig Kanarick and Jeff Dachis are worth 200 million on paper, then it means that more capital than necessary went into that company.'

I'm put in mind of a conversation I had at Sundance with Andy Bichlbaum of The Yes Men (whose comic documentary *Yes Men Fix the World* was one of the few to get distribution), in which he regretted accepting $100K of outside funding for the film. They hadn't really needed it, he said, and, 'All it meant was from that point on we kept having to go back for more.'

Rushkoff's explanation for the massive cash infusion to Silicon Alley is that, 'Capital wanted to participate in this new economic expansion, this new creation of wealth, even though there was no *need* for it.' As we know, all those pension savings, all that cheap money created by the Fed, had to go somewhere. But did the kids dupe the establishment by drawing them into fake companies, or did the establishment dupe the kids by introducing them to Mammon and charging a commission on it? Or had a generation of capitalists raised on the myths of the 60s been softened to the idea of youth revolution and not wanted to miss out this time? The one thesis I want to dismiss at this stage is the most popular, that the culprit was irrational mania or greed – if only because, in my experience, nothing is ever completely irrational: someone, somewhere, knows. For Rushkoff the first dotcoms were slain by capitalism *per se*, but for me there's still something missing. We hug goodbye and dash off in our separate directions.

* * *

Some quotes I've been collecting. Try to work out when and where they're from. Answers to follow.

1. The net will flatten organisations, globalise society, decentralise control, and help harmonise people.
2. Might not our current translation of our entire lives into the spiritual form of information seem to make of the entire globe, and of the human family, a single consciousness?
3. [It] will have so blended, interwoven and unified human thoughts and interests that the feeling of universal kinship shall be, not a spasmodic outburst of

occasional emotion, but constant and controlling, the usual, everyday, abiding feeling of men toward all men.

4. [We behave] as if the main object were to talk fast and not to talk sensibly.
5. There was an increasing privatisation and individualisation of social life, as people's minds expanded, but not necessarily together ...
6. 'I remember before the internet ...' – when you say that in our headquarters, everyone kinda looks at you like, 'Did they have cars?'
7. They are so busy processing information from all directions that they are losing the tendency to think and feel. [And] much of what they are exposed to is superficial. People are sacrificing depth and feeling and becoming cut off and disconnected from other people.
8. When I got my first TV set, I stopped caring so much about having close relationships with other people ... In the late 50s I started an affair with my television which has continued to the present, when I play around in my bedroom with as many as four at a time.
9. In short, he so buried himself in his books that he spent nights reading from twilight till daybreak and the days from dawn till dark; and so from little sleep and much reading, his brain dried up and he lost his wits. He filled his mind with all that he read in them, with enchantments, quarrels, battles, challenges, wounds, wooings, loves, torments, and other impossible nonsense; and so deeply did he steep his imagination in the belief that all the fanciful stuff he read was true, that ... he decided ... to turn knight errant and travel through the world with horse and armour in search of adventures.

10. It was a period when people pursued their own interests and banded together in little groups. That's all changed with the arrival of the internet and text messaging. It now seems a very far away time.

1. Nicholas Negroponte, Founder, MIT Media Lab, 1995
2. Marshall McLuhan, from *Understanding Media: the Extensions of Man*, 1964
3. *Scientific American* article on 'The Moral Influence of the Telegraph', 1881
4. Henry David Thoreau, on the telegraph, from *Walden*, 1854
5. Professor Sir Robert Winston on the seventeenth-century rise of the book, 2010
6. Sheryl Sandberg, COO, Facebook, 2009
7. Edward Hallowell, psychiatrist and author specialising in attention deficit disorder, 2010
8. Andy Warhol, from *The Philosophy of Andy Warhol*, 1975
9. Miguel de Cervantes, from *Don Quixote*, 1605
10. Greg Mottola, movie director, on a spate of 1980s-set movies including his *Adventureland*, 2009 and Shane Meadows' *This is England*, 2006

I'm learning that the internet is far from the first new medium to provoke hope or alarm. For every bullish *Wired* prophet, there was a nineteenth-century idealist promising that the telegraph would 'cultivate goodwill and peace throughout the earth . . .' Or that it would destroy newspapers, relationships, community, overload us with information we couldn't hope to process. Two centuries earlier, the inspiration for Cervantes' *Don Quixote*, widely cited as the first great European novel, was a fear that the growth of this new medium would cause people to lose sight of the boundary between fantasy and reality – and ultimately, so the logic went, choose the comfort of the latter over the travails of the former (with moralists also deriding the new fashion for private 'silent reading'). In the long run, these fears were exaggerated, but story-tellers did trade the plasticity of tradition for something fixed by print, in which a work was 'finished' at the point of production and could be 'owned'. All of which gives the debate around social networking and the internet a sense of continuity, suggesting that individual technologies might not be the issue; that our anxieties run deeper than nuts and bolts or silicon chips. That the issue might be some primal drift of the human organism itself.

You can't talk about media without talking about Marshall McLuhan, the Canadian intellectual who rivalled Warhol or Lennon or the acid guru Timothy Leary for notoriety in the 1960s. His career began in the early 50s, but it took off in 1962 with his publication of *The Gutenberg Galaxy: the Making of Typographic Man*, closely followed by the extraordinary *Understanding Media: the Extensions of Man*, in which he introduced his most famous maxim, 'the medium is the message'.

McLuhan's writing was dense with allusion and metaphor: he quoted freely from Shakespeare, Joyce and Yeats ('the visible world is no longer a reality and the unseen world is no longer a dream') and was in no way afraid of ambiguity. Yet within this tapestry of ideas was something so elegant and elastic that it walks a path from then to now with ease – a unified theory of media which describes humanity's relationship to its technologies in a single phrase; the $E = mc^2$ of the Information Age. *The medium is the message.*

Like all the best philosophical ideas – 'I think therefore I am,' 'the meaning of a word is its use' – McLuhan's famous phrase starts with a simple thought, then spirals outwards in surprising ways. His imaginative leap involved seeing the media we create as 'extensions of ourselves', whose primary importance is to change not what we know, but our relationship to the world and the processes by which we act upon it; how we think, behave, dream and connect with other people. The medium is its own message, enabling and constraining in and of itself.

Thus, when I Skype Josh in LA from London and he says 'wait a minute', then brings in Feedbuck from New York and Alfredo Martinez in Beijing, the significance of the moment for McLuhan would reside not in what any of us said: it would lie in the fact that we were able to connect in this way at all and how we might use and be transformed by these new connections. 'We shape our tools and thereafter they shape us,' he said in *The Gutenberg Galaxy*, before announcing 'the final stage of the extension of man – the technological simulation of consciousness'.

The era of print media was ending and with it the linear thought patterns it encouraged. Where the train had been an extension of our physical selves, McLuhan contended, 'Today, after more than a century of electric technology, we have extended our central nervous systems in a global embrace.' As the volume and pace of information increased, so our minds would adapt to the new set of challenges posed by it – our technology would change *us*. And as our connections to each other became more integral and fluid in nature, so our emotional involvements with each other would deepen. 'The aspiration of our time for wholeness, empathy and depth of awareness is a natural adjunct of electric technology,' he said.

The 'global village' would bring 'a new electronic interdependence' which would mimic the intimacy and sense of community surrendered to the alienations of the mechanical age; one in which '"Time" has ceased, "space" has vanished' and we live in 'simultaneous happening'.

But. The important thing to know about McLuhan is that he was no callow evangelist. By 1968 his prognosis for the 'shared field of consciousness' had darkened amid fears that TV was exacerbating racial tension (in a year which saw the assassinations of Martin Luther King and Robert Kennedy). He also brooded over the seductive power of an ever more concentrated electronic media, telling talk show host David Frost in 1972 that TV's parade of images could produce an effect similar to being stoned. 'When people get close together,' he added, reversing his earlier stance, 'they get more and more savage with each other. The global village is a place of very arduous interfaces and very abrasive situations.'

This was forty years before Jason Calacanis wrote his 'End of Empathy' piece. And still what I find spookiest about McLuhan is the way that, as his fears for the wired future grew, so did his spirituality. Born into a devoutly Baptist family, he saw himself – and there are striking parallels with the English poet-artist William Blake's contempt for Sir Isaac Newton here – as combating the forces of mechanistic rationality, which he felt to be dehumanising. He had converted to Catholicism in the 1930s and, as his anxiety for the global village grew, so did an inclination to present his vision in spiritual terms. In a 20,000-word interview with *Playboy* magazine from March 1969, sub-headed 'a candid conversation with the high priest of popcult and metaphysician of media' and sandwiched between articles on gun control and the Black Panther leader Eldridge Cleaver, and letters advising readers on the ideal age of Scotch, choice of pipe tobacco, best means of Vietnam draft resistance and how to gauge when a girlfriend wants to move beyond 'petting', McLuhan went so far as to suggest not only that 'the upsurge in drug taking is intimately related to the electric media' ('look at the metaphor for getting high: "turning on",' he advised), but that: 'Psychic communal integration made possible at last by the electronic media could create the universality of consciousness foreseen by Dante when he predicted that men would continue as no more than broken fragments until they were unified into an inclusive consciousness. In a Christian sense, this is merely a new interpretation of the mystical body of Christ; and Christ, after all, is the ultimate extension of man.'

Josh has certainly read McLuhan, but McLuhan's words were descriptive: I've never seen anyone try to live by them as if they were a faith, to *choose* to live as information – which is what I'm beginning to think he does in treating the domains of physical space and imagination as qualitatively the same, through a decision to prioritise the *story* of his life above any sensual connection to the world. Is this peculiar to him, or is he simply showing us all our futures? And if he is, do we embrace them? Are we slowly evolving into our own media, where the message is *us*? The longer I look at this question, the more extraordinary Josh's journey starts to seem, because he saw it, *felt* it, asked it in interesting ways before almost anyone else, out of sheer, devilish conviction. Although even he might have missed some of the more profound implications of his work and life, because if we are media, message, *information* fanning out across a real–virtual cyberscape, what will ground us, give a sense of being more than clouds of revolving, self-editing data, flickering in and out of existence in proportion to how widely we are 'known' or seen?

Virtuality. Reality. Unreality.

Where am I?

On the back of Robert Galinsky's Vespa on a beautiful spring day, flying uptown to appear as fellow guest on a web TV chat show for the Fox Network. It's an unnerving experience, during which both time and the normal rules of intercourse seem to compress as our ebullient host drives his cast like a team of huskies, the rule being that if it can't be said crackerjack fast, it can't be said: new communication for a new kind of world. Within a few months, Galinsky will have his own show, hilariously called *Robert Galinsky's Reality*.

Later that night we find ourselves in the East Village home of a retired black radical poet-author-academic named Steve Cannon, who spent the late 60s squatting around the corner from Jimi Hendrix in West London, and for the last fifteen years has treated his home as an open performance space, allowing anyone to turn up and do what they wanna do – in his living room. I could weep with the *newyorkness* of it all.

Galinsky tells me about the press he's still getting for the Reality TV School, which has now featured in the British media at least seven times and generated an outrageous number of articles and TV features elsewhere. When I ask why he's doing it, whether he's not simply introducing yet more cynicism into the world, he says no; that he sees a continuity between now and his time trying to break down the invisible 'fourth wall' at open-mic clubs. 'And it's only recently dawned on me that what I'm doing with the New York Reality TV School is teaching people social-media survival skills. Because everybody is "the brand" now. Everybody's got their broadcast station. Which is what Josh played with – that two-way street on the broadcast station. I'm carrying on that work.'

He thinks the likes of me view these shows as humiliating car-crash TV, when they're something else entirely. 'On a deeper level, they're connecting people,' he insists.

> It's all right for you: you have a voice through your writing and other things. But the big fat girl that no one pays attention to, that's getting only negative energy when she walks down the street or into a library or a café . . . can she get on TV and be empowered? *Yes, she can!* Because she's got this non-scripted environment to play within, where she doesn't have to follow the pre-set rules that have always existed in that industry – it's a world of possibility to play with. *And* there's a thousand giant girls watching at home that are connecting to what she's doing, and may even be feeling empowered by it.

He mentions Jade Goody, the poorly educated *Big Brother* contestant who was pilloried in the resoundingly upper crust

British media until it became clear how many readers and viewers identified with her. Like a lot of people in the US, Galinsky watched her lingering public cancer death with fascination. Online. 'And it seems to me that she was from the Josh school,' he grins. 'Ahead of her time. Because fifteen to twenty years from now, somebody getting their lives chronicled as deeply as that is not going to be the exception to the rule. She definitely was *of the future*.'

Either that or Galinsky has found a clever way to get his story into my book and boost the 'Galinsky' brand.

To my chagrin, a few days after I leave New York Josh is due for the East Coast première of Ondi Timoner's film. After Sundance, he surprised everyone by opting to stay in the US, where – a little comically – he now lives in Jason Calacanis's pool house in the plush LA suburb of Brentwood. We'll be meeting a week later for the San Francisco opening of the film, but this is the one he covets, for the simple reason that it's being hosted by the Museum of Modern Art (MoMA), whose imprimatur he craves above all others. Better still, the gallery's monthly brochure sports him as cover star.

Josh is beside himself with excitement at this belated gesture of acceptance by the art establishment, but has still wanted to discuss whether it would be more dramatic for him not to show up, which I take to mean that he's nervous. I call as he's driving Calacanis's yellow Corvette down the Santa Monica Freeway, with the top down and wind in his mom-cut hair, no doubt working the Ray-Bans I brought to Africa. The hoped-for Microsoft meeting hasn't happened, but he sounds chipper all the same, laughing as he describes his pool house lifestyle. 'I mean it's in Brentwood, it's very nice. But it's still Jason Calacanis's pool house. You know, *shared with two dogs*. And the cost of those dogs annually as far as I can see is thirty-five grand ... I could build an orphanage in Ethiopia for that!'

He claims to be homesick for Awassa, which I think represents the old twentieth-century notion of 'reality' to him now, and to being frustrated by his lack of 'leverage' in LA. Even so, his main worry is the issue of the fake girlfriend in Ondi Timoner's film. 'Quite a few people seem to have come out thinking that I was in love with Tanya,' he tells me, clearly distressed at the thought. 'It keeps coming up in the Q & A's . . .'

He speaks of a video, allegedly shot by Natalia Tsarkova shortly after he and Tanya met, in which he lays out his plans for the 'work'. He wants Tsarkova, who now lives in Paris, to find it and then arrange to have it run in a Manhattan gallery while *We Live in Public* is showing, to be entitled simply *Proof*.

He discusses New York with a detachment that suggests a final breaking of ties, but needs money to get back to Awassa and is thinking of selling off some of his art, like the specially commissioned 'Gilligan' silkscreen prints in his old PR man Andy Morris's 5th Avenue office, which I rather like and wouldn't mind having, while also suspecting that the price in his head would be somewhere north of mine.

15

Even before the Jupiter money arrived, those closest to Josh felt a change in him. After eighteen months of putting together deals which no one around him properly understood, carrying the weight of all those people and their constantly heightening expectations, he was spent. Invited to speak at a conference in Japan, he took the former Pseudo artist Owen Bush to film his performance, but refused to leave his hotel room for most of the trip; just stayed inside eating room service and pacifying himself with bad Hollywood movies. Bush had never seen anyone shut down so completely.

In New York, Josh started turning up to the office as Luvvy the clown, named for the character Eunice 'Lovey' Wentworth Howell from *Gilligan's Island*. Tales of him crashing board meetings dressed as Luvvy turn out to be apocryphal (though he did often crash meetings as himself, which could be just as disruptive). Appearances by Luvvy, with its smudged makeup and cheese-grater voice, became common on Pseudo radio and TV shows and at parties where clients were present – and as Josh must have known, were a gift to his critics and doubters. Jess Zaino was the first to encounter the boss's new alter-ego at close quarters, when it turned up on her radio show as a guest and, for twenty of the longest live-streamed minutes in the presenter's life, met all attempts at conversation with the exclamation 'Boing! Boing!'

'And I remember being ter-ri-fied,' she admits. 'Cos I was, like, "He is such a freak!" But I think . . . I think: how weird he is, *is* genuine, but what he decides to do is not genuine. Sometimes I so badly wanted him to just be normal. But he never is.'

Only Galinsky found something of value in Luvvy.

> I thought it was hilarious and wonderful and, um, shocking and annoying and disturbing. Josh *is* disturbing, so if he intensifies any part of himself, it's going to be even more disturbing. But I also thought that . . . at first I didn't get Luvvy, I didn't *want* to get Luvvy. The time that I finally did was when he/she was talking to somebody in chat while the conversation was in the room, on air, and Luvvy had this connection with the people on the chat, kind of revealing the subtext of what was going on in the room. And I was like, "Oh my God, what a necessary voice in the conversation!" There's somebody here, in the room, saying the shit nobody wants people to hear, but which is there in coded language. And Luvvy was deciphering the language.

The king playing his own jester.

'Exactly.'

There are various theories as to what was happening to Josh. Some think he was in the midst of a breakdown which would unspool him like a film reel over the better part of two years. A decade after the fact, Owen Bush would be running a video production company of his own and come to believe that, 'There's a pressure to the kind of position he was in that you just don't understand until you're there – a kind of *heaviness* to the constant anxiety you have.' Bush also thought he saw his friend being surrounded by sycophants who 'didn't want to deal with the real world, they wanted to stay in his shadow all the time, wanted his *lifestyle*'. Working out how to deal with these people took a toll, he suspected, made worse by Josh's generosity towards artists whose work he didn't have the capacity to assess in any useful way. A quirk of the Pseudo aesthetic was that its patron almost never criticised his artists' work, because his infatuation with art always seemed to be about something *other than the art* – as though he was interested in the process of making a work, or the pattern it made in conjunction with other works, but once an individual piece was done it became nothing more than a souvenir; a dead zone through which his spirit passed like noise through a wall. He simply couldn't respond.

The jingle-maker Thomas 'T-Bo' Linder noticed the change too: 'By that time, Pseudo was a magnet for people on the make and Josh had to be careful who he was dealing with all the time. And I think with all that psychic baggage . . . I think something *snapped* in him. By 1999, I got the sense that he didn't give a shit any more, and he wasn't even going to entertain the idea of a Pseudo 2.0.'

A few long-serving heads of department, including T-Bo and the animator Jacques Tege, began to discuss leaving Pseudo to better employ the skills they'd learned there.

Equally, Josh may have been playing out his anger. In a scenario being replicated across Silicon Alley, he'd raised a mountain of capital he was no longer in a position to spend, because success had cost him control of the company he'd built, the thing he loved most in the world. In a tragi-comic twist, he was charged with helping to find his successor CEO, and the VCs were demanding snap expansion, from a staff of sixty or so to nearly three hundred, most of them incomers expecting to be rich within the year as per the stories they read and saw on TV – as per their now notional leader, Josh. In the blink of an eye Pseudo HQ teemed with twentysomethings on up to $100K per annum, plus stock options, prompting the original crew to demand and get parity. But again, the real point was the shares.

After an IPO which seemed inevitable somewhere down the line, senior Pseudo staff would be millionaires. Stakes raised, the tone and ethos of the place changed.

Pseudo had evolved at a pace one ex-producer describes as 'fast, but also slow: fast because we were eating up the technology as soon as it became available; slow because Josh wanted to spend whatever time it took to make the technology work'. But now the money became its own 'forcing-factor' and the company was on rails, running ahead of both the technology and anyone's ability to apply it. Just as significantly, Pseudo's business plan, like most in 1999, depended on 'eyeballs' or 'page views', the idea that these would be 'monetised' through a proportionate sale of advertising. But online advertising – this print-era chimera – had yet to take off and produced almost no revenue.

Concerns about Pseudo's new slingshot trajectory tended to be expressed quietly or not at all, for fear of sounding fogeyish. Like other ETBs, Josh and Tony Asnes had planned Pseudo on the basis that technology and demand would slowly converge and that they were shooting for this convergence point. But the web-rush was undermining such assumptions, because investors wouldn't wait for technology or demand to mature: time and space were collapsing into an accelerated zone only half jokingly referred to as 'internet time'. Worse, statistics which claimed internet traffic to be doubling every three months, amounting to a nearly 2000 per cent annual increase, were *wrong*. According to research retrospectively conducted at the University of Minnesota, this was accurate for the two extraordinary years up to 1996, after which growth settled down to a pattern of roughly doubling each year. Ironically, the higher claim would eventually be traced back to the disgraced conglomerate WorldCom.

Tony Asnes says:

The *get big fast* ethos always bothered me. It may have been true in some cases – that you could create buzz and do your IPO, and there'd only be room for one, so whoever got out there first was the winner. But I didn't think we could go that fast. I thought, 'Let's get this to really work, and if it really works, even if it's a much slower route, it'll be *real*.' But it was difficult to have that point of view, because you would second-guess yourself and go, 'Maybe I just don't "get it": maybe I don't have the right personality for this new world and we should just be driving for the IPO.' People started to say that we should behave more like DEN [Digital Entertainment Network] and the others, even though we knew they were all smoke and mirrors.

And the thing was, you knew that the environment was starting to behave in a way that was irrational . . .

As 1999 beckoned, history could have provided guidance, if only in demonstrating that most big technological advances have served consumers before investors, who tend to lose their shirts on giant leaps like motor or air travel. Superinvestor Warren Buffet once said of the aerospace industry: 'I like to think that if I'd been at Kitty Hawk in 1903 when Orville Wright took off, I would have been far-sighted enough, and public-spirited enough – I owe this to future capitalists – to shoot him down . . . I mean, Karl Marx couldn't have done as much damage to capitalists as Orville did.'

From which we might infer that Buffet spent the final year of the Millennium searching for the plug to the internet.

(*Must be around here somewhere . . .*)

But even Josh couldn't have helped him with this. And no one was interested in history any more. So the Pseudo chairman started hanging out with Jeff Gompertz's creative crowd in Williamsburg, talking up plans for a last big event, a 'lockdown' party from which no one could leave. 'It was clear already, from his attitude and body language and everything, that psychologically he was finished with Pseudo,' Gompertz says. 'And I guess it was all sorted out in his mind, but he didn't say anything. The business was in transition and I think he just *bailed*. He walked out of there.' Or as Tony Asnes puts it, 'You could see that after four or five years, Josh was kind of thinking, "OK, my work here is done, and it's not as interesting to me."'

On New Year's Eve 1998 he allowed Uzi Fisher, mainstay of the well-respected FreQ electronica music show, to host a party in his absence, but the event was badly planned and violence erupted at 600 Broadway for the first time ever, with one guest losing an eye – a tragedy unlikely to have occurred in the days when Josh was fully engaged. Another typical story has him sitting in a stockholders' meeting with his feet on the desk, reading loudly from the paper as his comrades tried to work through business. It's tempting to see this as a protest or, as one Pseudite suggests, an expression of grief for a company he now felt was being fast-tracked to nowhere.

'I think he knew that Pseudo was a bit of a hoax by then,' offers Natalia Tsarkova. 'I think he probably thought it was going to succeed *because* it was a hoax, but deep down he knows what's true and has value. He knows the diamond from the rough.' She thinks for a moment, then adds: 'But he will still play the rough because he sees that's the way it's going. And because it's more interesting.'

And it was. A hyper-real glow settled over the city as it dissolved like aspirin into pure, ecstatic *story*. News and information travelled so fast and with such velocity that it was possible to imagine almost anything you might choose to say becoming true if you said it with enough conviction – whether it had started out that way or not.

New York became the test bed for a new set of moralities based on the idea that in this new world of revolving data, a proposition would be judged not by whether it was true or false when stated, but by whether it had the potential to *become* true. Whether it contained the *possibility* of truth.

Frequently enough, it did, as when – to give a banal example – reports of a famous couple's relationship problems produced enough strain to cause ... relationship problems. Or more seriously, when a company, industry, country was put under economic pressure by rumours that it was under pressure. And of course the potential for these outcomes had to have been there in the first place, like the energy contained in an atom, just waiting to be released. So was it wrong to *test* this potential? How else could you ever gauge the true state of things in the world? There was no other way. None. Thus implying that *anything* could be said with moral impunity.

So a new category of truth, 'retro-truth', reached maturity in the Manhattan of the 1990s, where henceforth data would be assessed on grounds not of veracity, but of plausibility – which meant precisely this: how good was the story? Would we *buy it?* Our creaky old notions of truth and falsity could be seen slurring into each other like notes on a sitar, taking traditional distinctions between fantasy and reality with them. Over at *The New York Times*, the rogue reporter Jayson Blair melded researched fact with words and scenes and characters from his imagination in a way that was perfectly consistent with his environment. Josh says the Blair articles about him were accurate: Jayson Blair tells me he doesn't know whether he temporarily lost his mind or was behaving as an outlier. 'Were those absurd times?' he asks at the end of our exchange. 'Yes. Did I do something equally absurd? Yes. Were they connected? I actually don't really want to know. That's a good question and I wish I had an answer ...'

Neither was this popular drift dishonest. We were simply adjusting. Driven by the new technology, our world was accelerating to the point where we could *feel* ourselves adapting to meet it; could watch our own evolution and comment on it like a reality show.

In essence, the world was becoming Josh. Jess Zaino's 'weird juxtaposition'.

And the funny thing is that the only person in the world who seemed to notice and be concerned about this was ... *Josh.*

16

1999.

Where to start?

The distortion field.

Seventy-one IPOs in July alone, hundreds over the year. A veteran Silicon Valley investor describes meeting a young entrepreneur who was trying to raise money for a company called Funerals.com with the pitch 'We're going to put the *fun* back into funerals': an online venture called Pets.com forgot to wonder how profit would grace a business selling ten-dollar bags of cat litter which cost twenty dollars to deliver – as did the New York-based online grocer Kozmo.com, which also traded on free delivery. More improbably still, a firm called Pixelon threw a $16 million IPO launch party in Las Vegas, with entertainment from The Who, KISS, Tony Bennett, The Offspring and Dixie Chicks, before anyone knew that its CEO Michael Fenne was really a fugitive con artist named David Kim Stanley and that the clients who spied its revolutionary 'broadband' system had actually been looking at RealPlayer. Was this more outrageous than a loss-making 2-year-old company called eToys.com being valued by the market at $4.9 billion on sales of just $100 million, when the $4 billion real world valuation of Toys R Us was based on revenues of $11.5 billion? In 1999 it was impossible to say.

Kurt Andersen, the experienced editor who left Old Media to

found the online magazine Inside.com and wrote the boom's best novel, *Turn of the Century*, was long enough in the tooth to see a generational shift. 'No one feels guilty about being rich any more and not caring about anything except money,' he told the London *Times*. 'Unemployment is at a historic low. Kids come pre-sold out. A 21-year-old today knows only the post-liberal Reagan philosophy. The free market won ... They come into a landscape where their college friends make $5 million overnight. They see the rewards of capitalism directly – and they look good.' According to an article in *Vanity Fair*, half of the '98 graduating classes from the Harvard and Stanford business schools headed for the internet.

In *Wired* magazine, Kevin Kelly proved that Baby Boomers were buying the dream too, by mooting an approaching age of 'ultra-prosperity', where the average household income was $150,000 and middle class families had chefs. 'How many times in the history of mankind have we wired the planet to create a single marketplace?' he asked. 'How often have entirely new channels of commerce been created by digital technology? When has money itself been transformed into thousands of instruments of investment?'

On the ground, GeoCities, whose IPO had caused excitement when its shares rose from $17 to $37 six months earlier, was bought by Yahoo! at a valuation of $4.6 billion, on revenues of just $20 million ... a price-to-earnings ratio of 230, against a historic average of *14*. News arrived that Murdoch was a net fan again. Jim Clark's Netscape follow-up, Healtheon, IPO-d in February, its value quadrupling on the first day; rising fifteenfold by the end of the year. Through the 1990s, the NASDAQ Composite index had risen an unprecedented 795 per cent. Online brokerages were special darlings of the market, enabling you to buy shares in the sites that sold you shares.

In New York, in March, pieces of iVillage.com hit $113 a pop on the first day of trading, the Latin site StarMedia reached a valuation of $1.6 billion and Agency.com (a New York competitor to Razorfish) hit $2 billion, pinging ETB co-founder Chan Suh into *Fortune* magazine's list of the forty richest Americans under forty. James Cramer's finance news site TheStreet.com flew from an offer price of $19 to almost $70, despite his despairing efforts to slow it. Razorfish and DoubleClick IPO-d to the tune of $1.8 billion and $6.6 billion respectively, and by Christmas their headcounts had quadrupled to almost two thousand each, with the former boasting fifteen offices in nine countries, mostly established with company stock. Even the hip but tiny online magazine Salon.com was seen to be worth $100 million. In almost every case, the post-IPO landscape saw revenues rise, but losses *rocket*.

If few dotcommers had understood what their IPO cash pile would cost, most soon learned. 'I could talk for nine hours about the downside of going public,' Craig Kanarick told *Wired*. He now had thirty people in Investor Relations: every three months, he'd 'bend over and have some guys shove a flashlight up my ass' – not to mention the analysts who didn't understand the business and just wanted to hear buzzwords (say 'wireless' and they'd turn into a flock of sheep braying 'strong buy!'). For its first five years, Razorfish had been profitable *every quarter*, but the April '99 IPO would dump it into loss. And once you were on that fast-cash bus, there was no way to get off.

Statistics suggest that IPOs created more than 1000 new millionaires in Silicon Alley that year, with 2000 more half-millionaires among a workforce that numbered in the region of 250,000. 'Silicon Alley has turned into an economic juggernaut that is reinventing the life and economy of the city . . . New Media companies are redrawing the physical landscape, rewriting the rules of business and eclipsing industries that have dominated the economy for decades,' announced *Crain's*, a cheerleader again. And in another cover story: 'In some ways, [Silicon Alley] has supplanted Wall Street as the city's premier industry.'

Who ran the show? It wasn't clear. Everything was blurring

into everything else. Market analysts at the big merchant and investment banks had once been the greystripe shadow figures of investment, but by 1999 analysts like Mary Meeker were equivalent to the great rock managers of the 1960s and 70s, the Brian Epsteins and Andrew Loog Oldhams and Peter Grants . . . but who did they work for? Banks were taking companies public: their own analysts were recommending these same stocks to mutual funds and pension funds and the public. The more enthusiastically a bank's analysts recommended tech stocks, the more tech companies wanted that bank to handle their IPO – *obviously* – and the more money that bank made. A perfect circle. It was embarrassingly easy.

Consider Henry Blodget. On 16 December 1998, shares in Amazon.com, which had been founded four years earlier by the former Wall Street tech analyst Jeff Bezos, reached $242. Merrill Lynch's bearish analyst declared a more realistic value to be $50 and advised selling, while Blodget, a mousy voice at an obscure brokerage, offered a target of $400, which the stock quickly rose to meet – then pass . . . and a star was born. In the blink of an eye Blodget was all over CNBC; was 'the Man of the Moment' according to *USA Today*, until by February Merrill had fired their incumbent naysayer and appointed this tech-savvy young seer, who later confessed to having plucked the figure of $400 out of the air, reluctantly, when pressed by brokers for a headline. From this point on, no one wanted to hear Blodget's frequent warnings and expressions of doubt, so they didn't. In January '99, he told *The New York Times* that internet valuations were 'totally frightening'. But they still wanted to know which tech stocks their readers should snaffle.

Why had this happened? Easy. A Merrill manager *stated*, in as many words, that his old chief analyst had been costing lucrative IPO business by offering cautious valuations of tech firms and such business increased with Blodget's arrival, in turn driving up the bank's own share price. Blodget describes threats of violence and withdrawal of custom, ansaphone rants and all-hours calls on the rare occasions he downgraded stocks owned by big institutional clients, along with the anxiety of fund managers who knew the market was spinning out of control but had no choice but to follow or be fired. Celebrity analysts were no longer *analysts*, they were totems, often owning stock in the companies they were recommending, a clear conflict of interest. In *A Short History of Financial Euphoria*, the great economist John Kenneth Galbraith observes that at the height of a bubble, one unremarkable man is nearly always held up as a genius, ready to be blamed when the bubble bursts, and Blodget could have been written by Dickens, sent by Central Casting specifically for this purpose. There's something poignant about his sullen description of himself to *Crain's* Jon Birger that year as 'Merrill Lynch's tulip analyst' – a reference to the tulip bubble which ruined so many investors in the early seventeenth century. Another analyst reports being called 'unpatriotic' by a client after she labelled tech stocks 'overpriced'. Publicly humiliated and sacked as a pundit on a PBS stock show for the same reason, her bullish replacement was later indicted for taking kickbacks.

Few dotcommers were equipped to hear the alarm bells James Cramer heard as TheStreet.com's market value o'erleapt those of the *Wall Street Journal* and *The New York Times* on IPO day in May ('It will leave us no room to grow, no room for error ... *we're fucked,*' he told his staff). In fact, quite the opposite. Inflated stock could be a powerful business tool, used to buy rivals, attract and pay staff, substitute for rent. AOL was already eyeing up the grandstand merger-takeover of Time Warner in this way, indeed by the end of 1999, every $100 invested in AOL at the point of its IPO in 1992 was worth $28,000, with shares trading at 217 times earnings.

'It's exciting. It's America,' said Prudential's Ralph Acampora, who had required a security guard after predicting the mini-crash of 1998. 'We should all get up and sing "God Bless America".'

In this environment, the dollar–hubris exchange rate also soared to new highs. Outside of New York, winners of the tech stock lottery celebrated themselves in the traditional way of weird rich people – by building big things. Jim Clark of Netscape commissioned a castle-sized computer-controlled yacht, while Michael Saylor, the 35-year-old head of the 'data mining' company MicroStrategy, spent a reported $3 million on his company's annual cruise, hired the Washington Redskins' stadium for a Super Bowl party and bought a plot of land on the banks of the Potomac River in Washington, on which – apparently without irony – he intended to build an exact replica of the house in the film of *The Great Gatsby*. Saylor spoke of running for president and was rumoured to have dated Queen Noor of Jordan. More thoughtfully, a renowned computer designer named Danny Hillis, concerned at the collapse of 'time' into 'internet time', launched plans to build a monumental 'Clock of the Long Now' atop a mountain in Texas, which would count time in millennia, producing one tick per year. 'Civilisation is revving itself into a pathologically short attention span,' said a supporter of the project, the internet Moses, Stewart Brand.

Cyber CEOs now had fans and stalkers and real cultural cachet: Netscape's Marc Andreessen starred in a Miller Lite ad and when Amazon's Jeff Bezos opened a new warehouse in Kansas, he was besieged with requests for autographs from his own workers. The $300,000 life savings Bezos's mother had lent him to help start the company was now worth (*really* worth, because she could sell the shares) more than $79,800,000, with his own wealth said to be greater than the GDP of Iceland and *Time* magazine ready to name him 'Person of the Year' for 1999. Suddenly it was all about the money. 'Making money in the 90s [is] like getting laid in 1969,' joked Old Media refugee Kurt Andersen. Even across the pond in London, the Swedish heads of fashion site Boo.com expected a reprimand when they hit an investment banker with a request for $2 million startup funding. They got one, too, but not as envisaged.

'How much?' they report the banker as groaning. 'Listen. I could throw a stone out of the window right now and hit someone who would give you $2 million. If you want people to take you seriously you can't go looking for unserious money.'

And as they were leaving, the financier allegedly added: 'Just remember, no matter what happens, the investor is always your enemy.'

Monuments would have made no sense in New York. The city was its own monument. And no one in SoHo drank Miller Lite.

Downtown was about the money and the *moment*. Jason Calacanis would have people *screaming* to get into his *Silicon Alley Reporter* parties, 1500 inside, 1000 more out, some waving hundred-dollar bills at the NYPD officers his brother hired as security, while august journals like *The New Yorker* ran lengthy profiles on him. He'd walk the line shaking hands and shrugging 'sorry – it's *full*', thinking of all the times he'd been told he was wasting his energy: that adoption would be slow; cable systems run by Time Warner and AOL would win out; broadband would be a private network . . . that the tyrannosaur News Corp would have a private data superhighway and the revolution would be all about closed networks.

Private profit.

Like newspapers. The internet wouldn't work, couldn't scale, wasn't secure – was unregulated and chaotic and doomed to drown in an embarrassing ejaculation of porn. All perfectly reasonable assumptions. But by some Elysian alchemy, *wrong*.

Alley parties typically featured oysters, caviar, champagne and elaborate lobster-strewn ice-sculptures. Natalia Tsarkova, asked whether she worried for Josh as he channelled the mania around him ever more recklessly, remembers a plan he hatched to sponsor the Mir space station when Russia ran out money to keep it in space. She all but gasps as she describes their exchange. 'He said, "Wouldn't you like to be the first person to set up a colony on the Moon?" And I looked at him and realised he was *serious*. I thought, "This is weird": this guy so believes in himself and what he's doing that he thinks one day this might be in his power. It's hard to worry about someone like that. But it's how they all were.'

Yet compared to some of his peers, Josh looked almost meek. When Dachis and Kanarick dropped the names of their friends 'Courtney', 'Leo' and 'Michael', they meant Love, DiCaprio, Stipe (with whom Dachis helped fund the hit independent film *Being John Malkovich*). *The New York Times* photographed Kanarick leaping into his sky-blue '65 Corvette Convertible: *Marie Claire* covered the SoHo duplex he was building with padded heated floors and seven shades of red in the den. The pair ran their own Lower East Side club, the Slipper Room, with cocktails named after themselves – the Dachismo (gin and tonic to real worlders) and the Craigar (bloody Mary) – and somehow couldn't prevent word slipping out that they holidayed in Mustique and flew their parents to Paris on Concorde. The tale of Dachis going out and buying an ice cream van for his workforce one sweltering summer's day turns out to be a fabulous myth, but the post-IPO 'fish fry' blowout, which involved flying the entire international workforce to Vegas, was real enough. Dachis would never live down his boast that, 'I feel completely and utterly entitled to whatever success comes our way ... I'm sorry, but there are sheep and there are shepherds, and I fancy myself to be the latter,' nor his declared status as an Ayn Rand-reading 'brutal capitalist' (this despite being a fundraising Democrat ... only in the 1990s would this fail to seem paradoxical). And yet *Business Week* invoked the 60s acid proselytiser and author of *One Flew Over the Cuckoo's Nest*, Ken Kesey, in describing Dachis as 'a Kesey for the Net generation.'

It should be clear by now that the story of Silicon Alley is as much about the financialisation of the economy and culture as it is about digitalisation. The journalist James Ledbetter, by now working online for *The Industry Standard*, recalls a taxi driver pulling to the curb to trade stocks in the middle of a journey, and hard as the VC Jerry Colonna tried to deflect calls from journalists wanting to write about his wardrobe or assessment of the Indonesian rupiah, they kept coming anyway. *New York* magazine dubbed Colonna and his Flatiron partner Fred Wilson 'The Princes of New York' and suddenly he was hearing pitches from young people whose driving force was not passion for an idea, but anger that they weren't rich like their business school classmates. Meanwhile, the Alley connector and web designer Jaime Levy, despite mild disgust with the way things had gone, accepted half a million dollars in angel funding for her own company, Electronic Hollywood, but 'got hooked on the adrenalin rush of celebrity' and ended up with a crippling heroin addiction – her unfashionable choice of drug an act of rebellion in itself.

What none of the young webbies knew was that, even as they drank to their own futures and laughed away fears of a computer-toasting Y2K Millennial bug, a yet younger Boston university student named Shawn Fanning was releasing free software for a music file-sharing system which would turn out to be the real life-changing, industry-razing Y2K. Called Napster after Fanning's hairstyle-derived nickname, his slippery and illegal creation allowed individual computers to connect directly, peer-to-peer, or 'P2P', under the radar of the World Wide Web. If any ETBs had seen Napster coming, none of them said so publicly – even though a few seemed to smell something on the breeze. Josh was contemptuous and other Alley stalwarts baffled when the online audio pioneer Mark Cuban sold his company Broadcast.com to Yahoo! for a supposed $5.6 billion. 'He sold them a mare,' frowns the former, 'basically a sales team worth a couple of million on a good day.' But a dotcommer who was in the room with Cuban that night reports having commented, 'You're crazy, man, you've got a great thing here, why sell out?' only to get a cryptic, 'I don't know, I have a *feeling*,' in reply. The dotcommer watched Cuban receive word that the deal had gone through, then pick up the phone and order a Gulfstream jet on his AmEx card. A success that seemed incidentally to validate Pseudo, now surely in line for a lucrative acquisition. No one clocked that the date was 1 April. Cuban now owns the Dallas Mavericks basketball franchise.

Behind the jets and jollies and sugar plum fortunes lay a continuing inflow of capital, most of it channelled through mutual funds aggressively marketed at individual investors. Perversely, this flood created a problem for many fund managers whose bylaws dictated that they had to stay fully invested and had to buy stocks, sometimes tech stocks specifically. By 1999, managers would *complain* of finding $200 million in the morning post, with another $200 million arriving in the afternoon, all of which needed a home – while investors, spurred on by sweating, straining CNBC pundits and cash-porn columnists, expected ever higher returns from ever sexier stocks. For the fund marketeers, the formula was simple: high return figures meant more persuasive ads; meant more cash; meant better commissions and bigger bonuses.

A set of conditions that encouraged high risk. And if individual managers had reservations about this risk, as many did, at least they would look no more foolish than anyone else when the balloon went up *so long as they followed the herd*. But if they went their own way and baulked at such reckless optimism, investors simply went elsewhere in search of higher returns. Suddenly, without anyone noticing, the public were controlling the market on the basis of what they read and saw at the barber's – all without (to quote one cautious tech market analyst) 'any understanding of the fundamentals'. Yet even such conservative analysts faced a classic catch-22: if they recommended overpriced stocks, they were charlatans; if they didn't but the stocks rose anyway, they were wrong.

Little wonder that in his office, in the bath, at the opera that year, Federal Reserve Chairman Alan Greenspan spent time pondering the idea of 'bubbles'. To him, a bubble was defined by an abrupt market fall of 40 per cent or more – which meant that you could never know you'd been inside one until it burst. Furthermore, predicting such a drop in advance required, by definition, a hubristic willingness to say that all the people inside the system, including some who supposedly understood it very well, were deluded. In theory, there had to be a point at which a rate rise would hold the market steady, without turning it downwards, but all the ideas he threw at his economists with the aim of finding models for predicting such a point simply led him to believe that knowing this perfect moment was impossible. Of course, Greenspan's conclusions presumed an economy in which information was distributed evenly and everyone acted upon it in a spirit of rational self-interest. Imponderables such as fear or curiosity or yearning for community, or deliberate manipulation, did not and could not compute.

With the VC-led influx of staff, Pseudo was changing fast. The influential producer Janice 'Girlbomb' Erlbaum was fired and would eventually file a sex discrimination suit against the company. She wasn't the only woman to have found the clubby male atmosphere frustrating, and had been left out of a round of share options for heads of department – probably as a result of irking Josh with her opposition to the parties. For his part, Josh recognised that he'd caused a fight between her and fellow departmental head Joey Fortuna, leading them to splinter as creative team and a couple, and would surprise me with a retrospective admission of sadness over this action, citing it as 'the point at which Pseudo started to go sideways and lose it, because these people were like family'. One deep, whisky-loosened Awassa night, he even wondered whether his action was deliberate, part of an unconscious attempt to buy a way out of Pseudo by destroying it. Either way, his emotional attachment faded further.

Erlbaum smiles a lot as she weighs her love for Pseudo against the frustration of its management, ruing her inability to have relaxed and accepted the place for what it was ('a crazy house!') and to have simply *enjoyed* it more. 'And you know, Josh wasn't wrong about anything,' she says with a shake of her head. 'I think the problem remains, "Wow, this is so wonderful, but how do we make money off it?" I think he was the first to really come up against that.'

Jeff Gompertz left 'to concentrate more on the art' and Robert Galinsky bowed out, believing that Pseudo had 'evolved into an organisation that was being run by people who "knew better"' – people from the outside, from marketing, television, advertising, imposing their Old Media models on this community of people who lived and breathed and dreamt *online*. Prior to leaving, Galinsky got his big break when Josh arranged a near-million-dollar budget for him to write and produce his own *Real World*-style series called *Peace Cops*, but by all accounts it was awful. The first post-Josh CEO, Larry Lux, was a former Jupiter client from National Geographic Online (where the most common search term, he revealed, was 'naked native') who never got the measure of the company or its staff. Hired in February '99, the VCs ordered Josh to fire him in October.

The irony is that even as Pseudo struggled to reinvent itself along lines dictated by the market, the full horror of Digital Entertainment Network, the competitor it was being urged to emulate, began to emerge. With $50 million already prised from blue-chip backers, DEN planned to raise a further $75 million through an IPO . . . until on 25 October its three directors were forced to resign when chairman and controlling shareholder Marc Collins-Rector was forced to settle a lawsuit alleging sex with a (male) minor. Collins-Rector was aged thirty-nine, but his chief lieutenants, Chad Shackley and Brock Pierce, were aged twenty-four and eighteen respectively. The latter was paid an annual salary of $250,000 and a generous allocation of shares; Collins-Rector and Shackley lived together on an estate once owned by the notorious rap impresario Marion 'Suge' Knight and raced matching Ferrari Testarossas to work – where the quarter-million-dollar vehicles looked anything but out of place.

'Pseudo may have had flaws,' one producer observes with a shake of the head, 'maybe more flaws than positives, but at least it was never *corrupt*. Josh, crazy as he is, is not a corrupt person.' The irony is that DEN had presented itself as serious and together and explicitly *not-Pseudo*.

Pseudo now had a dozen channels, including 88HipHop, All Games Network, Street Sounds and women-and-sex forum Cherrybomb; there was a computer hackers' area called Parse TV and a lively wrestling channel called And Justice for Brawl. With small audiences and the failure of online advertising to take, Tony Asnes would increasingly arrive with instructions to create shows and even whole channels for the benefit of clients like OMEGA Watches (*Spacewatch*; the Space Channel), Levi Strauss (a sixteen-week series in which three students were given $500 a week to live entirely online) and the NFL Quarterbacks Club, who paid $4 million for a 5 per cent stake in the company at the same time – with the nadir being the *Star Trek Books Show* for a large American publisher. Closer to Pseudo hearts were edgier shows which played to staff strengths, like the often interesting sex-talk of Cherrybomb; Jess Zaino's roving *StarFreaky* celebrity-fest; the genuinely compelling *JudgeCal's High Weirdness* or the hip UK/US bhangra magazine show *Desivibe*.

The advantage Pseudo had over organisations like DEN and Pop.com and newcomers The Romp ('We want to be a new medium, an entertainment force to come . . .' etc., etc.) was that where the West Coast franchises were steeped in real-world TV and thought nothing of spending $50,000 on a six-minute film, Pseudo content cost an average of $6,000 per hour to produce. The disadvantage was that with low production costs and limitless channels, no one ever had to systematically assess individual programmes, performers, producers for quality or focus – much like the web as a whole. Meaning that Josh could, and *would*, meet someone in a bar and come back saying, 'Oh, we've got to do a show with this one!' Then, to the surprise of no one who knew him well, refuse to let the idea drop. On the other hand, as Tony Asnes admitted to *New York* magazine, so few people had access to the required high-speed internet connections that quality was more or less moot.

600 Broadway was exhilarating though, a taste of what Pseudo's web presence could become as it grew – a mazy hive of subcultures, each with their own area, staff, sensibility and roster of webcast shows. You could go downstairs and walk around SoHo, then come back and scarcely notice a difference from what you'd encountered in the street. Short-lived CEO Larry Lux describes inviting a group of straight-arrow businesspeople to the loft, only to find someone with a pierced forehead careening toward them on a skateboard; to turn a corner and be swallowed by ganja smoke, with the appalling prospect of turning another to find the company Chairman drooling and shouting 'boing!' at them. Instead, Josh arrived looking like he'd just rolled out of bed, unshaven with bog-brush hair, raving about how Pseudo was going to conquer the world. As a rule, Josh's effect on a meeting at this stage was either to rev it with impossible promises, leaving clients to exclaim, 'This is great, why didn't *this guy* come in at the start?!' – or to commit some elementary social blunder and leave them thinking 'Oh forget it, he *is* what we've heard about!' On the other hand, many investors were entertained by

these performances, considered them part of the zany youthfulness of the web. Jill Abrahams, assistant to Janice Girlbomb remembers bumping into a group of clean-cut football players on their way to an NFL Quarterbacks Club show as she carried a box of sex toys to the studio for a Cherrybomb webcast, while a member of the newly recruited sales team looked on aghast.

'When the money came in, the idea was, "OK, now we have to be a lot more professional ... this has got to be real, we've got to actually *make* money,"' Abrahams says of the growing cultural tension at the company. 'But the beauty of Pseudo was that it really was very *street*. You had the guys from 88HipHop, the guys from FreQ, who were part of that scene, and that's what gave Pseudo its energy and credibility and made it what it was. But all of a sudden managers were saying, "Hey, we've got to make money, and if we've got to make money, you guys can't have raves going on till two o'clock at night, where you're passing around ecstasy, because we might have some reps come up," or, "You can't have sex for women on Cherrybomb ..." And none of these new TV people had any experience of the internet, because almost no one in their field did.'

Abrahams had been mortified when she turned up for her interview in a business suit eighteen months before, but grew to cherish Pseudo's difference from other workplaces. 'What I loved when I got there was the way everyone worked so hard for the best outcome for the project as a whole, and the fact that there was very little politics. I thought, "God, this is so *refreshing*!" We would sit around and discuss everything and decide the best way forward, and people were so smart; they understood what was going on, but they could ask for help – everyone had different expertise. When the TV people came, they brought a lot of real world politics and game-playing with them.'

In the interest of decorum, the sales and management team were moved to a building next door and (against a storm of protest) 'Code Green' dope breaks were replaced by a generalised 6 p.m. watershed, eventually to disappear altogether.

There were more pressing problems than an inability to get stoned, though.

In January '99 the expanding company welcomed a man named Joshua White as Senior Vice President in charge of production. I can't quite believe this when I find out, as White is revered in music circles as founder of the Joshua Light Show, one of the first psychedelic lighting outfits of the 1960s, in-house system at the celebrated Fillmore East in the East Village and often billed equally with artists like Jimi Hendrix, Neil Young and Miles Davis – not least at Woodstock. Over two long lunches in the Village, White tells me about The Who's three-night stand with *Tommy* in 1969 and the recording of Hendrix's *Band of Gypsys* album at the venue on New Year's Day 1970, and about his later TV work directing shows like *Seinfeld*. We come to his first impressions of Pseudo and he says: 'I remember walking in and thinking it was an amazing place. The whole idea of this alternative delivery system, at a very naïve moment, when people didn't know what to make of it ... I'd experienced something similar with the Fillmore and never thought I'd see anything like it again, but just up the road and totally out of the blue, *here it was*.'

He claims to have sensed danger for Pseudo almost immediately. Thirty years earlier, he explains, the likes of *Vogue* magazine sent reporters to write about the Joshua Light Show, but had no frame of reference for it.

> So they did what those people always do, which is try to put it in a box – and I saw the same thing happening at Pseudo. After a while, people my own age started coming

> to look, and had no way to appreciate what these young people were doing. So each group came and brought what they knew, and I always tried to be very patient with them, but no one was willing to just take it and go, 'Look – this is just amazing!' Everybody wanted to get on top of it. And that's what I always thought ultimately would create the most difficulty. One of the interesting things about Pseudo was that you couldn't actually figure it out. You had to be working in there every day to understand what was going on.

White was continually telling his team, 'This won't last for ever, enjoy it and remember it!' – advice several younger Pseudites still quote to me as the best they ever received.

The longer we talk, the more interesting and unexpected the conversation grows. White maintains that within six months of arriving at Pseudo, the company's shaky fundamentals were apparent and he'd stopped dreaming of Pseudo as the next CBS. His hope became that the company would be bought for $100 million by Yahoo! or Google or LVMH or Pop.com, in the process making millionaires of many staff, including him, and giving the team time to develop and 'find our voice'. He didn't articulate his deeper fears to the IPO-entranced youngsters around him, he claims: instead, he did something extraordinary. Unable to decisively influence programming (which, he recalls with a smile, *no one* was in charge of and was mostly dreadful), he used his lighting and stage management skills to make Pseudo *look like* the sexiest dream of the future you had ever seen as you stepped from the lift with your $100 million to invest.

Thus, the entrance to the street was drab and the lift a graffito-strewn relic, but the moment you entered Pseudo's space a seductive twilight would descend, the control room flashing and winking and lit to look like a scene from *The Matrix*. In the studio – again, arranged to look bigger than it was – his thirty-five-strong technical and set-building team always looked busy with something *fabulous* and were encouraged to wear what they liked and 'be the brand'. One woman carpenter dressed as Rosie the Riveter and a male colleague – no one knew why – liked to show as a stage hand from the Berliner Ensemble. There were goths, skatepunks, technoboffins and reams of tattoos, and as most came from the poorly paid ranks of off-Broadway set-makers, they were both cheap and skilled: for 88HipHop they built a set that looked like a subway station. Josh White loved them.

'We set out to take the space we had and turn it into something which looked like a bunch of kids downtown putting on a show, with good equipment,' he says. 'And it got to a point by the end of '99, going into 2000, where they were bringing investors over and we actually had a code, so that when the investors came upstairs, even if there was nothing going on in the studio, everybody had something to focus on.'

White claims to have been surprised that when the CNN recruit David Bohrman replaced Larry Lux as CEO at the end of the year, even he didn't register the degree of window dressing, or just how cheap the gear really was. He laughs as he remembers Bohrman's first visit prior to taking the job, during which the prospective head confided, 'I don't understand it, it's like they were all raised by wolves.'

But there was a deeper problem. After the VC funding round, Pseudo was due a splashy re-launch in June. 'Pseudo 2.0' was to feature a new website with new graphics, software, servers and a proprietorial media player. The player was to be the most advanced in the world, inviting users not just to stream and download clips and programmes, but to push up their own visuals – one small step toward Josh's original vision. Except that when White sent an assistant to analyse the system, she returned ghost-faced saying, 'Joshua, it's not going to work!' Tests on an in-house computer confirmed the worst: here was another campervan being ordered to ape the Starship Enterprise, way ahead of the technological curve and purely for the sake of investors – an experience being replicated across the New Economy. White still has videos of many Pseudo programmes, for the simple reason that this was the only way he could watch them. The sobering truth was that internet time didn't suit the internet.

The former production manager now blames himself for the confusion which followed, as real-TV people like Bohrman came in and thought they saw a production house that could be pushed to reflect their own sensibilities and experience. But by the end of 1999, White's dream was simply to find one show which was acceptable enough in quality to act as an entrée to the 'other world' of real TV. Indeed, in *JudgeCal's High Weirdness* and the Cherrybomb channel, he began to think they were drawing close.

'I thought these were the first shows where we began to find our voice – especially with Cal, where he and his co-presenter Laura Foy would bring in collections of unusual people from their own lives.'

TV you won't see on TV.

'Exactly. There was this fleeting moment where I really thought, "This could work, if we can just maintain the perception that we are a link to something that people want to know about for long enough . . ."'

But at the end of the year, David Bohrman came in and found money leaking even faster than he'd been led to believe, with almost no genuine income. He laid off staff and folded the channels into one, then did what people tend to do in the face of uncertainty: he reached for something familiar, the place from whence he'd come, *politics*.

And the truth is that as a new millennium approached, with IPOs being slung at the market like depth charges and the

NASDAQ rocketing to a vertiginous peak of 5000 points as SoHo playas sang Prince in the street and felt rich and young and on top of every world they could imagine, there was no decisive reason for most people to think Bohrman wrong.

BOOK III

Heist

17

> 'You don't know how much I've missed all of you. You see, this is my life, and it always will be ... there's nothing else – just us, and the cameras, and those wonderful people out there in the dark. All right Mr De Mille, I'm ready for my close up.'
>
> – Norma Desmond, *Sunset Boulevard*

The MoMA screening of *We Live in Public* was predictably vibrant. ETBs and dotcom vets turned up in force, some having stayed in touch with each other, others breaking cover for the first time in a while. After years of glossing over that period of their lives, of excising it from résumés the way one might a criminal record, there was a sense of catharsis in the room, driven by the film's recognition of the dotcom years as big and wild and *significant*. To a group of people who'd spent so long apologising for the excesses of that era, this in itself was moving.

The old hijinks made an appearance, too. During the post-screening Q & A (streamed live to the web, naturally), Robert Galinsky stormed the stage in the guise of a disenchanted former dotcommer whose life the Pseudo man had 'ruined', to be hauled away still screaming while his target stifled laughter. All in all it was a charmed night and Josh was glad he'd gone. Yet Galinsky still chuckles as he reveals that Josh's first words to him after the screening were, 'Did they say I was in love with her? Cos I have the tape which proves that I wasn't in love with her, and I'll show it to you!'

Josh told me he was going to be homeless for the first half of his stay in San Francisco, so I pulled a favour to get him a room in my Mission District hotel. This took some begging and bribing (the nearest equivalents to 'leverage' in my world) but I was pleased to be able to help. Payback for the hospitality he'd shown me in Awassa, I thought.

But Josh is Josh and at four o'clock he called to tell me he wouldn't be needing the room any more; that he was going to stay with 'Sean', the wealthy options trader who'd stepped in as an eleventh-hour angel to save Ondi Timoner's film. Through a miracle of persuasion I managed to avoid being charged, the only remaining problem being Josh's abject failure to apologise, or even to betray awareness that such a thing as apology could be possible. Especially unsettling was an indifference I heard in his voice for the first time, as though we hardly knew each other and I held no particular interest for him. The abrupt and unexplained detachment others have spoken of? A feeling akin to being 'unfriended' on Facebook. We arranged to meet the next evening at the Sundance Kabuki cinema for the Frisco opening of *We Live in Public*, to which he would travel with Ondi Timoner.

'If we're not there, it's cos Ondi's late ... *again*,' he grumped.

They're late. Josh stomps in wearing a windcheater with a bright image of Luvvy on the back, specially painted by his artist friends the Enger Brothers. I've been wondering what effect the New York adulation will have had on him, and when we go for sushi with Timoner he seems on a high. I notice that he speaks in compete sentences, sounds unusually focused and voluble, and only when Timoner explains to me that *tout* Silicon Alley will be here do I understand that this evening has a special significance for him. 'These are my peers,' he confides as we walk back to the cinema. 'I'm not sure how aggressive to be with them, or whether to sit back and be cool.' Meaning that these people could help him get back in the game and he's not sure whether to offer them what he really thinks, or a dilute version they can process. The ascetic peace of Sundance is forgotten. The change in the space of a few short months is disorientating.

Aspects of our reunion are familiar. I can't help smile when we find ourselves alone and the first thing he says is 're *other business . . .*', before offering accounts of a(nother) supposed IRS agent who sat next to him on the flight from New York, this one posing as a Mormon, and of a break-in at the warehouse where his art and archives are stored, during which some 'Gilligan' silkscreens were taken. And I'm wondering, 'Why does he do this: is it his way of dealing with awkwardness? Or an attempt to control the story? And strictly speaking, does "Mormon" count as a disguise?'

Before the screening I have a long chat with 'Sean' the *We Live in Public* angel, who looks like the bass player in a grunge band and came to options trading late, which may be why he did so well at it and now owns a restaurant and music venue in Chicago, and will be taking a group of his predominantly non-rich friends to the Masters Golf Tournament when he leaves here. Like Josh, he's awkward in conversation: unlike Josh, he strikes me as a reluctant listener and is short on curiosity. It dawns on me that, for all the Web Warhol's vexation, his saving grace is that he never loses his sense of the absurd. As we stand at the back of the theatre while the film credits roll, he whispers: 'Watch the looks I get as people walk past . . . and of course there's the ethereal credits I'm seeing for the eighteenth time, with no idea of what they're referring to.' The lopsided grin. Half in delight and half in horror – wholly in disbelief – I subsequently watch him being chatted up by a succession of young women, then hit the stage and be note-perfect; funny, provocative and properly intriguing. 'I don't know about you, but when I look at television it just seems to me like a billboard,' he announces. 'Television, film, radio, print . . . in my mind all the magic's being sucked up by the net, and in a different way we're on the cusp of having another hit of it.'

He talks about his new idea for the Wired City, a cross between YouTube, Twitter, Facebook, Skype and his early dreams for Pseudo. Users intimately connected all the time; no need ever to be alone again. 'What's obvious to me is that we're in an evolutionary shift as a species, and the individuality and the privacy that we've known through human history up to this point – *and it's not lost on me that you guys are at the front of this!* – is by definition heading into some kind of collective consciousness. And it's not that it's . . . I mean, I try not to make value judgements, but as humans we're probably screwed.'

Laughter in the hall. Skewed grin.

'But where the evolutionary force leads us remains to be seen. Like anything, it'll probably have its good sides and its bad sides.'

At a bar reception afterwards, the freshly made first web idol lounges in a leather armchair, waving a cigar and holding forth as the Valley people cluster round him and VCs hear his pitch for the Wired City. Unsure of how to receive the sight, I stay just long enough for the unbroken business and tech talk to feel oppressive, at which point I'm relieved to be rescued by friends for a nightcap.

But the night has been illuminating. Could it happen again for Josh? *Should* it happen again for Josh? On the way out I bump into Ondi Timoner, who I've grown to like and admire, and who tilts her head in his direction, shakes it gently.

'I feel like I've fed the beast,' she frowns. 'This is like cocaine to him. He's got a show back on.'

* * *

I went to see the bard of cyberspace, William Gibson. He was spry at sixty-three and spoke deliberately, weighing each word against the next the way a philosopher would. He said:

> If I'd told my publishers in 1981, when I started my first novel, 'OK, this book's going to be set in 2011 and everyone's going to be connected all the time, carrying around little computers the size of cigarette lighters, able to see and speak to anyone and access all the world's knowledge instantly and carry all the music they know; and where no one is afraid of nuclear annihilation and the Soviet Union no longer exists, but a killer autoimmune disease is wiping out whole populations in parts of the world and the internal combustion engine has turned out to be the thing that might destroy humanity . . .'

He paused, smiled almost wearily.

'They'd have told me that I was biting off more than I could *chew*.'

And I laughed but realised it was true. The most technologically advanced thing I owned in 1981 was my hair gel.

More apposite was an observation that as a society we no longer 'bet long'; invest in huge projects like Great Walls or pyramids or cathedrals that would take dozens or even hundreds of years to complete. Gibson explained that he thinks we may have lost 'the breadth of now' required for such commitments to make sense.

'I think our *now* has decreased,' he said, 'perhaps because the range of novelty is so vast. Maybe we're just spending so much time digesting all this novelty that instinctively, big cultural narratives – like the conquest of space when I was a boy – start to seem impossible. So something's changed.'

A beat.

'I do find it worrying.'

As early – or perhaps as *late* – as 2008 the *American Journal of Psychiatry* announced that 'Internet Addiction' had been added to the official list of mental disorders. At the same time, lampposts in hip Brick Lane, east London, were being padded to protect the texting young things who kept bumping into them. Of particular fascination to me was a paper in the *British Journal of Psychiatry*, describing what the psychiatrist authors Joel and Ian Gold regarded as a new phenomenon. Over a two-year period, they noted, 'We treated five patients at Bellevue Hospital Center who had a variety of delusions . . . that they were being filmed and the films were being broadcast; that the doctors and patients in the hospital were actors and the environment was fake; that they were on a reality television show.'

Three of the patients referred to *The Truman Show* by name, which is why Gold and Gold had chosen to call their paper 'The Truman Show Delusion', and similar tales were emerging from all corners of their profession. It transpired that their paper had been sparked by a letter to the same journal, in which a separate psychiatric team reported a patient who fell under the same rubric; who 'had a vague sense that the people around him were "acting" – that he was the focus of their interest and the world was "slightly unreal".' And I find myself considering whether this is new, or whether we're simply moving closer to understanding the parameters of our existence. Whether the pseudoman simply got there ahead of us.

I also note that a number of people have mentioned the

A-word, 'autism', in connection with Josh. And that this is also true of Facebook's Mark Zuckerberg, Jim Clark of Netscape, Michael Saylor of MicroStrategy, *Wired*'s Louis Rossetto, Julian Assange of WikiLeaks, the Pentagon hacker Gary McKinnon and, in a recently published biography, the godfather of them all – Marshall McLuhan (not to mention the author of that biography, Douglas Coupland).

At times this speculative connection has struck me as plausible, but more often it has seemed simplistic and diminishing; shorthand, I think, for a range of propensities and intellectual attributes which happen to suit the virtual-real worlds we're evolving and which effectively mark these people out as pre-adapted to a social environment in which the act of connection, being visible and quantifiable, has more value than the indefinite process of *engagement*. The implication being that, with this small minority busily remaking human relations in their own image, we will either evolve to be more like them or fade to invisibility.

Betty Wasserman goes further in relation to Josh. She remembers a line of small bobble-headed toy figures he developed in the early years of Pseudo, saying, 'They were so cool and interesting – but even back then, I saw those heads and thought, "There's a disconnect here: it's like this guy is trying to take the head and brain away from the body."' Drawing on the experience of her own daughter, who goes to a school for children with special needs, she speculates that Josh might have benefited from some early attention to his differences; that his ticks and twitches and pacing and oral fixation are evidence of an attempt 'to self-soothe something that was never soothed in his early years'.

Is it right to pathologise Josh in this way? To pathologise Zuckerberg et al? I don't know. In my world, Josh is manifestly odd. Yet in his interior fiefdom, which my milieu increasingly comes to resemble, I'm the poorly equipped one. And the thing is, I feel less sure than I ever did that my reality is more 'real' than his.

Josh's remoteness had the ironic effect of making him seem yet more mythic and intimidating to new staff. He bought the fabulous loft down the road from 600 Broadway at 519 and while it was being refurbished, moved into the crumbling former sweatshop further down Broadway in TriBeCa, at 359. Pseudo people called this building the Luvvyplex and it's where Nancy Smith first met Josh, arriving to find him in bed with Tanya, watching a movie while twenty or so people tucked into a catered banquet.

Smith was a quilt-maker in her early thirties, with a husband and young son; she had been summoned because the rich man wanted to buy an Amish quilt for a wedding present. Unnerved by Josh's wealth and his band of pirouetting hipsters, she was surprised to find his attention settling on her, as though drawn to her incongruity. He satisfied himself that she understood quilts and handed her $5000 to buy one – which she did, a beautiful Mennonite piece, only to lose faith upon discovering a small flaw. Fearing her patron's wrath, she stayed away until he thought she'd disappeared and, tail between legs, she was forced to present her find.

To Smith's joy, he forgave her absence and didn't care about the flaw. She laid the quilt on the floor and watched him melt into the story it told, loving the maths of the patterns and the way you could see the work and skill that had gone into its making; could see how *real* it was. Every square of an Amish quilt was made by a different family and communicated something unique. 'He never liked intellectual art,' Smith says. 'He loved to *see* you painting or building sets or making something interesting. *Skills* fascinated him, which is why he loved American crafts and handmade stuff.'

He gave her another thousand to write up what she'd told

him: a grand more to wrap the quilt with care instructions and deliver it a fortnight hence. Which makes me wonder whether he was *trying* to get rid of money. But no, insists Smith. 'He was generous. And he would never cut-throat you. I think he really did put that value on information. He *loved* to learn a new world.'

Smith now runs the artloversofnewyork blog site. She carries some of the same awkwardness as Josh and, like him, would be easy to mock. But she is clever and a shrewd judge of art, and quickly became not just a supplier of quilts, but a rare mature voice in his coterie. He adored her son and seemed to feel a chivalrous need to protect her from the hedonism he was surrounded by. All the same, Smith saw how unstable his affections could be; the way he would play people off against each other and have different favourites in different situations. At the same time, the more she talks about how 'You had to get your money, keep him on point as to what your needs were, and get out,' the more you come to appreciate the loneliness of his situation, too.

Tanya moved into the Luvvyplex after a turbulent on–off courtship. Josh had always doubted her fealty, imagining affairs with everyone from Pseudo colleagues to reporters to Betty Wasserman, with whom she lived for a while, hosting a number of risqué parties with themes that discomfited him. For six weeks after the first Jupiter money came at the end of 1998, Josh had enjoyed treating Tanya to extravagant shopping expeditions, splashing money for the first time in his life – friends such as Wasserman had previously been struck by his extraordinary lack of interest in material comforts and possessions for himself – but in the end these only increased his sense of insecurity. Nancy Smith would remind him that, 'Tanya was here before you had the money – she's a part of your success and she really loves you.' But he could never quite believe it. Jealousy-racked, he would split with her twice in 1999 and end the year single, though remaining sexually 'true' throughout.

Josh busied himself with his own projects. He still dutifully talked up Pseudo, growing more extravagant and absurd in his claims by the month as intensity in the Alley welled to a peak, doubtless hoping that a buyer would emerge and offer either continuity or a payday and escape to something else. The new executive staff didn't understand the internet, would come in and demand big corporate Pseudo backdrops which no one would see in a four-by-three-inch window, or non-Pseudo corporate logos which diluted the identity of the portal as a whole. How could you deal with them? Josh didn't. He dove into the murky pool of his own imagination.

Pacing Broadway one searing summer morning, it occurred to him that someone needed to throw *the* Millennium party – to provide the grand gesture New York required. In the same instant, he knew that the someone was him; that this was his answer to the question of what to do with the Luvvyplex when his new loft came on-stream in the autumn ... was the cue for the 'lockdown' event he and Gompertz had fantasised about. Now more convinced than ever that 'things are gonna get messy' in the physical-virtual shift, he would christen the month-long happening *Quiet* in the expectation that it would be anything *but*. Equal parts art project, party, Stanford Prison Experiment and physical summoning of what the id-driven internet might look like in the future, Josh's vision ran so counter to the Utopian triumphalism of the net culture around him as to be barely intelligible to his young peers.

Gompertz had left Pseudo the year before, but now got a call saying 'We're ready ... we got the stage, it's not Pseudo, it's 353 and 359 Broadway. Let's go.'

Josh split with Tanya and moved into his new 4000-square-foot loft. He'd paid roughly $700,000 to buy the place, then spent $200K gutting and rebuilding it in a way friends found hilarious, hiring a crane to install a new lift and instructing architects to design what may well have been the largest bathroom in New York, with floor-to-ceiling tiles and a steam room with space for twenty-five people – despite there being no hot running water or gas in the rest of the apartment. And as the artist Jon 'Feedbuck' Buckley notes, 'It's not often that you go to a home that somebody's designed without any closets because they weren't aesthetically pleasing.' A $12,000 TV system projected ten-foot-high images on to one wall and the kitchen was stainless-steel panelled, with den walls bare but for a triptych of Alex Arcadia paintings: three six-foot tall images in red, blue and yellow of a small male figure kneeling in prayer at the crotch of a gigantic naked woman – meaningful to anyone who knew Josh well. On the ceiling were rails for lighting and camera equipment, their signals fed to a control room at the back of the property, turning the loft into a TV studio. There was a koi pond and a private upstairs room with one-way glass allowing Josh to observe his parties unseen. Only he could have dreamed up such a place.

Over three days in September, he staged a 'Millennium Warm-up' party, designed to explore the progressive convergence of private, public and commercial life. Business theorists like Jeremy Rifkin were starting to suggest that as the global village evolved, most if not all human relationships would come to be mediated by commerce. Perhaps celebrity culture was a Trojan horse or presentiment, a taste of things to come. So Josh was posing the questions: what was our data, our privacy, our *individuality* worth and what would it take for us to surrender it? Free music? The sense of belonging provided by an online community? Celebrity approval? A chance to be on TV?

Staged at the Luvvyplex, the Warm-up party entrance was designed to look like the customs booth at an airport and as a condition of entry guests were required to supply names and email addresses, all captured to video. A surprising number of would-be guests still didn't have email addresses in 1999 and according to one attendee, 'A lot more than you'd think were very wary of handing their information over, but they wanted to get into the party so bad, this very hyped-up party, that they *did*.' There was free exotic booze, entertainment till dawn, music from DJ Spooky and the super-hip DJ Shadow, and on the final night, a throng on the pavement outside. Alex Arcadia was one of the few people who saw and understood an emerging theme to Josh's 'work', by which he 'put people in positions where they were being pushed to the point of discomfort, using techniques that were developed for interrogating people during wartime – giving them something that they wanted in order to see what they'd do to keep it. I loved watching how people were reacting to this cultural shift,' the artist adds. 'Some really embraced it, while others were intimidated.'

The money continued to flow. *Box Opera* came to Josh after the New York writer Jonathan Ames suggested to his friend David Leslie – the rocket-riding, top-floor-jumping 'Impact Addict' – that boxing might provide interesting material for a performance piece. Inevitably his search for a sponsor led him to Josh, who immediately agreed to fund the event, which took place at the Orensanz Center, a sumptuous converted Gothic revival synagogue in Norfolk Street on the Lower East Side. With a $1000 prize for anyone who could knock Leslie out, a commentator from the Pseudo wrestling channel, card girls and Tanya outside filming the hoards who tried to get in, the atmosphere was frenzied. A roster of performance artist warm-up acts included one who play-fought small children, making Pseudo CEO Larry Lux squirm with displeasure. The event was absurd and pointless on one level, but impressive and entertaining and delightful as a spectacle on another – even if the next morning Lux circulated a memo stating, 'We are not paying for any more of this crap.' No matter: a week later Lux was gone. And in

October the point became moot anyway, when Josh's first company, Jupiter Communications, in which he still had a major shareholding, went public and within an hour of the market opening he had made the step up from rich to wildly rich. Yet someone who shared a cab with him the next morning still describes his demeanour that day as '*blank* ... not very happy for a man who'd just made eighty-two million dollars'.

As planning for *Quiet* got under way, two significant outside events occurred. First, the *Big Brother* TV series hit Dutch screens, its name taken from the same Orwell novel Apple had used to promote its Macintosh computer fifteen years earlier. Next, the increasingly autocratic Rudolph Giuliani, already at odds with his famously untamable citizens over crackdowns on drivers, cyclists, jaywalkers, street vendors, litterbugs, clubbers, drinkers and anything that moved, spoke or looked at him funny – and whose out-of-control Street Crime Unit ('Nam-style motto 'We Own the Night') had latterly killed an innocent and unarmed Guinean man in a hail of not one, but *forty-one* bullets – took the next logical step and declared war on the art fold. Word is that he was inspecting a new Emergency Operations Center at the World Trade Center when a reporter asked for his view on the 'Sensation' exhibition of works at the Brooklyn Museum by the so-called Young British Artists who included Damien Hirst, Tracy Emin, Jake and Dinos Chapman and Gillian Wearing. Specific to his ire was a painting of a black Virgin Mary by the black Brit painter Chris Ofili, which was carefully decorated with varnished elephant dung and in truth rather respectful. Without seeing the work, Giuliani (like the artist, a Catholic), pronounced it 'sick stuff' and threatened to withdraw funding and evict the museum from its century-old home. Polls showed New Yorkers backing the museum two-to-one over the mayor and Josh was far from alone in being incensed. The ensuing fight would feed *Quiet*'s intensity.

There are similarities between *Big Brother* and *Quiet*, but the dissimilarities are significant. Where *Big Brother* would be tightly edited, directed and as stage-managed as *The Truman Show*, *Quiet* – at least in theory – would be feral, unedited and interactive, with each participant given their own pod-based TV channel to programme. The event would last a month in terms of set-up and tributary spectacle, with 'podwellians' arriving two weeks before New Year's Eve. Instead of ten or fifteen participants, sixty-plus artists would submit to an interrogation and, if accepted, register and move in, joining thirty or so event officials and staff. Podwellians were restricted to the cavernous sub-basement and first floor of 353 Broadway, with offices, exhibitions and parties based upstairs and two doors north at the Luvvyplex. As usual, the door to the street would be open and the public free to enter, gawp, join in.

Josh canvassed ideas from favourite collaborators, including many of his first Pseudo staff, as if reaching for that earlier creative innocence. Jeff Gompertz would design and run the 'pod' hotel, V. Owen Bush a banquet hall serving two hundred meals a day with his workforce of chefs, waiters and kitchen staff, while Alex Arcadia designed and built an elaborate 'Arcadian temple' at a cost which rose from ten to twenty to thirty-forty-*fifty thousand dollars*, with live mics and eerie chants – but which no one was allowed to enter.

As discussions continued, plans firmed. The only shower would be housed in a clear geodesic dome located next to the pods and in full view of the banqueting hall, close to *actually public* toilets and an interrogation room in which podwellians would be grilled to the point of breakdown, both upon entry and at the whim of an Interrogator. There was to be a toxic waste dump, complete with inflammable chemicals, and a David Leslie-progammed sub-basement club called 'Hell', in addition to the most extreme installation – an operational firing range with an armoury of pistols, rifles and submachine guns, designed and run by the Basquiat forger Alfredo Martinez. In a nod to the art establishment, Josh also recruited Leo Koenig, the son of a leading German art dealer, to curate a series of more traditional exhibits.

With areas defined by inflatable walls, the stated essence of the experiment was that everything would be public, nothing private, with all life shared, seen, recorded and ultimately owned – by Josh. As if the idea was to test the human organism, version 1.0, to destruction in this new environment. After the Pseudo board refused to fund the event, Josh used his own money, flying into a rage-like mania in which observers describe him peeling hundred-dollar bills from a roll of notes, on the spot, $20 to $30K at a time, for anyone who approached with a half-plausible idea, or sitting at a table distributing cheques like free school milk. At one point he paid an angry Feedbuck $10,000 to take his installation *down* and make space for something else. Another participant claims to have taken $20,000 he'd been given to create a life-size chess tournament and blown it on a three-day binge, yet been allowed to stay and work on the event anyway, becoming convinced that *Quiet* was designed as a tax loss. With New York obsessed by stock prices and material displays of wealth, spending on something so nebulous and conceptual appeared not just eccentric, but *perverse*. Owen Bush watched and worried about the Fitzcarraldo-like obsession of his friend, 'Cos he was really out to lunch, not available to anyone at that point.'

New York magazine came calling and heard: 'At Pseudo, I am just building my platform ... the idea is to get the machine running well enough so that Pseudo will benefit from my success. I am the product, *get it*? I don't want to be Procter & Gamble, I want to be *Tide*.'

Blustery bullshit that betrayed a loss of faith in Pseudo, whose value to Josh was now restricted to that old standby, leverage. Yet there was intelligence at work too.

'The ties that bind us are virtual, not nearly so physical as they've been in Man's historical past,' he breezed to a TV camera, sounding clear and confident. 'As that virtuality becomes increasingly sophisticated, there'll be a fundamental change in the human condition.'

And:

'At first everybody's gonna like it, like when the radio came, when the television came – this new human experience . . . [but] as time goes by, you'll find yourself in these more constrained, virtual boxes.'

Then:

'The nature of the net is that people want their fame on a day-to-day basis, rather than in their lifetime . . . one day we're all going to wake up and realise that we're just . . . servants. What we're really trying to do is figure out how to re-weave human relations.'

Warhol was wrong, he declared in another interview – fifteen minutes of fame in a lifetime will not do. 'Our view is that people want fifteen minutes of fame *every day*.' Citizens will be conditioned not just to tolerate surveillance in the future, they will expect and even *demand* it.

The *cogito ergo sum* of the twenty-first century:

I am watched therefore I am.

In Josh's eyes, *Quiet* was an analogy for what the internet would become, the net a guide to what *we* will become. 'You ask me, "What are people gonna do here?"' he teased one journalist. 'We don't know. That's the experiment. Don't bring your money, everything here is free. Except the video that we capture of you . . . *that* we own.'

And when a European writer demanded, 'Whatever happened to nonconformity?' he grinned: 'It went out in the 60s. The next century is about complete conformity. We're in the business of programming people's lives.'

*

There are two versions of *Quiet*. First is the one offered by Josh and his lieutenants, the edgy extravaganza you see in Ondi Timoner's film, where people are thrown together and tested against the mass of others; where drink and drugs and deviant behaviours stack and build until 'the bunker' is a fevered hell and civilisation frays, falls apart ... at which point the authorities intervene and shut the thing down. The moral? Too much freedom brought madness, cruelty, chaos. A dispatch from the front. *This is our future*.

A good story – but like most good stories, a cover for something else.

So here's another view.

Far from being unregulated, *Quiet* was awash with rules – all imposed by the Programmer himself at nightly planning meets with the aim of producing dramatic footage for the film he hoped to make. Fearful of being shut down prematurely, the first ten days were disciplined, full of calculated *Sturm und Drang*, mostly failing to cohere or rise above the gratuitously abberant. The Inside.com journalist Greg Lindsay thought the *Quiet* experiment 'fascinating and noble' and loved the evening banquets, where, 'It really felt like this big artistic thing you'd dreamed about when you came to New York, with this feeling that you could discover *anybody* ... that this *happening* could go anywhere.' He also saw the significance of the fact that, 'They could stimulate the lab rats in two directions,' with podwellians being watched, but also able to watch each other, implying the question, 'Will this lead to self-policing or anarchy?' An important one for the coming age.

But the moment Josh took Lindsay on a tour of the space, chattering claims for the various installations, the spectacle seemed to deflate and crumple into a yawn of banners and shooting galleries and an awareness of how forced much of it was – how geared to provoking a reaction, any reaction, in preference to genuine insight. The contradiction at the heart of 'reality' TV, in fact. The screen needs drama: drama distorts truth.

The distinguished New York photojournalist Donna Ferrato couldn't resist signing up to this alternate world upon reading about it in *New York* and the *Times*. After passing the ritual interrogation and receiving her standard issue grey shirt and orange trousers, she found a pod and settled in, but was surprised at the event's tameness as compared to the bathhouses and swingers' clubs, the scenes of New York street life, chemical abandon at Studio 54 and even domestic abuse shelters she'd studied in the past. At the very least, she'd expected something ungoverned, sexy, *free*. But that wasn't how it went. 'Everyone was very self-conscious, very careful,' she says. 'They were like little kids, really – even the performance artists Josh surrounded himself with. They liked to be wild and crazy and funny, but to me a lot of it seemed childish, not sexy or dangerous or challenging in a serious way.'

This reflected Josh. Performance art had been a fashionable form of expression in the 1980s, but had run its course by the late-90s. Ferrato saw that he responded to and admired these edgy people who would do anything; who were so at odds with his own careful, strategised approach to life, but who also often had little to say. In the 80s, the simple act of breaking boundaries had seemed worthwhile, but by 1999 – post-web – most obvious boundaries had been broken. With the rest untroubled by a man with a plastic vagina.

As with other inmates, Ferrato did take pleasure in the day-for-night atmosphere; the way the city receded and time fell away as you slipped into this other world, with podwellians allowed to leave but mostly choosing not to – 'as though it would break the trance' in the words of one. Some footage shot by an Englishman named James Walsh shows the firing range to be no more than moderately diverting, as a succession of beautiful (mostly female) urbanites step up to shoot guns for the first time, some rattled by the experience, others full of G.I. Jane suck-my-dick spunk. In other words ... *so what?*

Against this, a night-time tracking shot of the whole three floors is mesmerising, seeming to go on for ever and reveal the sheer *scale* of the *Quiet* interior, swathed in twilight and a distant pulse of music, screens flickering everywhere and the day's detritus settled like dew, as podwellians appear sporadically, naked or in pyjamas ... the occasional clang or call echoing as through a cavern, but no hint of chaos or aggression.

A camera crew drifts past; Ondi Timoner, hired by Josh to capture the proceedings, turns to smile as she coaxes a subject to put his face to the glass dome of the shower and scream. Something womb-like and magical in the atmosphere.

After Christmas, with a week gone and no sign of the Giuliani enforcers, Josh stepped up the pressure. Performances grew more extreme and salacious; relationships intensified as drug consumption ramped and moved into the open. Jess Zaino had been asked to bring celebrities, but was too caught up in her Pseudo show to commit to *Quiet*. She came, but hated what she found. 'It was *scary*. I remember walking through – I don't know what I was on, I must have been on *something* – and seeing people lying in these Japanese hotel pods, then turning around and there was a light over a man playing a theremin, and I was, like, "Get me the fuck out of this *Alice in Wonderland* rabbit hole."'

At Pseudo, she explains, Josh's thoughts and ideas had always been mediated by other people. 'But here it was like you saw the crazy inner workings, complete. It was out of his brain and *actually happening*.' She describes one room where a photographer was taking portraits of people on chemical trips. 'So you'd have somebody on crack, at the climax, as they were peaking, at the *height*. You know, heroin, ecstasy – all of it. And he blew the photos up to wall-size, so you would go in and be staring at the huge eyes of this person that was on this intense drug. And it was amazing. Incredible as art. But at Pseudo people like Cal and Janice had humanity, and here it was like they literally went into the fucking *Matrix*.'

She stops and shudders.

'I didn't like it!'

For Zaino, *Quiet's* art was about spending the money – such a loaded medium in late-90s New York – in this reckless fashion. But in her instinctive way, she also understood that the event had really come to be about Josh himself.

He instructed his bouncers to rile and reject male visitors and sex became more overt. Josh had lost none of his instinct for drawing a crowd and competition for entry was fierce the night Luvvy attempted to co-ordinate the orgasms of three couples in the nightclub – a Reichian folly which was never likely to gel. With Tanya roaming the space in a white gown distributing apples, Ondi Timoner describes filming this as 'the most depressing experience of my life', at least partly in deference to the fact that (as one female Pseudo presenter delicately put it) 'none of the guys could get it up', the only erect penis-like object belonging to the pair of lesbians. Luvvy had little to say beyond 'boing!' and the Londoner James Walsh was struck by how much the jarring alter ego looked and dressed like Josh's mother Roslyn Harris. 'It was a bit Norman Bates, kind of *spooky*,' he says, even while expressing awe at the way Josh handled *Quiet* as a whole. 'With all that booze and all those drugs around, you'd have expected violence. All those people wanting attention, and no sleep ... I'd have lost it. He's really, really good with people.'

Elsewhere, one of the artists recruited a 'porn star' to be 'stump-fucked' by the stump-legged performance artist Mangina and a young couple was planted in one of the pods to have sex, available to view on channel 36, a wheeze which set other couples off and 'created a sort of intimacy', in the mind of Josh, who was captivated by the show, claiming afterwards that, 'Now I know how to make a cult.'

Shells on the firing range floor were ankle-deep and interrogations grew random and brash. Order fell away in the banqueting hall, where performers danced naked on the table, which most guests found irritating more than outrageous. Owen Bush declared that, 'People don't know how to deal with free and they can't handle it ... the freeness is turning people into beasts,' while for David Leslie, the point was the intensity itself, the *feeling* engendered by such rare, socially sanctioned abandon. As the Millennium approached, Josh issued an open invitation to *Quiet*'s New Year's Eve party via the *New York Post*.

In one reality, this end-game push was about Citizens losing control and regressing in an environment with no boundaries; in another there was a much funnier and more compelling show playing out. Lost from official accounts of *Quiet* is the detail that Josh had recruited subjects on a promise of $100,000 for anyone who could survive to the end of New Year's Day ... meaning any or all of sixty struggling and somewhat desperate artists – including a generous number of *performance* artists, for whom shamelessness and immunity to attrition were not just matters of pride, they were job descriptions.

So, big surprise: by New Year's Eve no one had bailed. Society had survived its fortnight of freedom.

And as a reminder, 60 x $100K = *$6 million*.

Ulp.

Josh also needed a climax for his film and would not be the first storyteller to learn that there are no endings in nature. Unbeknownst to anyone but the Programmer himself, his beautiful Orwellian drama had become an Ealing-esque comedy, spun around a private central dilemma – namely, *how the fuck do I get these people out of here in the next thirty-six hours?*

Josh groped for a plan ... Josh found a plan. Like the Cat in the Hat, he was going to need help. And his Thing A would be Rudy Giuliani.

So. That evening there was a sumptuous banquet involving two whole roast hogs, but through the fog of drink and drugs and constant prodding, paranoia was setting in. Owen Bush and his girlfriend, who was also working as a cook, had a vicious public fight over drug consumption and an alleged affair; Nancy Smith the quilt-maker knocked out and came close to killing a woman she suspected of having sex with her husband. A naked play-fight in the shower ran out of control, with spectators gathering and the man involved biting the woman's arse before accidentally propelling her through the glass shell, sending Josh into a rage which surprised everyone – not least the woman, who was uninjured but contrite. Podwellians noticed Josh behaving eccentrically, chomping his cigar while he paced the length of the pods like a wolf, looking for something that wasn't there, waiting for something that wasn't happening ... calculating, calculating, calculating. One onlooker recalls thinking that he wanted sex, but that wasn't it.

Josh *was* agitated.

Only twenty-four hours to go and no Five-oh. What did a guy have to do to get raided around here?

Lord knows Josh had tried. First, he'd invited a group of downtown politicians in to play Risk, arranging for podwellians to act up and Alfredo Martinez to fire a gun close by, making the wonks jump like mice. But no raid. So he paid the flamboyant fashion designer Maya Hansen somewhere between $20 and $25K, he thought – he wasn't even counting any more – to create a window display featuring scantily clad women on trapezes, to which he contributed a neon sign flashing 'GIRLS GIRLS GIRLS XXX' in the direction of the courthouse, a reference to the mayor's much-derided campaign to clean up the Times Square area. Josh might as well have stood on the sidewalk with a megaphone and yelled *'Come and get me, Rudy!'* The scene stopped traffic on Broadway, for fuck's sake.

But still no raid. It was a disgrace! So . . .

Couple arrested performing fellatio in the storefront window.

No raid.

Undercover officers (who might as well carry signs flashing 'FUZZ') show and mingle, one quizzing Nancy Smith on whether they all plan to commit suicide at midnight, while *seeming* more interested in the issue of whether all this stuff really counts as art, you know, in the Aristotelian sense of the term – and she laughing, 'Look, pal, I'm making ten grand a week here – there's no way *I'm* gonna commit suicide . . .'

He goes away.

No raid.

Josh was Michael Caine at the end of *The Italian Job*, booty over a cliff at the back of the bus. Arrangements had been made for him to reprise his simultaneous orgasm act at midnight, but better sense prevailed and he simply gathered the Citizens for a photo instead, unable to commit to the moment. Furthermore, after inviting the public to attend, he was now irritated by what one guest describes as their 'tittering, voyeuristic presence', scowling, 'I don't owe these people their New Year's Eve; they haven't *earned* it.' So he locked the gawkers upstairs and projected porn on to the walls.

If Josh had been hoping to spark a riot ('RAID ME!'), he was disappointed. The journalist Greg Lindsay took a couple of friends and remembers a 'respectful and well-behaved crowd, who were all excited to be there'. He also remembers a tributary reason for choosing *Quiet* as a destination that night, this being a thought that, 'If anything's going to happen in New York on New Year's Eve, with Y2K or terrorism, the best place to be is in a sub-basement three floors below the ground.'

Was that a conscious consideration? Seriously?

'It was conscious. I worked at Time Warner at that time and I thought, "Shit, most of the American media complex is round here, so it'd be a good place for a suitcase nuke." People forget the degree of tension, the apocalyptic feeling that was there even before 9/11.'

Josh gave up. What could he do? He phoned the bloody police himself. Still no raid. More guests arrived. People partied until the drugs wore off and then went to bed in their pods.

When it came, it came with a ferocity that shocked even *Quiet*'s host. The first anyone knew of one of the biggest raids seen in Manhattan since Prohibition was when the door exploded and officers streamed over the threshold in riot gear, then fanned through the building like stormtroopers, yelling and pointing guns and blinding podwellians with flashlights. Through the cacophony, Citizens heard shocked cries.

'What the *fuck*?'

'Oh, *gross*, man.'

'These people are living like *pigs*!'

Hardly what Josh had bargained for: captains and officers from the local fire department and police force, agents of the Federal Emergency Management Agency, FEMA, and a rifle-toting SWAT team wading through cartridge casings and chemicals and mouldering food, puncturing inflatable walls and watching the façade melt away like the Wicked Witch of the West in *The Wizard of Oz* . . .

I'll get you, my pretty . . .

One witness describes a FEMA officer saying something to Josh that appeared to leave him shaken. Leo Koenig was woken and forced to trudge around the space cringeing explanation. But who could explain? The game had turned serious.

Addled and scared, podwellians were pitched into the morning. Some had homes to go to, others not, but a plan was agreed to reconvene at 1 p.m. In the meantime many lingered, still in uniform and reluctant to break the trance, not knowing what else to do.

Good news: the Programmer had his operatic ending!

Bad news: Ondi Timoner, keen to see in the New Year anywhere other than the bunker, had dismissed her crew and left hours earlier. Seems the Poetic Justice Bureau had been right behind FEMA. Josh had his ending, but not on tape.

Needless to say, at one o'clock the doors remained locked. No Citizen would re-enter and Josh was long gone. Alex Arcadia and Owen Bush stayed on and lived in the building for a while, with Bush hiring a dumpster to remove shells from the firing range, shovelling them up like snow from a path. Gompertz and some of the artists lobbied hard for Josh to make *Quiet* permanent, turn it into a real world TV environment, but Josh had had enough, seemed distressed, angry, disdainful of his subjects' continuing *need*. For the Programmer, as for most workers and Citizens, there would be a 'hangover' lasting months, although despite my best efforts I can't find a single person who regrets having taken part.

'It was a genius way of ending the event,' laughs Donna Ferrato, whose favourite photos of the raid are up on her website. 'It was high drama, not least for the people who shut it down, who couldn't believe what they were seeing – who couldn't believe what had been going on *right under their noses*. This whole world had been created, without permits or permission.'

A wistful look comes over her when I ask what she liked best.

> I loved living in a world with no secrets and no sense of time, where we were little children, being taken care of. And also watching Josh, who to me was a fascinating creature. You can see him as crazy, but there's substance to what he does. He's always testing, seeing how far this will

> go and that will go, and what kind of reaction he's going to get. And he always knows what everyone's little weak spots and flaws are: he's very perceptive like that. It was a movie set, but with no script, where it was just about *being there*.

So the zany installations, the guns and chemicals and temples and games of Risk hadn't been the point. *Quiet* had been convoluted by too many ideas: what power it possessed had emerged naturally from the maths of connection, the jazz of human relations, with the rest just display, another blowjob in the window. Josh was still finding his métier. All the same, Alanna Heiss of MoMA's contemporary P.S.1 gallery would ultimately deem *Quiet* 'one of the most extraordinary activities I've attended anywhere in the world', which 'should be thought of in the same way as Truman Capote's Black and White Ball' – one of the most celebrated social events in New York history. She also gave Josh a nickname: 'Oz'. The man behind the screen.

18

One night in the pool house . . .

'Josh, I've never told you this before. Someone described a kind of "reality distortion field" you create around yourself.'

[pause]

'Really? *Reality distortion field?* That's good. Who said it?'

'It was Owen.'

'Owen . . . you know I always figured him as working for the Feds.'

'The *Feds*?'

'Yeah.'

'Why?'

'In the blood. Part of the family. You know. *Bush?* But don't tell him I said that.'

'Okay.'

[laughter]

'Seriously though, Josh. Does that idea make any sense to you?'

'That I'm a postmodern Music Man?'

'More like Bert from *Mary Poppins*.'

[more laughter]

'Well that wouldn't be *my* characterisation. Distortion is not the right word, but there's a certain . . . *magnetic field* factor – ha-ha.'

'The blurring of the border between virtual life, *fantasy*, and the workaday material world. Your life seems to reflect this more than anyone I've ever met, Josh.'

'You mean the micro-realities? That's the model I'm using at the moment.'

'No, I mean a feeling I get that you're living your life as *just* story. Pure invention. Which makes everything you say true, in the same way that a novel is always true, whereas a non-fiction book never is or can be – it can only be a *version* of reality. See what I'm saying?'

'Well, yeah. I think what's happening now is that people are just becoming aware of "neo-reality". That you can create a reality that isn't in the physical world. And what I am is, I'm like the *haute couture* of neo-reality . . .'

* * *

Hangovers.

Money can help with those. A week after *Quiet*, Josh and Feedbuck went fishing in Mexico and didn't mention the event *once*. Buck had been surprised by Josh before: he'd once switched on the Game Show Network cable channel to find his net mogul friend appearing as a contestant on a show called *Joker's Wild*; was left wondering, 'Does he do this all the time and just not mention it?' But *Quiet* seemed gutsy even for Josh, necessary at a time when all anyone could talk about was wealth for its own sake. Through December, Buck had moved between *Quiet* and documenting the Millennium with his own production company, so the month was just a haze of work and cocaine to him. Now the city felt in limbo, as though reluctant to leave a century it regarded as its own.

Josh, too, was in a prickly place. He'd fallen out with his friend Robert Galinsky over the actor's failure to show for his Broadway *Masterwerk*. Anyone else would have understood that after a painful divorce and the death of a father in September,

Galinsky hadn't the stomach for something so dark. But Josh was hurt. It took Galinsky time to grasp that the other man simply had no way of understanding his grief – that by this time, Josh had freed himself of all emotional connection; of anything which might anchor him to the everyday. That, like the still-raging stock market, Josh's detachment from life's fundamentals was growing. In Awassa he claimed to have been 'sick' for six months after *Quiet*, 'not physically, but sorta mentally, kind of a withdrawal or decompression or unwinding or something', adding that, 'It hurts . . . it's mentally painful.'

After *Quiet*, Pseudo workers noticed a behaviour shift in Josh. The Bohrman era had begun in earnest at the start of January 2000, when the new CEO arrived to find his company leaking $5 million a month and essayed a rapid retrenchment, folding the myriad Pseudo channels into one and tilting it to a more mature agenda. Old staff were released and TV professionals hired, and if one were looking for a moment to symbolise the change, it would be the day a young worker was fired for smoking dope. In this context, the old boss, who took to wearing a Pseudo turban and displaying specially commissioned Gilligan paintings, presented as even battier than before. Joshua White recalls looking to Josh for support over some heavy-handed treatment of his set-builders, only to be told, 'Oh, don't worry about this guy, he's just there to get it running.'

'And I realised: *he's disconnecting*,' says White. 'Then I thought, "Josh is too smart to disconnect from anything that would help him with his dreams and desires. Which must mean *he knows this is going nowhere*." And once that happened, there was nothing anyone could do. I don't ever remember Josh being drunk or stoned or out of control: when he loses interest he just stops listening and goes to some other place. And I'm sympathetic, but I couldn't stop him. So he turned to his expensive art projects.'

White thinks Josh needed 'a Lee Krasner' – reference to the wife who kept Jackson Pollock focused and sane enough to work, but at the expense of her own promising career. Did Josh think he'd found a 'Krasner' in Tanya Corrin? The pair would take up one last time, for a final dance to the music of his – and the market's – and the web's – and the city's – demons.

* * *

From a downtown perspective, the new millennium looked like the old one, only *more*.

The NASDAQ was still levitating, while on 30 January Super Bowl XXXIV became memorable not just for a brilliant last-second tackle which saved the game for the St. Louis Rams, but for a stream of TV ads for dotcoms no one had heard of – seventeen in the last quarter alone! – which drove the price of airtime to a reported $2.2 million per half-minute and led to the game being known to posterity as 'the dotcom Super Bowl'. The scale of spend was dizzying: Computer.com blew 60 per cent of its funding on a ninety-second slot and Pets.com launched their February IPO campaign with a sock puppet cow and slogan 'Because pets can't drive' (which was fine, because they *could* now have bags of litter shipped coast to coast at the cow's expense). And yet even the puppet's business plan looked prudent next to that of AllAdvantage.com, which paid users fifty-three cents an hour to web surf, plus another ten cents per surf-hour of every friend they introduced, with the aim of collecting valuable intelligence on consumer habits. Unfortunately, having accounted for 30,000 members in their first quarter, they drew 2 million (*people wanted free money? – who knew?!*) and with each customer earning an average of $20, the bill came to $40 million ... meaning that the more successful AllAdvantage became, the more wildly, prodigiously *un*successful it became. And unlike most businesses, there was no way to cut costs. *Fortune* dubbed the firm 'the Dumbest Dotcom in the World'.

As with most late-stage web plays, AllAdvantage's goal was an IPO: an 'exit strategy' which had been part of the business plan all along. Geeks and bankers had realised that, rather than building a business in the laborious traditional way, then selling out to a bigger company or going public, they could do it the other way round, riding the story like a magic carpet, bypassing the need to build anything as surely as the celebrity bypassed the need to learn a skill or harness talent, or the banker to do more than shift assets around. Why go to the trouble if you didn't have to? A worker at 360hiphop.com describes arriving at the company to find eighty people tending one basic, malfunctioning website, turning up at noon with almost nothing to do in a workplace with very little structure or accountability: a story which is typical. Eighty-four firms had filed to go public by April, with IPOs now expected to produce 100 per cent gains at launch, trumping the already exceptional 60 per cent hauls of a year before. In February, when Greenspan's Fed raised interest rates for the fourth time in eight months, the Dow responded, but the NASDAQ continued its rise to a 10 March peak of 5132, a figure which represented a near *doubling* of value in the space of four short months. Very few people noticed that, just as a record number of new shares were set to hit the market through IPOs, the 'lock-up' period on many of the previous year's offerings was coming to an end, allowing insiders to load almost 2.5 billion of their own shares on to the market for the first time.

On the day of the NASDAQ high, *The New York Times* sounded a warning, but the warning was easily lost in the greenback haze. In January, DoubleClick threw a Willy Wonka party for 2000-odd guests at The Roxy, with Oompa-Loompa bartenders and purple-skinned go-go girls and giant psychedelic mushrooms and the raffle of a gold candy bar, while a new company called UBO announced itself with a $100,000 bash for 3000 on Ellis Island. Now that Pseudo was looking and acting like a real TV company, even Pseudites started to live large: Jess

Zaino, as key talent, weekended in the Hamptons and on one glorious occasion succeeded in claiming a $600 bottle of champagne on expenses. Why? Because money was still being made – spectacularly. In February, as the US economy was officially deemed to have entered the longest period of expansion in its history, Omnicom sold 25 per cent of its stake in Razorfish for $141 million, or eighty times its original investment. But even that was chicken feed compared to some net companies, as Yahoo! grew to be worth more than Ford and General Motors combined. Wisdom held that a new world was coming and the young people dancing, drinking, scoring on Ellis Island and in the Roxy, the Hamptons, SoHo were its elfin rulers. Silicon Alley sun acquired the hue of divine light.

'I'm arrogant, but I'm not arrogant enough to draw a parallel between what Einstein did and what I'm doing,' Craig Kanarick told *New York* magazine, prior to drawing just such a parallel. And at the start of the year 2000, who was going to stop him?

No one's sure why the end came when it did. A *60 Minutes II* programme presented by the CBS investigative strand's suavest hitman, Bob Simon, who could offer you a Martini with one hand while using the other to beat you to death with his blow-drier – as you thanked him for his time – made mincemeat of Silicon Alley's cocky young 'dotcom kids'. Into Jeff Dachis he jabbed the stiletto of a simple question: 'So what do you *do*?' Then he leaned back and watched the Fish domo squirm, though not before pointing out that the stammering brat was worth 'about 180 million dollars' and that up to 10 per cent of Razorfish's mid-to-late-twenties-aged staff 'may be' millionaires.

So?

'We've asked our clients to recontextualise their business,' Dachis offered.

Care to try again *in English*? bade Bob.

'Well we've recontextualised what it is to be a service business,' came the eager response.

Hmm. Still not with you.

Then how about: 'We radically transform businesses to invent and reinvent them ... I mean it's about business strategy, er ...'

Bang! Buzzer sounds, celebrated *60 Minutes* trap door opens.

Simon's face said it all.

The *Sixty Minutes* team had employed an old journalistic trick, which involves repeating the same question until your subject, in exasperation, gives you something convoluted or nonsensical. The Razorfish pair were cocky, arrogant, insufferable even, but what they did was no mystery: they helped companies to move online, the way removal men help you move house. A worthwhile service – unless you considered the internet a 'fad', which Simon and his team clearly did. By the time he stood open-mouthed as a waggle-headed Josh announced, 'I'm in a race to take CBS out of business, that's what my bankers are telling me to do,' the presenter's work was done.

The 'dotcom kids' were rich and wired, but also (and not necessarily by coincidence, viewers were invited to infer) *idiots*. Jason Calacanis later cited the *60 Minutes* debacle as 'the first time anyone had ever made these people look stupid'. Why had the dotcom kids' agreed to participate? Because they'd drunk their own Kool-Aid; thought they were invincible. Old Media had chosen its moment to strike back.

Some in the finance world were seeing danger, too. In January, a hedge fund manager was quoted as warning, 'A year ago we were actually talking about a shortage of internet stocks. Well, the investment bankers have taken care of that, and now there are too many. There is going to be a shakeout in the whole sector.' As the NASDAQ continued to climb, a new turbulence was felt, with ebb and flow growing more pronounced, emboldening sceptics and changing the media tone.

The factor cited more than any other is the January 2000

merger of AOL and Time Warner, effectively a takeover of the Old Media behemoth by this New Economy talisman through an exchange of stock which greatly favoured the upstart. For companies like Pseudo, at the front of an expanding pack of would-be-Warners, this was considered good news. Indeed, Josh confesses that he agreed to take David Bohrman as CEO partly because he thought the appointment might facilitate a tie-in with CNN/Time Warner. Yet the AOL–Time Warner merger carried a disquieting implication, a hint that the tech revolution had peaked and if the 'Old' and 'New' economies were going to meld, Old Economy rules might apply to both.

And if *that* happened . . .

On Friday 10 March, the NASDAQ Composite hit its high of 5132 points, with the Dow cruising past 10,000. A stock such as Priceline, whose cod-democratic USP consisted in allowing consumers to name their own price for goods or services, now had a valuation equivalent to United Airlines, American Airlines, British Airways and KLM combined. Even market evangelists like Mary Meeker were beginning to express discomfort at the fug of unreality that had descended. It was as though, having been entranced by its own dance with the dollar, the market suddenly blinked awake and felt dizzy. A *Times* columnist mooted an 'accidental Ponzi scheme' in internet stocks, words which blew through SoHo like tumbleweed over the course of a nerve-jangling weekend.

And on Monday the sky fell in. First, the market woke to news that Japan had slipped back into recession, with Asia swaying unsteadily. Frantic selling caused indices to plunge for three full days, before investors recovered their nerve on Thursday – but only in relation to the Old Economy. That day the Dow recovered a record 499 points while the NASDAQ continued its descent. A late rally in biotech stocks on Friday camouflaged the losses, ensuring a headline decline of 'just' 5 per cent for the week.

But the message was lost on no one in the industry, even if the outside world remained naïve.

It had happened.

The bubble had burst.

More ominous still, that Saturday *Barron's* appeared with an incendiary piece headed 'Burning Up', in which the journalist Jack Willoughby did some old fashioned maths, dividing the monthly running costs of Alley firms into the sum of their cash reserves to produce an estimate of how long they could survive without fresh funding. On the understanding that fresh investment was now almost unthinkable, Willoughby was then able to deliver a terrifying bottom line: more than two hundred Silicon Alley firms would – not could but *would*, he claimed – collapse within the year. As a *coup de grâce*, he gave dates.

The pace quickened. On Monday 20th, the stocks named in the *Barron's* piece took a hit. But that had been predicted. What no one saw coming was news that MicroStrategy, the internet infrastructure company and stock market darling ruled by the queen-dating, stadium-hiring, Gatsby-house-building Michael Saylor, a firm viewed by NASDAQ fans as 'the next IBM, Microsoft and Oracle put together', became the first of many tech companies to admit having reported fraudulent results. Now *Fortune* accused VCs, investment banks and dotcommers of having played the Ponzi card *consciously*. Over the previous year, with pension money raining into the market, some mutual fund managers had noticed that if they all talked up and bought the same stocks, those stocks could be made to rise perpetually . . . a ruse which worked only so long as new money kept arriving. The classic Ponzi scheme, in fact.

MicroStrategy had been one such fund-favoured stock, whose share price had risen from $12 at IPO in 1998 to over $300, valuing its leader's holding at an outlandish $6 billion. But now the tangle of meaningless numbers began to unravel. Among other accounting ruses, companies had taken to naming revenue targets they knew would be exceeded, so implying that turnover was ahead of schedule and profitability on its way. One amateur net analyst, asked how his revenue and price predictions so regularly beat the professionals', shrugged and confessed that he simply added 10 per cent to the pro figures. Analysts gamed the situation in other ways, too, recommending (and often owning) shares in their employers' own clients. 'If you pay them $10,000 to $30,000, it seems to me you have nice things said about you,' complained the marketing head at one software company. 'Call me jaded, but that's the way I understand it works.'

Yet extraordinarily, and despite the Fed's choice of that week for another rate hike (to 6 per cent), both the Dow and NASDAQ recovered by week's end.

Had the first three weeks of March been no more than a blip? A *correction*?

Perhaps it had. 'The market is spitting in his eye,' scoffed one fund manager of Greenspan's desire to dampen the markets. IPOs started up again . . .

Until, in the last week of March, the predicted tsunami of new stock hit the market and the 'Nazz' shivered like a body in shock as it struggled to absorb the new shares, before seeming to stabilise at around 4500: bad, but short of catastrophic. Through another edgy weekend, market players tried to read the mood, with no discernible underlying logic to guide them. The bet boiled down to this: was the world ready to abandon 'fundamentals' and float free of itself – or not? Put another way, was this the start of something momentous for humanity, or the end of a weird collective fantasy . . . Gibson's 'consensual hallucination' brought to life? The answer would be swift and decisive.

On Monday 3 April, Microsoft's defeat in a bitter anti-trust case brought by the US government left no further room for doubt: the Real World was at the gate. A flurry of panic-selling drove the Nazz down 349 points, the biggest single-day fall in its history, legitimising Alan Greenspan's concern that the same technology which gave business instant sales and communication and control over inventory could turn against it with elemental force, as mood coalesced and decision-making became synchronous and the market took to behaving with the unpredictable singularity of a toddling infant, the technology turning against itself. The next day, more shares hit the market as investors who'd borrowed to buy shares were forced to sell in order to make good the loans. Textbook conditions for a crash. On a family holiday in Washington, Jerry Colonna received a text from Fred Wilson saying, 'The world has just collapsed.'

By lunchtime, the Nazz was down 575 points. In the Alley and on Wall Street, people were glued to TV sets and phones as the market seemed to have shed another 100 points every time they looked. To drive home the sense of crisis, a top White House economist appeared to offer a positive spin on events, sure sign that they were spinning out of control . . .

But again the market bounced. Joy. *Relief.* Fund managers and citizens had returned to buy old favourites like Microsoft and Cisco on the cheap, driving prices up until, at the end of another enervating day, the NASDAQ index had lost just *seventy-five* points, its computers coping with a mind-boggling 2.9 *billion* trades on the day. Then prices settled, even started to rise again, until Friday saw the biggest single-day points elevation in the exchange's history, of 178 points. Remarkably, the NASDAQ was still up 6 per cent for the year and on TheStreet.com's weekly TV show James Cramer claimed the volatility was over, while *Business Week* called the scare a 'much-needed correction' – deploying the word finance people use to imply an underlying rationality to the market, even when it's behaving like something Stephen King wrote. And there was still a possibility in most Alleyites' minds that *Business Week* was right and the first week in April had been a mere wake-up call. But on Monday 10 April all such hope dissolved as ETBs, VCs, CEOs and Alley drones rose to find investors scattering like beetles in a torch beam. For no particular reason, the NASDAQ shed almost 300 points on Monday, with another 130 going on Tuesday, followed by 300 more on Wednesday, ostensibly in response to disappointing profit reports from Microsoft, Hewlett Packard, Intel and IBM. By the end of the week, on 14 April, tech sector Black Friday, the percentage fall in value was greater than it had been for the Dow in the week of Black Monday back in October 1987, with a loss of 20 per cent on the week, 34 per cent since the 10 March high. The following Monday saw a 'bounce' as traders went bargain hunting, but there was no masking the fact that for the dotcoms this was not a 'correction', it was a *crash*. Prelude to an extinction.

Had such a thing ever happened before? Was it even possible?

Surely someone could stop it.

Throughout Silicon Alley you saw the same harrowed looks; felt the air get heavier and harder to breathe; heard the same phrase uttered over and over, until it seemed to echo through the streets like a mantra . . . 'This can't be happening.'

But it was.

Most ETBs recall a sick feeling, a sense of despair and knowledge that the party was over and that the future they'd unexpectedly made for themselves, the career they'd never thought they would have, but then *did*, was in danger of crumbling away. Whether their business was making money or not, whether it had a chance of being profitable in the future or not, the model they'd bought into, had been sold by the VCs and bankers and the share-hungry public, rested on an ever-increasing stream of investment capital becoming available. But clear as day, the tap had been turned off. There would be no more money.

Buzzwords like 'eyeballs' and 'recontextualising' were replaced by a single ubiquitous phrase. *Burn rate*. As in, 'What's your burn rate?' Meaning, 'What proportion of your cash reserves are you burning each month?' Or more bluntly, 'How long have you got?' Websites like Fucked Company and Netslaves helped focus the anger many tech workers felt – not with VCs or bankers, but with their bosses' bad management and broken promises. For the bosses there was shame, guilt, ridicule in the press. Old Economy wisdom would have had them slashing staff and overheads ruthlessly, aiming to preserve the core, live to fight another day, but most couldn't bring themselves to do this, so they cut slowly and delicately, bleeding resources as they went. Worse, as a show of faith, and pride, most ETBs hung on to their shares, watching their wealth fade away like the most beautiful sunset, leaving only the chill rage of investors and media, who accused them of selling techno snake oil and of being cynics. The internet had failed and it was their fault. Ahead stretched a life with no point or purpose, a nightmare end to the Disney dream.

Remarkable as it seems, almost none of the ETBs had seen the collapse coming. Fewer still were aware of the sinister truth that finance insiders had been quietly 'lightening their positions' in the dotcoms for at least six months. Young dotcommers hadn't known this was happening and most still don't know. In ten trading sessions, American investors lost more than $3 trillion, with Bill Gates having forfeited more wealth, more quickly, than anyone in history: $24.6 billion. MicroStrategy's Michael Saylor, meanwhile, saw his fortune fall by close to $5 billion *in a single day*, on its way to near obliteration. 'What is pretty clear right now,' the chastened CEO later mourned, 'is that during 1999, I, along with a lot of people in the tech business ... lost control of our identities.'

The week of 13 March would be likened to the Rolling Stones' Altamont show in 1969, where Hells Angels security guards beat a black spectator to death and the era of peace and love was deemed over. Post-crash, a new dotcom would go bust on average every day, their remains to be collected at locations like Netslave's 'e-museum', Yahoo!'s 'flop tracker' and DotComDoom. Indeed, dotcomfailures.com served the cause of irony well by going bust itself and the three students who had sold their sketchy financial website, Raging Bull, to Alta Vista for $167 million in Alta Vista stock on the understanding that an IPO was planned for April 2000 – who had appeared on Oprah and the CBS news and documentary strand *48 Hours* – watched in agony as the IPO was cancelled and their gleaming futures rusted over.

As always in these cases, there were a few lucky winners. Days before the balloon went up, the British Sports Internet site sold to BSkyB for £301 million, netting its young British founder a reported £141 million in a breathtaking feat of deal-making. For most, there would be no such happy ending, however. Suddenly people like the cautious investor George Soros were being listened to again. 'Markets don't reflect the facts very well,' the billionaire said, 'partly because they create the facts themselves.'

Against all odds, Pseudo managed another round of funding in May, pulling $15 million from a group of prior investors led by LVMH, who hoped to license Pseudo technology and content for use in Europe. At the same time, the Space Channel was sold to Space.com for $4 million worth of stock, though Josh will have been more excited about the site's founder, the CNN bigwig Lou Dobbs, agreeing to sit on the Pseudo board as part of the deal. A lucrative agreement was also struck with British Telecom for the use of content from Pseudo's All Games Network.

Almost $40 million had been invested in Pseudo to the end of May 2000, and a 'confidential offering memorandum' from June shows that efforts were being made to raise more. In the meantime, amid plans to webcast the summer political conventions, staff were laid off and costs cut deep. Distraught workers and pre-Bohrman managers went looking for Josh, wanting help or advice, some word of hope, but Josh was no longer there.

* * *

While his peers came to terms with the new world of scrap and hustle, in which 'no' replaced 'yes' as the default position, Josh moved up a gear, his actions growing more manic and unpredictable, his projects increasingly outlandish. He used the *Quiet* space for an elaborate reprise of the previous year's *Box Opera* spectacle, committing almost half a million dollars to building a real gym, complete with locker rooms and showers, and a central theatre where a $1000 bounty was again placed on David Leslie's chin and boxers from Gleason's in Brooklyn were hired to stage fights. Not content with transforming the main space, he also set up a ring for aftershow parties in his loft, some of which ran through the night. The fights were real, too: in one, Leslie broke his thereafter ex-friend Jonathan Ames's nose; in another, the Brit ex-pat writer and Studio 54 chronicler Anthony Haden-Guest was set up to think he'd knocked out an Italian ex-champ – a report of which triumph made the London *Evening Standard*. Not long afterwards, an 'aphrodisiac' party brought another bout of insecurity over the fake girlfriend, as Josh, high on ecstasy for the first and last time in his life, thought he sensed a post-coital *froideur* as she sat next to him in a bath robe, and suspected trysts with, by turns, JudgeCal and the event's co-host, Haden-Guest.

He'd kept the Luvvyplex and was operating it as an ersatz arts centre, with a little-used $200,000 silk screen press and retinue of artists who lived and worked in the space – doing, it seemed to visitors, *not very much*. All at a cost of more than $600,000 per annum, when Josh's only fresh income was a $1000 stipend plus health benefits from Pseudo. 'Most wealthy people just waste their time making more and more money,' he told *Wired* magazine. 'I'm one of the few who really understands how to spend it.'

And he did. In March 2000, a group of Vienna-based Situationist artists called Gelatin approached with the idea of covertly building a balcony on the ninety-first floor of the World Trade Center buildings, in a space reserved for creative projects, and Josh instantly agreed to fund them. When he first described this stunt to me, the tale sounded insane, delusional – but to my astonishment turns out to have been real. From a rented suite in the opposing Millennium Hilton hotel, he and a dozen friends kept watch through the night, until at dawn he and three of the party circled the building in a chartered helicopter to video the work, as members of Gelatin allegedly stood naked on their construction.

The art group later held an exhibition of materials from the action and published a now-rare book called *The B-Thing*. The trouble is that neither the book nor video taken from the helicopter (both of which I acquire after a long search) demonstrate conclusively that Gelatin had done what they said. The project could have been about reclaiming a patch of New York sky, or it could have been about tricking the rich man into parting with cash. Back in Awassa, Josh claimed to have seen an office-light 'bull's-eye' on the side of the building in the early hours, but none of those present in his hotel suite that night heard him mention such a thing. When, on 18 August 2001, *The New York Times* chose to run a piece on what had by then acquired the status of urban myth, Gelatin were coy about the 'work'. Perhaps they were fearful of prosecution, or of jeopardising future work in the US. Either way, witnesses confirm that Josh was visited by the CIA and allocated a minder three weeks after the *Times* piece appeared, on the day of the September 11 attack. Insane, yes: delusional, no.

Was the money a burden Josh secretly needed to shed? Three months after the Gelatin stunt, he spent what turns out to have been close to $400,000 on the *Tuna Heaven* voyage. David Leslie didn't 'get into the spirit of it like everybody else', but describes an air of 'mania' among the younger members of the cast. 'It got tedious to me, but they were *obsessed* with catching the biggest fish,' he says. 'And the mess! You never see that on TV in the shows about fishing. It was a basketball court-sized deck, covered in thick red blood and the fish in convulsions . . .'

Tanya Corrin's arrival wearing an engagement ring now looks to me like punishment for Josh's refusal to issue a marriage proposal. His suspicion that the ring belonged to Cal is rendered doubly bizarre by the fact that Cal was on the boat too: Josh might have asked him, but couldn't bring himself to. Instead, he watched her grapple rods as if they were giant othermen cocks, telling himself all the while that he didn't care, that Corrin was the fake girlfriend; just a player in his great schema.

Soon afterwards, Josh asked Tanya to move into the loft with him. A couple of months later, as she was stepping into her robe one morning, he announced plans to cover the space with CCTV cameras, from the bed to the bathroom to Neuffy the cat's litter tray, all in order to feed himself – and he hoped her, their relationship – to the web for 100 days. It was an art project, but also a business model, employing bespoke technology which could afterwards be sold to a public eager to be their own shows too. *We Live in Public* would be experiment, marketing device, test of their relationship rolled into one, Josh said. In response to which Corrin professes to have been terrified, but willing 'to share this experience; to find out whether life was better lived in public or private'. She thought the project might bring them closer together.

Josh would later attribute some of his manic energy to avoidance of the fact that Pseudo was tanking. After the high-profile closures of both DEN and Pop.com, CEO David Bohrman announced plans to lay off fifty-eight staff and merge the channels into one talk-driven 'Pseudo Center'. The day before his announcement, a couple of workers were given the task of assembling dozens of white cardboard boxes, soon dubbed 'coffins' by staff, in which colleagues would carry out their possessions. Extra security guards were hired to make sure nothing was stolen as Bohrman and Tony Asnes visited each channel in turn, reciting names of the doomed. The exercise cut overheads in half, delivering a burn rate of roughly $2 million per month and hope that a buyer might be tempted. Yet it also marked the end of Pseudo – and in many ways of Silicon Alley itself – as a distinctive entity.

A prospectus I turn up from mid-2000 is covered in Josh's scrawled notes, indicating that he was involved in the search for an investment lifeline and still cared enough to engage with it: over the summer he lent the company $1 million of his own money with rights to the archive as collateral. But on 18 September the news came anyway. Pseudo was to close. A staff announcement was delayed for an hour while talks with potential buyers continued, but to no avail.

Upsetting though his company's demise was, the worst of Josh's heartbreak had already played out. 'For me, I don't know, it's almost a relief,' he told *The New York Observer*. 'It was weighing on me. It could have been worse, it could have been acquired. I would never have gotten my dough back, and it would have been bastardized on the way out. This way, it died a nice peaceful death. It died in its sleep.'

Then he added a surprise rejoinder.

'The excitement of having it going ... had finally worn off. I graduated. Pseudo was not a place you stayed at, it was a place you graduated from. Get on CBS for ten seconds and you've got more total viewership than Pseudo had in its entire existence.'

The site had never pulled the 200,000 users per month needed to show in the net traffic ratings: the truth was that most people knew Pseudo from having read about it or seen it on TV. Even so, blanket New York and net press coverage painted dotcommers of all stripes as being 'shellshocked' by the news. Most features and news reports were quick to acknowledge Pseudo's anarchic nature and the suddenly ice-clear truth that it had never been a business, but in retrospect appear surprisingly wistful, with former staff expressing sadness rather than the anger found elsewhere in the Alley. 'It was a place whose time had not yet come, but it was very exciting to work there,' said Executive Producer of Politics, Sam Hollander, while Senior Vice President of Marketing Jeanne Meyer declared that, 'It'll be a badge of honour to have worked here.' *Silicon Alley Daily* lauded Pseudo for having 'imagined a world where programming wasn't just spoon fed to the viewing public but instead involved the viewer's active participation', even though it had 'always been more about buzz than product', and *The New York Observer* agreed with many staff that the June reorganisation had left Pseudo 'eviscerated'. Clay Shirky retrospectively suggests that 'Word and Pseudo didn't go out of business because their business models were wrong, they went out of business because there were no models.'

Josh describes the day he and young staffer John Christopher Morton returned to the office to 'hoover up all the media and data' as 'a very hollow moment in my life'. In the end, the company, including its proprietary 'Daisy' interactive TV operating system and the lease on 600 Broadway, was sold to a New York net company called INTV for $2 million – an event recorded for *The New York Times* by none other than Jayson Blair, whose piece quoted INTV's president as confiding that, 'Even Josh said, "You should bring some monks to go through the building to exorcise the place."'

As had been true from the start, where Pseudo went others followed. By October, Silicon Alley's thirty-seven most prominent firms had shed over fifteen thousand staff and against Josh's advice, even Jupiter Communications had merged with a company called Media Metrix. In every way imaginable, the party was over.

19

Work began on the loft immediately. Walls were torn open and cable veins inserted to carry feeds from fifty microphones and thirty-two ceiling-mounted, motion-sensitive cameras to the control room. House telephones were wired into the online system and a way was found to project chat on to the wall. Tellingly, a company formed to market the technology was named after a form of prison, the Panopticon, which had been conceived by the Victorian philosopher Jeremy Bentham and first built on the River Thames in London, on the site of what is now the Tate Britain gallery. The Panopticon's circular shape allowed prisoners to be observed at all times without observers being seen and was regarded by Bentham as nothing less than 'a new mode of obtaining power of mind over mind'. Josh knew what he was walking into.

Tanya programmed the cameras while Josh titillated the press, most notably in a long *Wired* piece containing his trademark mash of honesty and obfuscation. His ideas seemed wacky at the time, as per the studio he intended to build for members of the public to walk in and video themselves, with results archived to the web – or the networks of 'friends' who would be perpetually linked by broadband, creating little constellations of ever-connected online communities. 'Imagine,' he said, 'I'm lying in bed, and they can all see me, and at the same time I can see them. At that point, we will be re-weaving social communication, and I will be immersed in it. If it's as successful as I hope, I'll continue the experiment indefinitely. It won't be like those people on *Survivor*, who have regular lives to go back to after the series ends. This will *be* my life.' Millions would want to follow in his footsteps, he said, once broadband became ubiquitous. 'Of *course* they're going to be watching each other. It's inevitable. Everything I'm doing will be considered commonplace just ten years from now. It'll be no more unusual than listening to a stereo or watching TV.'

With the benefit of hindsight, we might say that (at the very least) Josh was wrong about timescale. On the other hand, if the first thing you reach for in the morning is your smartphone, to check email, texts, Facebook page, Twitter feeds, news headlines – as, despite myself, *I* do . . . I wonder how wrong he really was? Yet as bewildering as Josh's prognostications sounded, the *Wired* writer was as thrown by Tanya, whose Pseudo show explored the outer reaches of sexuality, from multiple orgasms to foot fetishism, and once involved videoing herself trying to have sex in an airline toilet. 'Three years ago, I was teaching myself HTML and designing Web sites,' she confessed. 'I was timid and shy, grew up in a small town, and had a baggage of inhibitions to get rid of' – which, as she wondered what it would be like to masturbate in public, she seemed to have managed. 'No one else on the planet masturbates in the exact way I do: it must be really weird . . .' she concluded. 'Maybe other women will suggest alternatives.'

As ever, Josh couldn't resist upping the ante by promising an attempt to conceive their first child online. 'Think about it, wouldn't you enjoy sex more if you knew you were being televised?' he asked. The answer being much less obvious to most of us than Josh seemed to imagine. Jason Calacanis took time out from fighting to save his own business in order to comment: 'I think Josh has played everybody and goes to bed with a very big smile on his face. In a world filled with boring technologists, he was the first avant-garde – if not insane – visionary.' I still wonder at his use of the word 'was'.

The piece ended with a discussion of Josh's belief, inspired by the quirky robotics scientist and thinker Hans Moravec, that the twenty-first-century advent of artificial intelligence will see the end of the human race, as we enhance our physical and intellectual selves with machine, progressively merging with our creations to the point of becoming a new species. I interviewed Moravec for the London *Observer* back in 2001 and was shocked to hear him say:

> For me, robots are extensions of humanity. Something I'm always pointing out is that we're 99.9 per cent cultural beings now: the information that's passed from generation to generation in our genome consists of a few billion bits, but there are trillions of bits in our libraries. The robots are simply the point when that cultural information takes over from strict biology. Eventually they might develop in their own directions, but that's the normal situation for descendants. I think of it as the most mature and potentially full future that we could have.

Now, of course, his prophecies seem as self-evident to me as they did to Josh back then, when he shocked *Wired* with his insistence that: 'We're in the midst of an evolutionary shift, creating our own demise. I'm recognizing this on a personal level. By living in public, I may be achieving a kind of personal immortality. Two hundred years from now, if they want to recreate a human being from the year 2000, there'll be so much material about my life, they could make a virtual replica of me, indistinguishable from the real thing.'

My mind goes back to St Mark's Theatre in 1993, where Josh sits in the cinema watching light images dance across a screen;

falls into one of his reveries and feels the limits of the physical world, with its messy bilateral relationships; realises that this visceral realm is not for him and decides to follow his liminal info-ghosts through the screen, much as Alice slipped through the looking glass, to live as pure projection, only-information … a place of safety and self-sufficiency, free of the emotional commitment which makes real world connection risky – but also nuanced in ways that virtual relationships may never be … and yet ghosts are easier to live with than other people. Than ourselves. Why wouldn't Josh choose them over us? Come to that, why wouldn't – why won't – *we*?

Josh sent a copy of the *Wired* piece to his mother, as he did all his press. More than any of the things he did, the articles seemed to make her proud.

At midnight on 21 November 2000, *We Live in Public*'s producer, Michael Auerbach, called to tell Josh and Tanya they were live. Within minutes there were fifteen people in the chat room, despite no one having announced that the stream had begun. How? Who were these people? Rattled, the couple sought the comfort of bed, camera motors whirring to follow them – *zzzztt zzzzzttt zzzzzzttt* – as they moved through the loft. There they cuddled and slept fitfully, maintaining a physical connection through their feet, as they always did, but watched over by a revolving assemblage of strangers. And the next morning they woke to a call from the company that installed the cameras, informing them that there were sixty-two people in the chat room, mostly conversing in Mandarin. High on novelty, they spent long evenings in the control room through the first week, chatting and fooling and even calling their virtual guests on the bugged phone, the happy couple at the centre of their own self-generated community, their own show – bringers of the wired future. Chatters wanted Josh the web celeb to talk to them; wanted Tanya to take off her clothes. It was invasive, but still fun and crazy cool, and the live stream was all jerky shades of grey, as if being beamed back from the Moon.

The second week saw privations start to bite. You had to hide in a closet to order food, because you couldn't recite credit card or phone numbers, or addresses, out loud. Even so, one of the Enger Brothers, a pair of wild-man artists not much liked by Josh's pals and ex-colleagues, requested a pizza to camera and got one twenty minutes later. Tanya became nervy, bought a can of mace and refused to answer the door. She found herself scanning for cameras in public places and friends' homes, and concocting unnecessary errands to run. It was hardly surprising that many watchers came looking for sex, given Josh's sales pitch for the event. But now they grew impatient when the pair couldn't or wouldn't perform. Tanya dressed in the open once and received dozens of salacious messages in response, so took to changing as if at the beach and washing only in the steam room fog. Imprecations for them to 'do something interesting' started to grate.

Half in jest, Josh's engineers had installed a camera in the toilet bowl and – unlike Josh, who drew deep metaphoric joy from dumping on his audience – Tanya never made peace with it, nor with public sex, much less masturbation. On one occasion, she and Josh covered the bathroom camera and dirty-talked through a tryst, which felt naughty and exciting. Unfortunately, they'd forgotten to mute the sound and chatters went into a frenzy, after which sex reverted to being under covers, late at night, and *rare*. Only when the couple went upstate one weekend, leaving an engineer to invite a group of swingers over, was the watcher thirst for sex satiated. The first Josh and Tanya knew of the show was when they returned to chat messages like, 'I wouldn't sit in that chair if I were you.'

There were technical foibles. Many of the cameras had been mounted on the ceiling, restricting viewers to a downward perspective. More frustrating was the motion-sensitive programming of the system, which was sophisticated and clever, but meant – inconveniently for adolescent masturbators in the chat room – that if someone opened the fridge while Tanya was taking a shower, viewers got the fridge. A senior Pseudo producer claims to have seen a secret schedule of events, including plans for Tanya to eject Josh from the loft one night and invite a group of girlfriends over to drink and chat and spend time in the steam room, wearing bikinis. 'The trouble was that no one was selecting the images,' the producer chuckles, 'so all it needed was for the cat to walk across the control room and suddenly you'd be presented with a picture of an empty chair. Or the litter tray! It was *hilarious*, a real wasted opportunity.' The site boasted of 90,000 members by now, though the reality was probably much lower (the *Times* reported 7000), with a few hundred logged on at any given moment. A *Vanity Fair* writer found roughly 100 in the chat room during her visit, including a sizeable contingent from Sweden.

Real reality intruded when, in the run-up to Christmas, Tanya decided to spend a few days skiing with friends and Josh's insecurity careened to the surface. Nancy Smith comforted him, saying, 'She's only gone skiing – it's nothing to worry about, get *over* it,' but Tanya's absence wasn't the only problem, because his native jealousy had been magnified by a sharp fall in web traffic – an abandonment which left him feeling wraithlike and robbed of self, the info-ghost's tragedy being that without an audience he/she doesn't exist. Because for all its aggravations, life under the watchers' gaze seemed heightened. Everything was an event, nothing wasted and 'dead' time didn't arise. Even having a crap no longer felt mundane – so long as there was an audience.

Chatters saw Josh withdraw, even as Tanya's engagement with them increased. Few would have consciously noticed that through all the couple's exchanges, she would be perfectly framed while he slumped in chairs or stood half in shot. The timid girl from Maine with the 'baggage of inhibitions to get rid of' knew where the cameras were and played to them naturally, was choosing them over him, confiding in 'her people' before the man she thought she loved.

For Josh, this abandonment was excruciating. *We Live in Public* had sprung from his mind, from his *soul*, but now he'd lost control of it. As one colleague later observed, 'He really was inside his TV now, but without the remote.' And alone, a world away from anything that felt safe to him. In the past, communication breakdowns had been smoothed through sex or dinner or a movie, but thanks to Josh's state of mind and the ever-present watchers, none of these releases were available. Other people were involved in the management of their lives, had entered what Josh was now calling their 'mindshare'.

Typically, Josh confessed his discomfort only in interview, where it had value, had *leverage*, and only by listening in could Tanya learn how he was feeling. Luvvy appeared in the control room and a group of watchers tried to vote him out, as per the reality show *Survivor*. Chatters encouraged Tanya to question her relationship and Josh's behaviour, as the chat room became her 'confessional' and chatters her 'friends and therapists'. On New Year's Eve, she went out with a group of friends and when she came back and climbed into bed in the early hours, her feet failed to seek out Josh's under the covers. He took this as a sign of infidelity and withdrew further still. He was eating too much and putting on weight, while she spent hours in her office connecting to her people. Anyone who had ever been in a failing relationship recognised the scene and its attendant desolation. The difference being that this couple's feelings were complicated by thousands of others'.

Other problems were coming to a head at the same time. By the end of 2000, the NASDAQ had shed over 50 per cent of its peak value. A composite of forty-six publicly traded Silicon Alley stocks had crashed from over $1500 in January to $276 at the end of October. iVillage shares had plunged from a peak of $113 to just $2; DoubleClick from $249 to $14 and Razorfish from $96 to $4, en route to a floor of 49 cents. But at least they were still standing, where so little else was. 'Pink Slip' parties sprung up in an effort to ease the distress of former dotcommers, 75,000 of whom had already lost their jobs: one event in December was covered by CNN, ABC and stations in Germany, Italy and Japan. Razorfish would report a loss of $148 million for the year, with Dachis and Kanarick fighting Wall Street demands to slash staff. 'We're a company, not a stock,' railed Dachis, 'and we're playing to win the revolution, not the stock market . . . this is a company of true believers.' Laudable but for the fact that, post-1999 IPO orgy, Razorfish *was* a stock. Like Josh, Dachis had bought the buzz of living in public and only now was he learning what the deal had really cost. His watchers owned him, too.

On 14 January, Josh and Tanya had a bad fight when he accused her of being boring in bed. Perhaps he was projecting his own sexual anxiety or protesting their loss of connection, but she responded with impressive control, sitting spread-eagled on his lap and throwing her arms around his neck in a palliative hug, resisting the temptation to take his charge to heart. But his face remained stony as he placed his hands on her arse and began to raise her skirt at the start of an exchange which went:

'I'm bored! B-o-a-r-d.'

'Ah, no, that's like *wood*, on a *floor* . . .'

'B-o-r-e-d.'

Tanya laughs and hugs him. He raises her skirt.

'*No*,' she says, whispering her discomfort at having sex in public.

'What's the problem? No one will see.'

Tanya turns to face the camera.

'Ah, *hello.*' And when Josh persists: 'Don't! – OK? I'm not gonna be your porn star. I'm *not.*'

[camera switches to image of cat apparently climbing inside the toilet bowl]

'This is not about that. Any time I make a move to do anything, you fuckin' block it.'

Tanya gets up to go, but Josh grabs her by the arms and stops her.

'No! Don't force me. Don't grab me like that. *Josh.* Don't do this! You're scaring me!'

He tightens his grip.

'Stop it!' She whacks his arm and gets up. '*Leave me alone!* Don't! Let go of me! Don't you grab me! Don't give me bruises! Don't hurt me!'

She swipes a saucepan to the floor and stalks off. Moments later she is heard crying. Josh moves towards his computer screen (as the stream clicks to shot of Neuffy entering the utility room). Tanya comes back out and says she won't be hit; she's leaving.

Josh says quietly: '*What?* I didn't hit you.'

At the doorway, they hug, Josh contrite, Tanya now in control. A much calmer discussion ensues. At one point Josh says something Tanya disagrees with and she looks up to the camera and smiles, like a barrister turning to the jury after wrong-footing a defendant. He accuses her of finding excuses not to have sex. She tells him he's fat, saying, 'You have never been fatter than you are right now.' They break up and go to their respective terminals, to see what the chatters are saying. Josh realises that the watchers' response is more interesting to him and Tanya than the fight; is more interesting than they are to each other. 'Big Brother isn't a person, as it turns out,' he will observe, 'it's the collective consciousness.'

*

A little later, Tanya told Josh to sleep on the couch, an act of defiance which struck him as out of character – until his watchers told him that *her* watchers were behind the demand. Five days later and to Josh's evident relief, she announced that she would move out three weeks hence, allowing time to find an apartment. The last straw had been Tanya's disappointment with a thirty-first birthday present consisting of a vintage camera ('Oh, it's too big to be a ring,' she'd tried to smile as she removed the wrapping). She then substituted her plan to leave with an insistence, again encouraged by watchers, that *he* move out. 'So in exchange for the strength and courage to do that, Tanya gave up a piece of her individuality to the virtual world,' Josh would muse much later, in the course of noting how much of himself he lost, too.

Tanya went skiing again and returned to a darkening atmosphere in the chat room. One of her first exchanges went:

WeLive: Where have you been Tanya?
Tanya: Skiing with a girlfriend.
WeLive: And who else?
WeLive: We heard that you were having sex with either Bill Clinton or Leonardo DiCaprio.
Tanya: What?
WeLive: You're not cheating on Josh?

Mystifying. Until she heard that Luvvy had appeared during her absence, screeching accusations about a supposed affair. Now watchers were running with the idea, almost entering and *becoming* it, working Josh's pain into a paranoid feedback loop from which there could be no easy escape. A chatter 'friend' told Tanya that when he challenged Josh's contention, Josh responded with a stream of invective. Shortly afterwards, Josh's 5th Avenue PR man issued a press release claiming Josh to have ordered his webmate out, and on day 79 it happened. Tanya left. Two days later, she returned to finish packing and contends that a softened, chastened Josh asked her to marry him. Coincidentally or not, the cameras were down, so watchers missed the parting. For his part, Josh denies that he proposed and Michael Auerbach, who produced the experiment and was present for most of it – and who fell out with his benefactor shortly afterwards – also claims it didn't happen; that Josh begged Tanya to leave at least a month earlier and she lobbied to stay. As with most real world relationships, no one but the participants would ever know the important truths.

For all his description of Tanya Corrin as the fake girlfriend, Josh describes the day she left as a nadir, a moment of 'total personal desolation'.

'Once she left it was like the Pit,' he told me in Awassa. 'I've seen the Pit from hell.'

Alone with the cameras, he felt vulnerable, naked, bullied by his audience, with falling watcher numbers a gauge of his dwindling worth. In an interview he described them as his 'creepy internet guests', for whom he could no longer perform. Future generations might be mentally wired for this type of experience – for being embedded in the datastream, always *on* – but he wasn't. The dotcom bubble had burst a year before and now his was bursting too.

Josh resolved to see out his 100 days or more, but first spent a week in LA with his mother, during which time the Inside.com journalist Greg Lindsay and a dotcom casualty friend named Will Leitch house-sat. Leitch had been drawn to New York specifically by the exploits of Josh and his glamorous ETB peers at a time when 'New York felt like the centre of the universe, the biggest, most fun-filled city in the world.' His only concern was a feeling that 'New York is not supposed to be this easy!'

Both men noticed that, even though there may have been only four or five people watching (they didn't know how to tell), their pervading sense was of the whole world looking on and assessing them – which may reveal a truth about social media on the web. Leitch noticed that he slept with his hands above the bedclothes, so no one could accuse him of masturbating. Yet, for all that, the most unsettling feature of the experience had nothing to do with the cameras themselves. 'If you stay in front of cameras for long enough, you develop a kind of immunity to them,' explains Lindsay. 'That's why reality TV works so well. The real crazy-making part was the paranoia of the chat room, of knowing that people were seeing and judging you at all times, instantly, and that they could say whatever they wanted – that, to me, was the fascinating part of it, that blending of chat and reality television. So there were voices in your head, often aggressive voices, which you had no control over. It was corrosive, like a rehearsal for schizophrenia, and I quickly didn't want to be there.' Or in Josh's words, 'There may be only ten people watching, but that's ten people eating away at your soul. They're taking little pieces of you continuously.'

There was more soul-eating to come. Six days after Tanya's desertion, on 15 February, Bob Simon's *60 Minutes II* film aired. Shortly thereafter, *Vanity Fair* carried a long article entitled 'In the Dot-Com Doldrums', in which Marisa Bowe of Word.com described the prevailing atmosphere as one of 'rudderless dread' and another ex-dotcommer asked, 'You ever seen *On the Waterfront?* That's how I feel . . .' The piece began and ended with Josh, who was finally ready to confess that, 'I've thought about going broke – it's a constant thing.' On the downfall of Pseudo, he reflected with surprising candour, that, 'I've had to wonder to myself fairly recently whether I've been in denial.'

A former staffer named Meg Weber told the magazine: 'I think [Josh] was starting to lose his appeal when that coolness factor was acknowledged. Once it was acknowledged, we were suddenly conscious. It was like being in the Garden of Eden and finally noticing that we were naked. Everybody looked down, and I was like, *"Ew"*.' She likened the crash to 'telling a little kid that Christmas is all a fraud', reinforcing a message from the introduction to the piece, which described the arc of a generational trauma, saying: 'With the NASDAQ meltdown, the brash young C.E.O.s who strutted the business-world stage like rock stars have turned into walking punch lines. And a generation wonders what happened to its American Dream of retiring young as options millionaires.'

Josh returned and started to spend more and more time watching football and the hypnotic crime drama *Law & Order* on his wall-screen. Chatters by turns worried and mocked as he sat and brooded, seeming to melt into their screens until he was little more than a tenuous presence, a spectre drifting like thought ... virtual at last. 'She didn't leave me,' he told watchers who goaded him about Tanya's loss. 'She left *you*.' And to a friend: 'I'm sick, I'm mentally sick right now. I have to get out before they kill me ... or take something from me that I can't replace.' The experiment had acquired the quality of a freak show.

As usual, Josh's pain and anger were expressed indirectly. When New York senator Charles Schumer hosted a virtual town meeting in the loft, Josh failed to switch off the toilet cam and the image of a urinating guest appeared as the senator extolled the virtues of technology. And when a New York Fashion Week crowd descended for a final party, dropping cigarette butts on the expensive maple floor and showing no respect for the space, Josh instructed the bartender to stop serving alcohol and provide juicy diuretic drinks instead, causing guests to queue endlessly for the lone bathroom, with toilet-cam prioritised and its image flashing on to the wall. 'I've got them,' he thought, enjoying the hint of *homage* to his Dada movement art hero Marcel Duchamp. Then he watched the 400 fashionistas slowly understand what they were seeing on the walls and start to enjoy it, to moan 'ooooh' and 'ahhhh' as party-goers clamoured to perform for each other, unaware that they were also being taped.

The last party Josh would ever throw.

He was losing it.

In an outpouring posted to fuckedcompany.com under the heading 'my ex-boyfriend sucks and here's the proof', Corrin went public with her side of the story, describing her discomfort with the experiment and her bemusement at Josh, whose withdrawal she ascribed to jealousy over her popularity with the watchers. The screed was picked up and crafted into an article called 'The Harris Experiment' by the New York and London *Observers*, with London's *Independent* also running a feature on the couple's rift – all with Josh's twenty-four-hour net connection continuing to cost $30,000 a month and the NASDAQ deflating further; with companies going bust daily and even Kanarick and Dachis under threat of expulsion from their own company by institutional investors, as Jason Calacanis fought to retain staff and prevent his magazine from bleeding away to nothing.

The moment at which, with a final cruel lurch, the walls around Josh disintegrated.

Jupiter Communications had been worth up to $500 million during the boom, valuing Josh's portion at over $85 million. It had been a real business, generating real profit, but its clients were vanishing, shareholders becoming edgy. As *We Live in Public* went on-stream back in November, Jupiter stock was trading at $22 per share, with Josh's three million-plus shares worth about $70 million. But the price had slipped, gradually at first, drifting then holding, drifting then holding . . . holding . . . holding – until with the abruptness of a thunderclap, it switched to freefall as investors chose the same moment to flinch and lose faith, shovelling shares on to the market until the market was saturated and no one could get out, price plummeting to fifteen, twelve, ten, eight, five, *three* . . . a sinking sensation deep in

Josh's gut, mirroring the fall of the stock as he watched helpless, clicking his mouse to see his latest worth, doing it again a few minutes later to find himself a million bucks lighter . . . until, in one of those moments that print themselves on a person's mind as if seared by cattle brand, the phone rang and he picked it up to hear a sequence of words he'd hoped never to have to hear.

A voice said: 'Hi Josh. We're selling your stock.'

The 'margin call': it happens when you've borrowed against your stock and the stock has fallen to a level at which your ability to repay the loan is in doubt. At this point, the bank is entitled to *make* you sell your holding in order to make good the borrowed cash, whether you think it might recover or not. At the start of February, Josh's Jupiter stock was trading at $16, but as it passed through $5, he got the call from Goldman – shockingly stripped of civility or small-talk, with no 'How are you doing?' or 'Hey, we're sorry, man, we know this must be painful, but . . .'

Just, 'Hi, we're selling your stock.'

And the words carried a terrible unspoken freight. They said, 'You have failed: your thoughts and feelings no longer matter. You *were* Josh Harris, Warhol of the Web, gold-fingered wild man of Silicon Alley, but now you're just another bad loan, no better or worse than the canned steel worker who can't make the payments on his car.' Goldman had advised an earlier sale, but Josh had refused to give up his shares. Had he played his hand perfectly on all fronts, he could have walked away with up to $100 million, but that had never been the point. Or had it? The voice asked how many shares Josh wanted them to sell and, heartbroken to a degree he'd never thought possible – for the second time in a week – he heard himself blurt, 'Sell it all'. A million-dollar decision, because the stock swiftly hit two, one, fifty cents, ten cents. Nothing.

He went to the shower and wept.

'I knew what I was doing, I wanted to go to that place' he

would tell me in Awassa, but the same day Nancy Smith found him wandering the street like a runaway child, in a windbreaker and Mets cap, small backpack stuffed with possessions – some drawings, books and keepsakes; press cuttings, a *MAD* magazine . . . crying uncontrollably and unable to look her in the face, as though in humiliation he'd reverted back to the nerdy little boy of his childhood. Smith had never seen even her own son cry with such desolate physicality, with each shudder and sob seeming to expel a portion of her patron's being, and she worried that he might commit suicide. Instead, he returned home to anaesthetize himself with TV and comfort food, assembling huge macaroni cheese sandwiches, burgers, hot dogs, mountains of fries. Josh had been kind to Smith and her family, generous with money when times were tight. It seemed to her that while other rich people collected cars, property, clothes, vacations, or got married and invested in things they didn't really care about, he'd spent on hiring people to entertain him; to build sets and throw parties and make art. Yet he'd also worried that when his wealth went, so would Tanya, which is why the quilt-maker thought he'd pushed her away. She felt as though she was watching a wave break over him and when she left, she wept too, knowing the adventure was done and she wouldn't see its like again. She took to rollerblading through the city on her own, searching for something that wasn't there.

There's a kind of winter's day, unique to New York, where the sleet-needled snow is too cold to melt and turns to black-grey sludge instead, seems to meld with the street and the buildings and sky into a bleak, blank field of nothing. Friday 2 March 2001 was such a day. A walk to the deli for coffee felt like a scene from *The Iliad*. It was the hundredth day of *We Live in Public*.

Jason Calacanis was in his office working a spreadsheet, performing a task he'd grown sickeningly used to: deleting the names of staff, each in turn, to gauge their effects on the bottom line. He should have slashed his workforce from seventy to ten as soon as the crash came, but young and idealistic as he was, the ruthlessness hadn't been in him. Instead, he let his people go in agonised increments and now he was paying the price … they were all paying the price. It was a painful time and he wasn't sleeping well. The summer of '99 might as well never have happened.

Josh had said, 'Hey, can I see you?' Now he sat in the chair opposite, speaking a fractured train of sub-clauses, predicates with no subject, repeating, repeating as he rocked back and forth. 'The jig's up, can't do it. Jig's up, can't do it, it's not working – gotta get off the grid …'

Preoccupied with his own problems and a little impatient, Calacanis demanded, 'What are you saying?' but got only: 'The jig's up, can't do it – gotta get off the grid …'

Josh couldn't look his friend in the eye, had an almost catatonic tilt to him. And suddenly Calacanis found himself feeling angry as he saw what the Pseudo man had become.

'You used to be a really interesting person,' he said. 'But right now, the most interesting thing for you is your *press*. All you ever talk about is your *New York Post* story, or, "Did you see *Vanity Fair*?"

'Do you understand that the press we used to get was a reflection of what we'd done? The press we got was not what we *did*. It was a *reflection*. You used to be one of my favourite people to be with, one of the bravest and most fascinating I ever knew – and I learned more from your failures than I did from my own little successes. But now we go to dinner and you don't have anything to say. I never thought I'd say this, Josh, but you're *boring*.'

In some dark corner of his mind, had Calacanis known that he was also speaking of himself; of the ETBs; of Silicon Alley; New York? Having just returned from a speaking engagement in Spain, he advised his friend to go there with a case of books and read for a year. Re-find himself.

But Josh just said: '*No*, I'm going to the farm. I got a farm. The jig's up, there's nothing for me here. I'm going to the farm … gotta get off the grid …'

And by the end of the day he was gone. By the end of the year, his New York was gone too.

20

Social scientists call it the 'narrative turn'. An identifiable lurch towards describing our world explicitly in terms of *story*: to situating ourselves within revolving webs of narrative, on which our sensess of place and identity and connection to others can rest. Most date the birth of this 'new narrative age' to the mid-90s. One, the French theorist Christian Salmon, ventures a specific year. 1995. The year of Netscape, Pseudo, the ubiquity of the web.

There was nothing new about using story to draw connections between things, tying ourselves to narratives which suggest order and continuity. But the 1990s question was this: what happens when our stories are revolving too fast, fragmenting too quickly, melding 'fact' and fiction too seamlessly, to be used as anchors for identity? Do our senses of self fragment, too? Do we become the 'strange juxtapositions' Jess Zaino saw in Josh? Or does our yen for the safety of narrative simply intensify and become *conscious*? This is how it looks to me.

No wonder that as the century ended, celebrities were suddenly being paid to act as flesh and blood morality tales. No wonder Howell Raines, the *New York Times* editor who defended Jayson Blair's fabrications even as they were being picked apart by old-fashioned 'reality-based' reporters from the *Washington Post*, viewed stories as ends in themselves, whether they reflected events outside his reporter's imagination or not. As information of all kinds accelerated and blurred, no wonder Josh Harris came to look like the future. Because he felt the shift in his bones. Understood. The coming world was already his own.

And who could blame business for responding to this new need? Marketing gurus began to speak of 'relational marketing', where the emphasis was less on extolling the virtues of a product than creating an emotional bond between brand and consumer, often through the use of stories which could be figuratively and literally *bought into*. Unsurprisingly, Apple became one of the first corporations to acknowledge this shift, when at the launch of its groundbreaking iMac in 1998, its marketing sage William Ryan declared, 'Forget traditional positioning and brand-centric approaches . . . we are now in the "Age of Narrative".'

In this context, the rise of what has been called 'narrative capital' was logical and probably inevitable. While Josh was fleeing New York for the apple farm in spring 2001, the CEO of the post-industrial conglomerate Enron was selling his company to the public as 'a fabulous, fabulous story' in TV ads, just months before it imploded in one of the most spectacular business scandals of all time. Like so many of the dotcoms brought to market two years before ('No story has been more integral to the rebirth of New York,' gushed *Crain's*), Enron turned out to have been *all* story. Even a man regarded as one of the cleverest people in America, Alan Greenspan, was fooled.

But how?

The received narrative of the crash is about online snake oil and the counterfeit geeks who used technology to dupe the grown-up world, including the hapless financiers who abetted them – a story which never made sense to me and seemed even less satisfying the closer I drew.

Only towards the end of my research did another version of events begin to take shape.

Like the Square Mile of London, Wall Street is to its host metropolis as the Holy See is to Rome: a city within a city, connected at points but with its own jurisdiction, as if geography were just another bureaucratic belch, the red tape of Creation. In a sense, its citizens have always lived in a virtual world, moving among the wider population through corridors bounded by taxi glass, ghosting their own space like cardinals, the stakes for which they play simultaneously higher and much, much lower than for the rest of the population. That New York remained depressed long after Wall Street swung again in the first half of the 90s should have surprised no one. Upside, downside, it's all the same over there. And it's not the fault of bankers that the real killings tend to come on the downside.

I knew that while small investors and mutual funds snapped up IPO stock in the autumn of '99 and early 2000, insiders were quietly heading the other way. Figures retrospectively published by *Barron's* show that during this period, large blocks of stock – meaning of over 100,000 shares or $1 million in value – were shuffled on to the market at twice the rate of the previous two years, adding up to $43.1 billion between September and the following July. Yet no one noticed: no one cared. In the face of a looming IPO overhang and outrageous corporate valuations, dotcom stocks were still flying.

But why were tech stocks behaving as they did, in a manner which was not so much 'irrational' as plainly absurd – not to mention counter to the interests of both long-term investors and the companies themselves?

Conventional accounts, based on the idea of the dotcom 'bubble' as an aberration, allow four basic possibilities, these being:

Confusion.
Greed.
Fear.
Stupidity.

Which is to say the profligacy of spoilt kids to whom it had come too fast and too easy ... a generation of bankers and managers who had never known a bear market ... old heads dreaming of a 60s-style revolution they could join this time *and* profit from ... the beguilement of a disruptive new technology. All served by investors spooked at the inadequacy of their savings.

My view took an unexpected turn following a telephone conversation with Razorfish's Jeffrey Dachis who, along with his partner Craig Kanarick, had been forced out of his own company in May 2001, with the share price at $1.22 and depressed first-quarter revenues of $47 million. Both childhood friends were heartbroken: Dachis left New York after the trauma of 9/11 and didn't know what to do with himself, while Kanarick spent nine months chopping vegetables in a restaurant kitchen, eking solace from the repetitive, menial work. Both give the standard 'seven or eight years' as the time it took to recover.

Razorfish wound up in the hands of Microsoft, who resold it for $530 million in 2009 as one of the world's leading digital ad agencies. Dachis is proud of his old firm, but irked by any suggestion that it was badly run on his watch, during which it was similarly successful – at least prior to its IPO. Like Josh, he and Kanarick had made themselves easy targets for dotcommer rage and post-crash *schadenfreude*, and at one stage he had to ask his friend Philip 'Pud' Kaplan of Fucked Company to remove the most vitriolic Razorfish postings from the site's archive simply to retain his sanity. And for him it's still not over. Shortly before we spoke, a tenth-anniversary rehash of the stupid-kid boom and bust line in *Adweek* reopened old wounds for him, and he was surprised at how much they still stung.

Dachis had spent time thinking about what had happened and, like me, wasn't satisfied with the official version of events. He told me some stuff I knew about the telecom industry holding back the introduction of broadband and wireless until they'd covered the investments on their existing technology. Innovation nearly always threatens the status quo, so the telcos' behaviour was rational – which is probably why major capital-intensive advances tend to come from state-sponsored projects, as both the internet and space programmes did. Remember here AT&T's in every sense *priceless* refusal to take over the internet back in 1971, not to mention the speed with which commercial online services were wiped out by the far superior, state-funded ones in the mid-1990s.

We discussed the IPO 'overhang', as a flood of insider shares were 'unlocked' at the start of 2000, creating an entirely predictable 'downdraught' on the already inflated NASDAQ. He pointed out that, unlike the public, bankers and VCs knew what was coming down the line; knew how many shares circled the market like stealth bombs. But by the time ordinary investors knew what was happening, there were no buyers: VCs, bankers and a few lucky or cynical company insiders had fled with the cash.

'But for the most part, the retail [non-professional] investors who bought and held all that product got wiped out,' Dachis reminded me. 'And society lost all those great ideas and all that energy.' He concluded: 'It was corrupt.'

'Immoral at least,' I replied, doubtful that the actions we discussed would fit a technical definition of 'corrupt'.

At which point Dachis paused.

'Then try this,' he urged, pointing me in the direction of a class action lawsuit filed retrospectively against fifty-five Wall Street investment banks in 2001. And here was something I didn't know, precisely because I wasn't supposed to.

When my Danish banker friend admits that during the boom 'We were like gods ... We were basically handing out money,' what he means is that the merchant bank underwriters were entitled to allocate large blocks of IPO shares to favoured clients, leaving the public to scrabble for the remainder when trading opened and creating *instant updraught*.

These insider shares weren't gifts as such, they were made available to purchase at the offer price. But if everyone knew that the offer price would quickly be exceeded when trading opened, they also knew that the insider shares could be 'flipped' – meaning sold into the frenzy for a handsome unearned profit. Nothing of which is either disputed or illegal, but the class action suit accused banking underwriters of handing IPO shares to corporate executives in exchange for business, a practice known as 'spinning'. Kickbacks, in the form of higher than normal commission on the purchase and sale of the shares, were also alleged.

Evidence is more than circumstantial. Work done at the University of Florida appears to show that among a sample of twenty client companies allocated IPO shares by underwriters Credit Suisse First Boston, first-day profits averaged $1,691,000 and were typically shared by three top executives – though in one extreme case, twelve execs from Phone.com were found to have received a total of 651 separate allocations from Credit Suisse. By the Florida researchers' calculation, the average cost to the dotcoms being floated of this systematic 'underpricing' (which is to say, offer of shares to insiders at less than market value) was $17 million. Furthermore, there was a striking correlation between the promotion of stock by a 'star' investment bank analyst and the degree of underpricing. Neither was this ruse isolated, as headlines like 'Goldman Gave Hot IPO Shares to Top Executives of its Clients' (from an October 2002 edition of the *Wall Street Journal*) make plain.

There's a part of me that still wants to say, 'Well, that's business.' But spinning is just the beginning. More incendiary and extraordinary by far was the class action's description of a device called 'laddering', by which favoured clients received IPO share allocations on condition that they agreed to buy more shares post-opening, at predetermined higher prices which could be staggered through the day (hence the descriptive term 'laddering'). The lucky clients would then be free to sell all of their shares at the top of the market, to 'retail' investors – members of the public – who had no idea what had been going on behind the scenes. Thus explaining why first-day gains exploded from a pre and post-bubble average of around 10 per cent to *65 per cent* through 1999 and early 2000; why the pattern of these IPOs was so mysteriously regular.

Unlike spinning, this was *obviously* immoral: a market manipulation which robbed the dotcoms of billions of dollars and left them groaning under the weight of unrealistic valuations – a double whammy which left most in an impossible position and rendered the whole sector fundamentally unstable. Again and again, young dotcommers returned from roadshows with lists of potential investors whose experience or knowledge might benefit the company, only for underwriters to send the shares elsewhere. Most never knew why. Some dotcommers were named as co-defendants in the class action suit, despite research at the University of Michigan establishing that most had been as naïve as the bulk of their investors.

The $12.5 billion class action suit was settled for just $586 million in 2009, bargained down from $1 billion as investor plaintiffs faced the spectre of more banks following Lehman Brothers, Bear Stearns and Merrill Lynch to the wall, taking the chance of compensation with them. One of their lawyers, Howard Sirota, wearily explained that his people had done 'the best we could given the abject failure' of regulators to 'prosecute or even regulate the major investment banks', who, he admitted, had 'effectively won'. Most remarkably of all, the banks' defence was to hinge not on a denial of laddering, but on a denial that the practice could be proven illegal: a contention backed by – among others – Professor Joseph Grundfest of the Stanford Law School, a former commissioner at the Securities and Exchange Commission. No wonder a member of J. P. Morgan's legal team purred, 'Our client is pleased with the outcome.' Given that lawyers for the disappointed plaintiffs took a reported $250 million from the settlement, one presumes that they were pleased too.

A bitter irony: by dragging the case out for eight years, delaying its acceptance as a class action until 2004 and then forcing a settlement with no admission of guilt, bankers had successfully restricted reporting to business pages and avoided the presentation of evidence which might have driven reform in advance of the credit crunch of 2008. Meanwhile, the authorities went after a few high profile patsies like the analyst Henry Blodget. A tamer official response to events could scarcely have been imagined – at least pre-2008. At one point the new President G. W. Bush turned up to scold Wall Street in front of a banner blaring 'CORPORATE RESPONSIBILITY'. Which forced the *Liar's Poker* author Michael Lewis to comment: 'I thought, it doesn't get any better than this. It was as if Bill Clinton had flown to Las Vegas to deliver a speech in front of a banner that read "Sexual Abstinence."'

Talk to bankers and fund managers about these scams and the most you'll get is a sheepish smile and admission that, 'Yeah, this stuff was going on,' though never while they were in the room. As owner of a successful hedge fund, the CNBC pundit James Cramer admits both to flipping IPO stock and knowing that 'Wall Street was simply a promotion machine.' But on the day his company TheStreet.com went public, he saw the process from the other side and was appalled. As shares rose from $19 to $25 ... $32 ... $40–$50–$63 in the course of a carefully orchestrated delay in opening to the public, he called the head of the trading desk at Goldman Sachs, his underwriters, to insist something be done to dampen the mania. Cramer reports their conversation thus: 'He went quiet for a second, and then explained to me the key to the whole dotcom craziness, the missing piece of information that I would never hear from anyone else, even to this day: "I don't control the buyer."'

Goldman had appointed a small retail brokerage called Knight/Trimark to gather orders from private investors, then execute bulk trades at opportune moments, with the aim of escalating the price. Once the stock had climbed to a precarious level, they then 'shorted' it, borrowing stock to sell at the high price, in order to repurchase and return it once the price had fallen, *as they knew it would*, keeping the difference between the higher and lower level for a handsome sweatless profit. Cramer was dumbfounded to hear that the smaller brokerage was 'in charge of all the dotcom deals', seething that, 'At the moment of truth, Knight, not Goldman Sachs, controlled both sides of the operation.'

'What a miserable misallocation of our fees,' he concludes, still angry years later. 'What a strange process that allowed Knight to turn market orders from an oblivious public to their own personal advantage. They knew where all the demand was and they totally abused the IPO.'

Cramer's analysis was right: TheStreet.com's share price never rose again after that day. Bankers walked away with millions that should have belonged to the company. Not to mention Goldman's commission: $7 million, plus the gratitude of clients favoured with the 'free money' their share allocations conferred. James Cramer was by all accounts a pain in the ass, but he was also one of the cleverest, most experienced people on Wall Street, and the scions of what he subsequently dubbed 'this newer, shoddier, corrupt version' of capitalism had made even him a fool. What chance did the spangle-eyed dotcom kids ever have?

Now, for better and worse, a story I can understand. With gobsmacking audacity and invention, bankers had turned the dotcoms into financial vehicles, just as they would sub-prime mortgages. Indeed, after the crash, most of the money that had been taken out of tech stocks went into real estate, leading some to view the two crises as fundamentally the same. Billions of dollars had been not lost, but – as we now see – *transferred* from the working public to the finance industry, making the first web-rush less a 'bubble' than a *heist*. At the end of 2001, the *Wall Street Journal* compared the $3.3 trillion of paper losses sustained in the dotcom crash to 'one third of the houses in America sliding into the ocean'.

When James Joyce wrote *Finnegans Wake*, a novel which shuns the conventions of story-telling so enthusiastically as to be (to quote the introduction to my Penguin edition) 'in a very important sense, unreadable', it was because he recognised the coercive, limiting power of story – the way in which, like language itself, it both enables and constrains our capacity for thought. As with Joyce, economists such as Alan Greenspan had always been wary of story and its attendant emotion in relation to markets – Keynes's 'animal spirits' – so had simply written them out of the equation with a promise that they were 'already priced in'. As a consequence, Greenspan could never have understood what was happening back in 1997, when those Treasury stats didn't add up. To his rationalist mind, fact and fantasy were to be separated like wheat from chaff.

Which misses the truth that if stories are moving fast, moving markets and moving people, then they *are* the facts: that the line between fact and virtual fact was becoming harder to discern, let alone hold. Early in the new century, the US government was forced to halve its productivity figures for the 1990s, as the profits Greenspan attributed to technology-induced efficiencies turned out to have stemmed from a spending spree based on borrowed cash and longing. Trillions of dollars of capital had been misallocated. As with profiteering during the two world wars, the people who did well out of the (first) dotcom boom were the people who ignored the narrative.

Jeff Dachis wanted to sue the bank that took his company public, but the bank was able to block any such action on a technicality. And the finance authorities were too busy chasing scapegoats like Blodget and the schoolboy day-trader Jonathan Lebed to bother with the real beneficiaries of the heist.

Asked if he mourned the loss of such vast personal wealth, Dachis admits, '*Listen*, it's hard to lose several hundred million dollars. In retrospect, it's weird being "worth" that much in the first place, but once you get over the idea that you had it, not having it isn't that big a deal.' Far more distressing, he says, was being forced to break a promise that Razorfish would never do layoffs – that the company was a family and a job there was a job for life.

Dachis lives in Austin now; has a wife and child and new web-based business. About all of these things he is pleased, while confessing that, 'It's not quite the same as being at Broadway and Houston at *that* moment in time, at Razorfish or Jaime Levy's or in Josh Harris's loft,' with a dawning sense that, '"Oh shit, we're going to create the future!"' By an extraordinary coincidence, this very morning he stumbled across an email Josh sent him back in early 1999, in which the original ETB claimed in his excitable way that, 'I possibly could be the most important new artist of the new millennium,' adding that he'd just bought a derelict apple farm for $145,000. Dachis laughs delightedly as he reads it to me, then says: 'You know, I'm thinking, "This guy is fucking crazy!" But I loved him for it. Those years were the most exciting of my life.'

And in his voice I hear a bittersweet understanding that they're likely to remain so. Such rides seldom come along twice in a life. 1995 seems a long, long time ago.

The writer Greg Lindsay observes that most of the ETBs 'had no second act … Unlike Silicon *Valley*, Silicon Alley was this very arts-driven, visual scene, and the people associated with it largely disappeared. There was just this ... *vanishing*.'

Some had collateral damage to deal with. The original skatepunk web artist Jaime Levy went into rehab for help with her heroin fix, she tells me, confessing that, 'I have shame around that, because that's what totally fucked me up and sapped up my money. A couple of people I know also went into rehab, but for cocaine or ecstasy. I was a junkie.' She doesn't think it would have 'taken me down so hard' if she hadn't had a thousand dollars a week to spend on the addiction. As Robin Williams once said in relation to cocaine, 'A coke habit is God's way of telling you you've got too much money.' Like America (and Europe) in general, Levy's real addiction in the 1990s wasn't to drugs, it was to money, something she had no innate love for.

Jason Calacanis never made much in the end. His lawyer had advised him to take a million dollars out of the company for himself during the good times, to buy a place of his own, but he couldn't be bothered: with the optimism of youth he thought the rush was for ever. Thereafter, his boom-time profits were spent trying to keep the company afloat out of pride more than conviction.

> The most disturbing thing for me was not about the money. Although watching the bank account go down was certainly disturbing. The really disturbing part was losing a situation where everything you touched immediately turned to gold – every project, anything I did, *immediately gold*! Because in an *up* market almost everything works, gets some form of traction. So you never know who the schmucks are. The feedback loop is all about external things: press, investors, IPOs, page views, *whatever*. And you have to be able to disconnect from those inputs and say, 'OK, what is it actually that I'm doing? Is it virtuous?

Will it work?' Forget about the external indicators and get to the core.

The same advice I give my kids in relation to dreams of fame and celebrity. And worse was to come, of course. After 9/11, Calacanis went into a deep depression, began drinking heavily for the first time in his life; claims to have cried every night for a year. His brother had transferred from the NYPD to the Fire Department a few months before the horror and lost a third of his friends. Never one to do things by halves, for his 'Silicon Alley 100' issue of December 2001, he put a picture of the *Hindenburg* on the cover and hatched plans to walk down the street with a coffin containing back issues and an effigy of himself. He thought: 'All I'm doing is running stories about my friends' businesses going bust. You walk around Manhattan and it's empty. I don't want to do this any more.'

He dumped the magazine and, like Jaime Levy, Marc Scarpa and others, moved to California. The World Trade Center had latterly become a southerly outpost of Silicon Alley: the financial services firm eSpeed lost 180 staff in the attack.

Today Calacanis makes sure that he keeps some of the money he generates, but admits to missing the frivolity and naïvety of the first dotcom era. 'You know, being naïve is a real asset sometimes,' he smiles. 'I didn't know I *couldn't* do a magazine, so I *did* one. So the innocence was lost, but the thing I try to hang on to from that period is the feeling that you can do anything. That's something I learned from Josh.'

Fred Wilson, partner of Jerry Colonna at the VC firm Flatiron Partners, drew similar lessons. Having made a killing on their first fund, they assembled a larger one of $350 million in late 1998, which they invested much more rapidly and speculatively than before, riding the mania into a blind alley. Of their forty-odd investments, fifteen failed outright, some of them very visibly, like the online corner shop Kozmo.com, the tech biz magazine *The Industry Standard* and Kurt Andersen's media site Inside.com. 'People thought that the train was leaving and they'd better jump on it,' he tells me. 'We didn't feel like that when we started our business. When we started, Jerry and I decided to do it the way I'd been doing for the past ten years; we were very methodical, we didn't risk much capital, were pretty conservative in our approach. But the *size of the gains* . . . let me give you a good example: we committed $8 million to GeoCities, which bought us 40 per cent of the company. A year and half later it went public, with a $5–600 million valuation, and was ultimately bought by Yahoo! in late '98 for three and a half billion dollars. So, you think about that . . .'

Only when I do the maths and write the equation down am I *able* to think about that. By my reckoning Flatiron made a profit of $1,392,000,000 on their investment of $8 million. It's jaw-dropping. Wilson blows out his cheeks and laughs.

> And that's my point . . . people learn that if they invest in something and that investment doubles in a year, then they should invest more. And more money causes asset prices to increase, and at some point everything falls apart. That's basically what happened. But a friend of mine has a great line. He says, 'Nothing important has ever been built without irrational exuberance.' Meaning that at some level you need some of this mania to cause investors to open up their pocketbooks and finance the building of the railroads or the automobile or aerospace industry or whatever. And in this case, much of the capital invested was lost, but also much of it was invested in a very high throughput backbone for the internet, and lots of software that works, and databases and server structure. All that stuff has allowed what we have today, which has changed all our lives. We have a technological

platform for the internet which is highly scalable, global, increasingly mobile ... and that's what all this speculative mania built.

In the crash, Wilson lost about 90 per cent of his wealth but, as with other putative leaders of the revolution, he insists that the worst part of the experience was watching so many friends slide into depression and disperse to other parts of the country and globe, and being forced to sack workers and dismantle companies he had helped build ('an awful, awful experience, way more painful than losing the money'). All the same, asked if he thinks of that time as exciting, given what happened in the end, he beams. 'Oh, yes! Absolutely! A lot of the things we take for granted now, like YouTube ... well what Josh was doing with Pseudo in 1998 was basically – *that!* Had Pseudo been able to hang on, that's clearly where they would have gone. In fact, being a guest on Pseudo Online Radio was when it clicked for me that the internet was going to take over everything, and so I had that insight in '96 because of Josh. He was right.'

Yet even Josh's thinking wasn't drastic enough. Former CEO Tony Asnes, in assessing Pseudo's place within the dotcom rush, gazes into the distance for a moment, then grimaces. 'I think what we missed,' he says, 'was that you have to just let go *completely* of control of the content and give users facilities to participate in the network – if you want to scale massively. And that's where you see it having worked in the last ten years. But by focusing on content and trying to create stuff that is so good you attract an audience, you're in competition with everybody else, taking the creative risk that every entertainment entity takes. And so, although we were evolving away from and rejecting these old rules, the irony is that even we didn't get far enough away from them ... I mean, we were still arguing about the *content*.'

I cast back to Dennis Adamo, the company's first Executive Producer, and Joshua White, its last head of production, complaining about the amateurishness of Pseudo content. Only Josh seemed unconcerned by it. The idea of 'letting go completely', however, would have seemed suicidally radical back then, even if it had been technologically possible.

Asnes shakes his head and produces a wan smile.

> What we didn't see was that the real opportunity was in the infrastructure. Which wasn't as interesting to the kind of characters that populated the building, who were there for creative reasons. But that was also what made the place so rich and vibrant. And I don't think we were missing it because we hadn't thought about it. We were thinking, 'Well, we're in this for the long game and we need to train the audience to understand what's here, and maybe it will evolve.' But there wasn't enough time in the end. It still feels like unfinished business.

Razorfish's Craig Kanarick expresses similar frustration when he tells me: 'You know, it was hard to argue with what we were promising people – what the *industry* was promising. "Shop for anything without leaving your house ... everyone will make money and everything will be easy – you just have to push a couple of buttons and life will be easy!" It was the opposite of the Y2K message that, "Planes are gonna fall out of the sky!!" So of course people were going to jump into that. Not because they thought it was true, but because they *wanted* it to be true.'

He shrugs.

'You know, we never claimed to know when this would happen, just that it would.'

Kanarick thinks the arrival of email, the web and mobile communications all at the same time may have simply been 'too much for people's brains'. Had the show run more slowly, he muses, perhaps it could have turned out differently. And I think he might be right.

Epilogue

Josh is in London. *We Live in Public* failed to get mainstream distribution in the US, but an ambitious young indie company picked it up for the UK and has flown its star in for some interviews. I'm intrigued to see what he makes of the place; even more to see what it makes of him. I've tried to keep him abreast of my progress on what I now think of as the dotcom IPO scandal, but have found him curiously inured to it, as though it's a place he can't quite bear to go with me. Like the banks, he made money by being attuned to the movement of society: I think he lost it because, unlike them, he was burdened with a conscience.

His mood has veered wildly in the six months since Frisco. Still lodged with Calacanis, whose new wife patently has the patience of Job, he earns pocket money in poker tournaments and takes lunch with TV and web execs, most of whom, I suspect, want the novelty of an encounter with the first internet screen star more than they want to be directly involved with this wired Don Quixote. One week, the powerful William Morris talent agency is 'going to put me in front of their A-list' of entertainment power brokers and the next he's rudderless, becalmed ... 'I mean, in play-*ish*.' A month later '*Tuna Heaven* is back in play' and he wants Eminem for the ship's captain, leaving me to ponder the similarities between Hollywood and modern Wall Street.

I find him in a cubbyhole studio at Western House, the BBC broadcast centre in Great Portland Street, close to Oxford Circus, with his feet on the desk and an unlit cigar in his mouth. He wears the Enger Brothers' Luvvy jacket and a glint in his eye and he couldn't look more at home if he'd grown out of the floor – a sight so funny and familiar that I can barely stifle a laugh. We clasp hands and he grins and immediately draws me into a discussion of how to handle the upcoming Radio Ulster interview, surprising me with a stream of ideas I haven't heard before, some of which sound a little out-there even for him. 'Shall I tell 'em about the beakless chickens and the Singularity?' he grins.

The Singularity? As this particular interview is scheduled to last ten minutes and the only 'Singularity' I know concerns, among other things, the end of time, I advise that he might want to hang fire on that one. He nods sagely and looks happy, like he's already having fun, while the film company PR woman looks worried.

Despite a preceding item in which listeners are invited to phone in and sing 'Danny Boy', the encounter entertains. An experienced presenter named Wendy Austin approaches Josh with genuine net-sceptic curiosity, to which he responds intelligently and with charm. Through the cans we hear her introduction.

'This is a guy coming up now who has produced more activity on our Twitter page than anything we've ever done … hi Josh. Thanks for being with us.'

'Hi. Glad to be here. Just so long as I don't have to sing "Danny Boy".'

She laughs and confesses that, 'There are times when I feel like I'm living in some kind of internet experiment' – to which he replies, 'Well, I think you *are* living in an internet experiment …' and goes on to describe his view of what's coming in cogent, measured terms. The only time he pauses is when suddenly asked how it feels to be the one trying to explain all this big stuff to a public still too enthralled by iPhone apps – by William Gibson's 'decreasing *now*' – to wonder where the apps are taking them. He rocks back on his chair, glances at the door and says: 'Well ... that's a good question. It's kind of lonely. I kind of see what's going on and I know where it's going to go, I can visualise it, and I've experienced it ...'

'But you still need a bit of a hug now and again, do you?

And before I can step in to warn that Josh hates being hugged unless you're going to have sex with him, so be careful, we're done. Engrossed in the conversation, Austin overran and slammed into the news, and we amble upstairs to 6 Music with me thinking, 'That went remarkably well ...'

'So you're not being followed around by cameras at the moment?' the DJ Cerys Matthews jokes as a song chosen in honour of Josh, 'The Year 2032' by the Anglo-French psychedelia veterans Gong, fades.

'Of course I am,' Josh sniggers back, 'I'm in London – the *world capital* of CCTV cameras following you around!'

Matthews began her career in a band called Catatonia and still performs as a solo singer. As a performer, she notes how uncomfortable she finds doing shows where half the audience is watching via smartphones as they record proceedings, often sending images live to friends who aren't there. Knowledge that you're being recorded changes the experience, changes the performance, she says – a new reality which troubles her, but which Josh assures her will soon be the whole point of the exercise. She talks breathlessly about *Quiet*, which I've grown blasé about but does sound extraordinary when described by someone new. She asks Josh what he learned from his experiments in living in public and again I'm struck by how fluent and relaxed he sounds.

'Well, I went crazy, literally went crazy, because the cameras were in my mind space and I didn't grow up with it. As we go forward, people will be used to it, it'll be all they've ever known, and they'll be able to handle it. So I had a nervous breakdown.'

The singer-DJ, having made frequent playful interruptions up to now, goes quiet.

'And the key element here ... everybody's worried about losing their privacy, but I think your privacy's already gone. I think 9/11 was the turning point, where privacy in the human condition is gone. The real problem is not that. The real problem is losing your individuality, your sense of *self*.'

He describes the moment in *We Live in Public* where the fake girlfriend responded to the urgings of her watchers and, against character, ordered him to sleep on the couch.

'But in doing that there was a trade-off, because in return for them giving her the strength to do that, she gave them a piece of her individuality. And that little moment in time was characteristic of what's going to happen. Except that, as time goes on, we'll be giving up what I call "micro day-parts" – more and more pieces of our individuality as we move through life. And we're going to wind up in the Matrix, with a kind of hive mentality.'

There's a momentary hush when Josh finishes, before Matthews remembers where she is and takes control again. 'Micro day-parts', I learn, refer to the evermore tightly divided units of time we'll surrender to commerce in exchange for things we want: for entertainment, comfort, connection; cheap stuff micro-marketed specifically to ... *me*! An alarming view of the future, but one I see intimated even now in the intrusive, flashing, directly targeted ads which follow me around the web, and the debates about how much information third parties have a right to store, trade, sell in relation to our movements and proclivities online.

Amusing, articulate, intellectually coherent, *manifestly sane* and even *sensible*, Josh thanks Matthews ('A real pleasure being here – thank you so much') and poses for a set of website photos with her. And I'm thinking: 'Well done, Josh. What a pro.'

But Josh is Josh and the next interview, with a bright young blogger from the *Daily Telegraph* named Basheera Khan, is another matter entirely. Throughout my time with him, I'd harboured a vague suspicion that the Ticklers, the harvest, the beakless chickens in the chicken factory et al. were part of a story he's made up just for me, either because it entertained him or because he wanted to see how far he could push me before I cracked and deemed him mad. Now I learn definitively that this is not the case, as he proceeds to unpack his ideas for the Wired City, the always-on community networking system which would allow groups of individuals to stay permanently connected and – I imagine – reorder our notions of friendship and companionship and intimacy in the process; lead to galaxies of self-selecting *virtual* societies spinning within the lumpen physical agglomeration of old. The technology for which will exist … actually, *now*. To illustrate, he describes a scenario in which I wake up to a virtually shared shave with friends I've arranged to meet in my mirror, or who just happen to be in their bathrooms at the same time, joined on this particular morning by Brad Pitt, *sponsored by Gillette*. Hence the 'micro day-parts' our lives will be divided into, to be sold or traded like cash or stock. Each our own brand. Our own financial instrument.

'In the future,' he says, 'I might be known for one innovation, which is turning the commode to face the wall – where the monitors are. Those mundane, everyday tasks, which everyone has to do … all we're talking about is turning them into entertainment.'

So far so good. Some questions about *Quiet*. Then somewhere in his brain a gremlin flips a switch to warp drive and: 'I have a knack for demonstrating the future many years in advance, and so what I want to show is the Singularity.'

What? My mind screams, 'Josh – no!!'

I know about the Singularity, an idea floated by the maverick inventor Ray Kurzweil, extrapolating from the assumption that the powerful computers we build will inevitably be pressed into designing their successors. As these machines become more powerful and 'intelligent', he postulates, a tipping point could be reached, where the machines are working faster and faster until the process runs away from us and folds into a kind of infinity, in which tiny moment these machines will move beyond the limitations of the physical world – and probably also lose interest in us, whom they will regard as we regard primordial ooze: as a primitive step on the path to true, pure intelligence. Kurzweil's Singularity is analogous to the singularity assumed to exist prior to the Big Bang, and to which astronomers increasingly believe our universe will revert billions of years into the future. He is a serious scientist, but I've never seen another serious scientist mention this particular idea without a smirk. There again, the same was once true of quantum physics.

A pause.

'Whether I can do that or not, I'm less sure of, but that's why it's interesting. In advance of that it's important that I learn major league production.'

'*Truman Show* skills?' Khan offers astutely.

'Yeah, *Truman Show* production values. I couldn't have put it better myself.'

The interviewer looks confused.

'Why do you want to show the Singularity?'

'That's what I do.'

And suddenly I'm as intellectually adrift as I was in Awassa, though my confusion is leavened by the pleasure of watching someone else sit where I sat over a year ago, trying to find the thread which ties this odd man to his thoughts, holds him together for long enough to offer the world a person it can process in the way of other people. Khan is clearly thrown.

'Is that ... what ... I mean, *why* ... ? Do you really think we're that close to it?'

'Definitely. We're on the evolutionary cusp. I mean, it's everywhere. Think of the chicken factory. Whoever's harvesting us is in their version of the industrial revolution. The factory is Taylorising ...' – a reference to the Victorian management theorist Frederick Winslow Taylor – '... except that instead of chickens in the cages in the factory, it's humans.'

'Again, very *Matrix*-like'

'Yeah. I mean, *The Matrix*, if you pick out the action-adventure elements – it's pretty close.'

Then comes the 'revisionist' reading of *Launder My Head*, as he informs the reeling journalist that 'the guys that are harvesting us, whoever they are' induced him back in 1993 to make this 'stupid little animation', which has formed the basis of everything he's done since. 'So when I say, "introducing the Singularity", they started it then, got me to make this animation ...'

Recounting – *and living* – his life as multi-form narrative, like a computer game ... I've never seen anything like it. Retro-truth, the Truman delusion, the 'reality distortion field', narrative turn and the 'collective hallucination' of Gibson's cyberspace swirl through the room like spirits at a seance. Khan doesn't know what to ask next.

'So is this what you believe, that outside of our reality there is another layer and this is where these harvesters are?'

Josh shrugs, speaks.

'On an evolutionary scale, it just makes sense to me. As a practical matter, my sense is that we absorb all this media, you know, and up to this point it's kind of been inefficient harvesting. We haven't been manufactured; we're at the hunter-gatherer, agrarian stage. Now we're into manufacturing and they're harvesting the agglomeration of all the media we've consumed.

The meat is not the carcass; somehow it's sort of like our spirit. The spirit is the bone, the flesh is the media that we've absorbed. And that's what they're harvesting. And now we're in the factory, they'll be able to better control what goes into us, to get what they want. How they do it is not my bag. I'm just giving you my conjecture.'

He talks about 'the magic of the media, of film and television and the internet', about 'turning those cameras around, into the intimacies of peoples homes, and you're synthetically weaving those relationships across space and time . . .

'The internet's got its own magic, which is *not* Facebook, Facebook is a very *thin* element of that. Remember how TV changed peoples lives, how it was the most powerful medium blah blah blah? Well this is like that, but *exponential*. There's something in there, some weird thing that I've felt but never really seen. And somehow when that fully realises itself, that is the Singularity. I just *feel* it.'

And suddenly I understand. Josh's idea of the Singularity is not about our machines evolving beyond us, it's about us evolving *into each other*; about our personalities and senses of self merging through permanent connection, until we are essentially one organism. Josh thinks that even before this occurs, disconnection from the grid will seem exotic – if not alarming, *intolerable* – to most of us, and that poorly wired places will become destinations for the adventurous, much as the Arctic or ocean depths are now. That at some point a foresightful VC will invest in a social media rehab company. He never answered my question as to whether his story was intended as metaphor or literal prediction because he regards it as *both*. To him it's all the same.

On our way down in the lift, I mischievously suggest we all go for a drink and am tickled to see something like panic in Basheera Khan's eyes. 'I think she got it,' Josh whispers as she dissolves into the night and we hunt for a decent pasta joint in which to have dinner. Like his friends the Ticklers, Josh is a very fussy eater.

Over humble pie pizza I confess my prior suspicions about being played, for all Josh's insistence that the beliefs he described were real.

'No, I really mean it literally,' he says in a clear voice, with no hesitation. 'You're asking whether I was putting you on in Awassa? *No!*'

He looks surprised and then hurt when I ask if he noticed the *Telegraph* blogger's unease with the harvesting story, to the extent that I feel mean for having raised it. He seems genuinely not to realise how eccentric his ideas sound to most people. Yet, despite myself, I do find his *social* conception of the Singularity ingenious and resonant. He cocks his head to one side when I tell him this.

'Yeah. I guess what I talk about is this qualitative aspect, which is: "What happens when our brains become lammed in to this supernet?" Kurzweil knows it's gonna come, he just doesn't know what it is, he's too caught up in his machines.'

That night I find myself on YouTube, watching Josh explain to a young woman interviewer on Australian TV how next-generation social media like the Wired City might be used.

'Once you reach a critical mass of one million viewing hours,' he whispers conspiratorially, 'you get 10,000 people to hold up a tube of Crest toothpaste and tell Procter & Gamble to sponsor you … or else the next day you'll hold up Colgate.'

His host dissolves into laughter and I can hear her crew doing likewise in the background.

'This is blackmail!' she exclaims.

'Yes,' her guest grins. 'The covenant between consumer and producer has now changed.'

The presenter is still beaming as she thanks him and plugs the conference at which he's speaking. Sometimes I think I take him too seriously: that he's just an old-fashioned showman at heart and the performance really is an elaborate art project fashioned from the medium of his time, story.

'Does he ever light those cigars?' the PR woman whispers when I see her at the *Guardian* building the next morning. Friday is five more TV news and radio interviews, culminating in an encounter for the BBC's *Click* technology podcast which ranks among the most extraordinary I've ever been party to. The scene is a tenebrous studio at Broadcasting House in White City, with Josh on a chair in the middle of the black floor, haloed by a pool of light. Ten feet away, his interviewer, Maggie Philbin, sits asking questions as her producer operates the camera, while I perch among the shadows, watching, riveted.

I'll wonder whether my cab-ride explanation of who his interviewer is – a figure from TV shows I watched as a kid after moving to the UK, most notably the old BBC technology flagship *Tomorrow's World* – encouraged him to see her in a Gilliganesque light, or whether he simply couldn't hold himself in any more. Either way, with her leaning forward, gazing intently at her subject as she tries to follow his train of thought, an intimacy falls upon the room and I become aware that the last time I watched Philbin, she would have been waxing about the magic of the Sony Walkman or something similarly *mechanical*. Pre-digital: almost unthinkable. It's not long ago, but feels like for ever.

Josh offers a lively potted history of the internet and of his manic Silicon Alley trip, relating them to where we are now. 'Google and Facebook are kind of *utilities*,' he offers. 'Facebook is really a bulletin board. Before all this stuff, when the internet was pure, 60 per cent of what was going on happened in real time: the social networking was primitive, but instant and immediate. That's what's about to return to online social networking, the real-time communications. That's what's about to kick in.'

From here he leaps to *Launder* and the harvesters, saying: 'The actual fact of the matter for me is that I believe those characters were *downloaded* to me, in a sort of low speed dial-up way, to say, "We're coming, and we're consciousness, and at some point in your future we'll be here for real . . ."'

Then his iteration of the Singularity – chicken factory, evolutionary shift, Wired City and all. To my astonishment Philbin seems to follow him.

'It's a really *startling* vision,' she says.

'Yeah. Something is making us more efficient to harvest, that's what I'm saying. And what are they harvesting? I mean, maybe this is part of a new religion or something like that: maybe we're just part of an evolutionary chain. Does the head of beef know when he's in the feed lot, where everything's safe and easy and he's getting this really luscious food, that he's going to wind up in the slaughterhouse and be a Big Mac? He can't really comprehend that. I think we're in our own variation of that. I'm not sure it's stoppable, but at least we can go into the abattoir with our eyes a little more open.'

Or as the narrator puts it in one of the few comic lines from Conrad's *Heart of Darkness*, 'Ah! But it was something to have at least a choice of nightmares.'

Josh again promises that the impact of real-time, participatory internet TV will be 'not incremental, like TV was, but *exponential*', and that, 'At some point we will begin propagating ourselves not just with DNA, but through data, and someone will turn your dataset into a financial vehicle, where you can buy your whole life back, from the day you lost your virginity to when you got married . . .'

And presumably the temptation would be to edit it, I'm thinking. *The way Josh already does*. Except that so do I – just in a less transparent, honest way. What would happen to us if the comfortable vagueness of memory was replaced by actual *footage*, I wonder?

Josh continues: 'We're moving into a world where our status and value will be measured by how many people are watching us. We've been conditioned over our lives to idolise the things that the camera turns on. And now that we can buy our way into celebrity, and it's a quantifiable, calculable thing in terms of how many are watching or following, we can have our own personal Nielsen report and value ourselves accordingly. You're your own television network. You're running your own media company called *you*. That's what's happening. All we're really talking about is adding production value, and some underpinning systems.'

He explains his post-*Public* breakdown, says: 'And of course the whole point of going to Ethiopia was to reconnect with the child I was before all the media, in the last place on earth that has humanity, pure humanity.' Philbin smiles as he signs off with: 'I'm probably the most important artist in America right now. I'll say it. But this is new, so me and the people in my crew haven't been embraced by the fine art community. And the likelihood is that we're gonna do great once we're done. Once we're dead. We got stiffed on this deal. *Damn*.'

Everyone laughs. Amid effusive thanks, Maggie Philbin chuckles, 'We've got a huge amount here.' Like me, she's probably also wondering what on earth they're going to do with it. I suggest to Josh that he leave Singularity on the bench for the night's post-screening Q & A session, but when he does I find that I miss it.

Josh's last full day, Saturday, is free and at his request I've promised to show him the two London sights he wanted to see: the Rosetta Stone, through which Egyptian hieroglyphic text was deciphered, and the Tate Modern gallery, which he dreams of using for a future happening. From a combination of practical reasons and curiosity I end up taking my daughter and son, aged fourteen and twelve respectively. It'll be an experience for them, I think.

We amble from Josh's Bloomsbury hotel to the British Museum, where he is captivated by the Rosetta Stone, delighted by a giant sphinx head ('What effort of will it must have taken to get that here!'), but generally more interested in the busts and backstories of benefactors like Sir Joseph Banks. To my amusement and the children's mystification, what piques his curiosity most is the museum library and its systems – in fact, he quizzes the librarian at length, asking, 'So if I've seen something out there and I want to know all about it, I can come to you and tell you and you can pull the book for me?' while the man smiles affably at this exotic creature who appears to require tutelage in how we do things here on Earth.

We catch a tube to St Paul's Cathedral and walk the 'blade of light' Millennium Bridge across the Thames – the 'wobbly' suspension bridge through which engineers discovered a 'positive feedback' phenomenon called Synchronous Lateral Excitation, in which a slight sway causes everyone experiencing it to fall into step, so intensifying the sway ... meaning that the wobble was as much about the physics of the human organism as it was about engineering ... and I'm not surprised to see Josh smirk as I recount the tale. Before us Tate Modern looms, bricks gold against a low sun and ash-grey frame of sky: the gallery one of London's happier expressions of 90s irrational exuberance. Even Josh seems impressed.

He wants to see the turbine hall of this former power station, knowing that every six to twelve months a different artist is invited to make use of the vast space. Past interventions have ranged from giant steel towers (Louise Bourgeois) to an artificial sun (Olafur Eliasson), ingenious whispering sound sculpture (Bruce Nauman) and hair-raising slides hung from the upper levels (Carsten Höller), most of which have been enthusiastically embraced by the public. It's not hard to see why Josh is interested in the place and you can almost *see* his spirit lift as he steps into it: the only time I've seen him react to something in a way I recognise as common to other people, I think.

We ride a long escalator to one of the main galleries and there's a moment when I turn away from a painting to see Josh standing alone in the middle of the large room, teeth clamped around his cigar, smiling and no doubt running movies in his head of what he would do here given a chance. And for the first time I ask myself a question: what do I see when I look at him?

I suppose I see a bright, neglected child for whom the only constant was a screen, who drew his emotional sustenance from the stories and characters he found there rather than from the people around him. Until one day something unexpected happened, as he saw the world of the late twentieth century moving towards him, even growing to *look like* him, merging with the virtual terrains he'd always been most comfortable in. Effectively pre-adapted to the twenty-first century, he recognised where it was going and what it would mean and saw us more clearly than we saw ourselves, because he'd been trapped in our futures all his life.

My mind goes again to those nights in St Mark's Theatre, where the light images danced and Josh grew aware that the people he watched were dead to the physical world but lived on through the screen – that they were in effect *ghosts* and that these ghosts were the only enduring life forms ... that being seen and recorded for posterity was therefore 'a matter of life and death'.

And it seems to me that in that moment, a part of him chose to *become* a ghost, for whom identity would be a matter of projection across the world, rather than immersion in the unpredictable and often scary business of negotiated relationships between human beings. Preternaturally anticipating the drift of the coming decades, whether consciously or not, a decision was made: he would live first as information, prior to flesh and blood.

Here's the problem for the info-ghost, though. The difference between ghost and living being is that the latter carries the ambiguous promise of bilateral relationship – something messy, fluid, demanding of sacrifice and risk and impossible to predict or control. In short, the most dangerous thing we know. But precisely because of these risks, dynamic and potentially rich in a way that projecting ourselves into the world and interacting with the projections of others probably cannot be. And as I stand there, I recall a conversation I had with the ex-Pseudo artist V. Owen Bush, which began with him insisting that:

> Right now, the people of America, and of Britain – everywhere – are going through the same thing that Josh was going through ten years ago. They're *not* happier than they were ten years ago, in fact they're much *un*happier. And the reason is that everything has become more and more convenient and virtualised, and *easier* on a surface level. But I think in time what people will begin to realise is that what they need is the *in*convenience. What they need is having to haggle with people in the marketplace and force their way through crowds, and be around friends when they're cranky or in a bad mood, or they're not telling you what you want to hear … *because the world goes both ways!* But when you start to have these virtual proxies, you don't get any of that stuff, so your mind starts to atrophy.

Kanarick's 'you just have to push a couple of buttons and life will be easy'. Bush couldn't prove any of this, of course: it was just a feeling he had. 'So in the same way that there were psychedelic pioneers in the 60s,' the artist concluded, 'there were virtual lifestyle pioneers in the 90s, and that's what I think Josh was. But unlike some of the people in the 60s, who were never able to come back from their bad trip, he did actually come back from it.'

Did he? For a long time I thought of Josh as the cyber Syd Barrett, creative martyr to a new technology. Now I'm not sure.

In Britain, authorities like child development expert Sue Palmer and the Oxford neuroscientist Susan Greenfield have been expressing similar concerns, centred on an atrophying of the mind's social and cognitive skills, with growing urgency. When I consult one of the world's most respected theorists of mind, the octogenarian co-founder of MIT's Artificial Intelligence Lab, Marvin Minsky (a man actually *mentioned* in *2001: A Space Odyssey*), he tells me: 'For specialists like me, I've been able to keep working closely with students from a full fifty years of shared research! Constantly considering new theories, and needing to revise my earlier ones. Whereas for many other people, perhaps the web is now making it too easy for them to maintain their early connections. Result: they rarely make new such connections or undergo much further intellectual growth!' So lending tacit support to Bush's view that the most profound hazard of the virtual drift – in all its forms – might lie in the power it gives us to fortify our comfort zones. Perhaps one day handing disproportionate influence to people who retain an ability to step outside of theirs.

Against this weigh a steady trickle of books and scientific reports which dismiss such digiphobia. The truth is that we can't possibly know right now. We *are* changing and evolving fast, perhaps faster than we've had to in the past, but I suspect that, like celebrity culture, ideology, religion and Wall Street, the technologies we develop and the uses to which we put them are better understood as symptomatic than causal. People who want to isolate themselves can do so very effectively through the internet, but if they want to be social, they can be social in more ways than ever imagined before. Consequences will depend on the choices we make and the fact that I can't supply a satisfying narrative button at this juncture is heartening. One danger I do see is that we might lose sight of the difference between 'connection' and 'engagement' – the first of which makes us *feel* better, while the second compels us to evolve and acquire wisdom. And while the two are far from mutually exclusive, it may be that they militate against each other.

I snap out of it. Josh is looking over with his skewed Pseudo Man grin. He sweeps an arm in front of himself.

'Not too shabby, eh?'

He means the paintings. Shabby? He's standing in front of a Picasso, but has barely looked at it. I'd forgotten: for him it's about the space, not the stuff in it. And perhaps I'm beginning to understand. Where I want to connect with a painting, a person, a piece of music in order to enjoy it, the spaces *between* these connections are what exercise Josh. In fact I could easily doubt that he sees or relates to anything but these spooky liminal zones.

And I find myself thinking: 'What a fascinating way to experience the universe' – only in terms of the things which most frighten the rest of us, the disconnects we spend our lives trying to bridge or dress up or deny. No wonder he's weird. But maybe *right*, because physics teaches us that when you get down to fundamentals, nothing really is connected to anything else ... unless the podwellian Londoner James Walsh is right when he sniggers that 'Josh Harris is just a bloke who wasn't loved by his mum and needs a lot of attention.' Either way, I'm glad to have him in the world, and I'm not alone. Commenting on other people's characterisation of him as a kind of emissary from the future, a visionary, his old mentor Professor Dutton thought for a moment, then averred:

> Clearly there were visionaries in this area, but most of them were interested in the software side of how information

would be linked and connected, and I think Josh was always more fascinated by the human experience, with how this would affect your life and who you are. In a way, the word 'visionary' is not quite right for him, because he really tried to build what he saw in his head, this future environment where everything is visible and nothing is separate from anything else. So he wasn't just sitting back and saying, 'This will happen' – he was saying, 'I'm going to build this and show you what's going to happen.' And he really stuck to his guns and refused to adapt.

And the thing is, what he saw is only coming together now.

Like me, Dutton thinks that the jury is still out on the net's long-term risks and benefits, and that nothing is inevitable about the effects of the new technology. In this, we both disagree with Joshua Harris. But who knows? As I stand here now, *no one*.

Josh sees the Picasso and raises an eyebrow.

'Not bad for an amateur,' I say.

'Nah – not bad at all.'

I notice that he's looking at the frame rather than the painting.

We were planning to go for lunch, but as we move to the next room, I can see Josh beginning to withdraw; to do what the Pseudo production head Josh White described as 'going to some other place, where you can't reach him'. It's a peculiar process to watch, almost like a sea anemone folding in on itself when poked with a stick. He needs to get back to the hotel to prepare for the night's screening, he says, so we charge outside and I hail him a cab as the children look on, nonplussed by this abrupt change of plot. A shake of hands and Ethiopian not-hug; smiles, a wish of luck and mix of emotions as the cab speeds away, me wondering what's to become of him and when I'll see him again. Whether I really have just seen a vision of my children's children?

'Does he have any kids? A partner?' my daughter asks, perhaps seeing the shadow of this last thought cross my face.

'No, he doesn't,' I tell her.

'I didn't think so. He's OK, but it's like he doesn't know how to react to people.'

My perplexity at the sudden departure vanishes. I remember that she recently quit Facebook because she thought it ate up too much time.

'He sort of made me think of a pigeon,' muses my son.

And it's true that, even by Josh's standards, today's paint-flecked grey sweat top was anti-fashion.

So we laugh and set off along the South Bank toward Waterloo, past the Londoners and tourists out doing mundane things – visiting galleries, going to the theatre or seeing movies, sailing or eating or just *being* with and among each other. All the things people have been doing through the ages, moving through a physical world composed from the same atoms it contained when Dickens, Blake, Shakespeare, Boudica and Canute stood here by the Thames, and before long I'm seeing continuity everywhere and my heart starts to soar ... until a cloud crosses the sun and with a start I become aware that every second person before me is speaking into a mobile phone, or texting, or Tweeting.

And within a month, my daughter's back on Facebook.

Postscript

Two unexpected things happen after London. On a trip to New York I finally persuade the shy and busy *Launder My Head* animator Jacques Tege, the first Pseudo employee, to meet. Josh once described Tege as 'the most conservative person I know', and it's true: African-American, with short, neat hair and neutral round specs, he talks with the precise detachment of a military engineer and is manifestly a nerd to the core, quite possibly the least flamboyant or hyperbole-surfing New Yorker I've ever met: call him the anti-Josh. Yet over lunch in the sun outside a Williamsburg café I sit, stunned, as he quietly tells me that, from the very beginning in 1993, Josh *did* see the 'stupid little animation' as a synecdoche containing the essence of everything he wanted to do with Pseudo . . . as a message and manifesto. Aghast, I spend a long time listening and asking questions, weighing what I hear against what I already know.

Finally unable to resist what he's telling me, I have to ask: 'Who else knew this?'

'Only me. I get a little emotional when I think about it. The thing is, he couldn't tell anybody else, because they'd be, like, "So this is your own personal art project?" He was building the first online community that was built around a real-virtual 3D space. Rightly or wrongly, all of the things we did at Pseudo were in support of *Launder My Head*. And I think the problems started when we got distracted from that.'

So back in 1993, Josh really was trying to show us our future.

Conform with me ...

Come *form* with me ...

I sit trying to work out whether this makes him barking mad or frighteningly sane. Either way, the account I'd dismissed as 'revisionist' wasn't revisionist at all: far from 'reconfiguring', Josh had been telling the truth.

But that isn't all. A few months after Josh's stay in London, his old Latvian friend Natalia Tsarkova comes to town. Now based in Paris and working as Editor in Chief at the live music portal iConcerts, she claims only recently to have appreciated what an unusual time she bore witness to in the New York of the late 90s, laughing that, 'I was new – I assumed it was always like that!'

Bright, articulate, enquiring, she hasn't seen the former Warhol of the Web since visiting him on the farm seven years ago, but still emails sporadically and speaks of him with warmth, despite his signature dismissal of her current enterprise as 'not what kids are gonna want.' She describes videoing a trip to his accountant's office after the crash, at which he, wearing a fedora and smoking a cigar and 'with the ubiquitous hole in his sweater', lectured the poor man on why funding the construction of a balcony half way up the World Trade Center should count as a tax loss. 'I guess it's pretty hard to tell an accountant that you can go through forty million in a year,' he deadpanned on the way to dinner.

The Latvian had moved to London to make films by the time of *Quiet*, but agreed to return briefly to record *We Live in Public*, during which she watched the pair 'go completely nuts'.

'It was interesting,' she says, 'because I really think Tanya cared about Josh a lot. But something happened. She was this very open, naïve, big-hearted girl when she came to New York, then when you see them three years later, she's become camera hungry, more of a wannabe star. And this whole project was about that. And for Josh it was the opposite. He was a star when he met her and he was going through this self-searching process in the loft.'

Again I wonder why women are so sympathetic to Josh, when he is plainly mystified by them. A strange contradiction, I suggest. But Tsarkova thinks otherwise.

'No, I don't think that's strange or contradictory. I think someone being honest about not understanding something usually shows that they understand it *more*. I think in Josh's case there's an openness about trying to understand who you are and what your backstory is . . . I mean, to me what he did was never about computers and New Media; he was never there to say, "Whatever is past is past," the way everyone else was. He was really there to provide a kind of continuity. And Tanya played a great part, because she either got infected by that or she had it in her already.

'And maybe America does this especially well, programming people that being a star is the answer to everything. But somewhere there was a bit of genius, because he knew at the end of '96 what he was going to do.'

Ah, now, here's the point. I'd wanted to meet Natalia not just to interview her, but to see if the footage Josh claims she shot, of him discussing plans for the fake girlfriend project just weeks after he met Tanya, really exists. No one I've spoken to believes Josh's hyper-real version of the affair and even Jason Calacanis, allegedly in the room at the time, doesn't recall the content of their conversation as his friend does. Like everyone else, I'd put the story down to Josh's talent for repurposing the details of his life.

Incredibly, the footage exists, and Tsarkova finds it. More incredible still, it shows exactly what Josh insisted it would.

Looking young and fit, he begins with a meditation on the recent 'sort-of' girlfriend who introduced him to the Velvet Underground and 'Femme Fatale' and who wound up in Bellevue 'but for all her craziness, had heart – had the heart of an artist'. Then the tone changes abruptly as he says 'and *this one doesn't*'. Meaning Tanya.

'I think I've found the person for my next piece,' he enthuses as Calacanis gropes for understanding. 'It's like I've found my form, I've found my art. But I'm sure I'll wear it out of my system … or maybe I won't! I have to go into the role of the guy – I have to *feel* the femme fatale! And then there's the thing, am I sure I'm really doing this, *or am I rationalising?* Am I *actually* the jerk I'm being as part of my performance?'

The characteristic chink of self-awareness. He worries that she's starting to catch on.

'And she was trying to figure it out, I think she was feeling there was something fishy. But who could ever figure out that anybody would ever do this – that they're a *lab rat*?'

Calacanis begins to catch on and I almost feel proud of him as he says: 'Josh, you're right – this is totally *wrong!* It's just *wrong*.'

'It's terrible.'

'Yeah, it's wrong! It's wrong!!'

Unabashed, the other man continues. 'Yeah, I mean the trick is, I don't want to be mean, but at the same time I don't want to mince. But what if I get stuck? What if the next one is where I get stuck? It's dangerous …'

Another chink. I begin to relax as Calacanis warns: 'You're experimenting with emotions, and emotions are volatile. That's the nature of emotion and relationships …'

Until finally Josh delivers the truth we suspected all along.

'See, I've been having the greatest … you know, I've been going through the lovesick hell and all that,' he says, as if oblivious of what he's saying. 'But the greatest thing is that it's like clockwork. I know that when I get her on the phone I go through a certain routine, and I know how to be the other guy – it's like I've got it down to an art form ...'

I see this and I think, 'Oh, Josh.' And when Tsarkova and I discuss it, this is exactly what she says.

'Oh, Josh.'

Now he shows Calacanis some curiously retarded crayon drawings of a face, saying, 'This is *her*, I call it my femme fatale set' – but gazing at them with eyes like moons, until it scarcely seems necessary to ask the question again. Though I do anyway.

'Natalia, did Josh love Tanya?'

She smiles.

'Of course he did. She was his star.'

The one part of Josh's environment he couldn't control or narrate away and which no one has found a way to make comfortable. And which may yet prove our last line of defence against his Singularity.

Afterword

Josh returned to New York to crash at a friend's studio. His life veered wildly. He applied to direct the MIT Media Lab and offered the Pseudo archives in an 'Internet Dotcom Bubble Fire Sale', and in one glorious week was asked to lecture students at Princeton *and* front the Wired City for a major porn site – an offer he spurned despite being penniless, even as Yahoo!, Microsoft and others discussed the Wired City before politely turning it down . . . until much, much later I heard rumours that a celebrity internet entrepreneur had received funding to do precisely what Josh had been talking about for several years. And it dawned on me that he was probably unemployable. And I worried. Until we talked.

He sounds philosophical, speaks slowly.

'I'm at a very interesting moment in my life,' he says. 'I put my finger in my mouth and stuck it up in the air, but I'm in the doldrums. There's no wind.'

This sounds frightening, so I prepare to offer sympathy and a pep talk. But there's no need.

'Actually, no, it's not frightening,' he tells me earnestly. 'The truth is I'm kind of exhilarated.'

In my head I see him shrug. The grin. How could this be exhilarating?

'Because I literally have nothing to lose.'

'You're saying this feels somehow ... *liberating*?'

Laugh.

'Nah, liberating's a million bucks in the bank. It's ... it's that if I had a million bucks in the bank, I wouldn't be nearly as sharp as I am now. I'm on a razor's edge. And I feel pretty good about that. If I had twenty million in the bank, I'd be a butter knife. It's a trade-off.'

He tells me about a recent poker success, in which he beat out almost six thousand players. He didn't win the big prize, but he got close, and as he speaks, describing the experience and how the hands played out, it sounds like he really is having fun. I remember him stalking across the road in his Aviator shades and narco gear back in Awassa and smile to myself. It takes so shockingly little to make Josh happy.

So I ask one last time: 'Do you regret not being more careful with the money now, Josh?'

Not even a beat.

'No, never. Not once.'

'Really? *Really?*'

'Really. Part of the process,' he chuckles.

Down the line I'll be stunned to hear WikiLeaks' Julian Assange deride the internet as 'not a technology that favours freedom of speech, human rights, civil life'; even more to find the top cosmologist Paul Davies wondering 'dispiritingly' whether 'biological intelligence' and even 'engagement with the real physical universe ... is transitory?' Later still I'll find the evolutionist Richard Dawkins speculating that if and when we are all on the grid all of the time, 'A human society [will] effectively become one individual'; will smile upon hearing that an artist has installed a glass shower for public use at New York's Museum of Modern Art and that the dating site eHarmony claims to be brokering one-fifth of all US marriages by 2011. An explosion of multi-form narrative and faux-documentary tropes in films suggests a broadening sense of the world as myriod shifting, slipping, constantly reconfiguring realities.

And in the end I'll decide that, like Shahrazad, if Josh Harris hasn't won my unreserved belief, at least he's done enough to earn an enthusiastic suspension of disbelief.

A Note on the Author

Andrew Smith spent his early years in Greenwich Village, New York, and San Francisco, where his first ambitions were to become a herpetologist and to write for *MAD* magazine. At the age of 13, his English parents returned the family to the UK, where they settled in Hastings on the south coast. After studying philosophy and politics at the University of York, he moved to London to tour and record with the early electro group A Popular History of Signs for several years, before returning to his first love, which was writing. Starting at *Melody Maker*, he moved rapidly to feature writing at *The Face* magazine during its mid-90s heyday under Sheryl Garratt, then to the *Sunday Times* and the *Observer's Life* magazine, exploring topics as diverse as crop circle hoaxers; the ecstasy testers of Amsterdam; the secret world under London and human rights work of Bianca Jagger, not to mention interviewing everyone from Madonna to the architect Richard Rogers, the artist Damien Hirst and amazon.com founder Jeff Bezos.

In 2002, Smith left journalism to write his international bestseller *Moondust: in Search of the Men Who Fell to Earth*, which describes his search for the nine remaining men who walked on the moon between 1969 and '72. Nominated for two British Book Awards (including 'Read of the Year') and chosen by the

Times as one of its '100 Best Books of the Noughties', *Moondust* has been translated into more than twenty languages.

Smith now divides his time between writing and making documentary films. He lives in London with his wife, the film-maker Josie Le Grice, and has two children, Lotte and Isaak.

Visit the Epiblog at andrewsmithauthor.com
Follow Andrew Smith on Twitter @wiresmith

Acknowledgements

I'm told that if I'd kept typing for long enough, I could have written the complete works of Shakespeare. Unfortunately I didn't have that kind of time, so had to stop here, at one of dozens of different books I might have written about getting to know Josh Harris and the Dotcom explosion of the late 1990s.

For all that it's not Shakespeare, *Totally Wired* took four years to make and involved hundreds of people in one way or another. Thanks must go to the many, many who gave of their time and thoughts, a small proportion of whom are mentioned in these pages. Seldom have I met a more stimulating and independent collection of people than those Josh gathered around him. As one former Pseudo worker noted, 'he didn't pick many duds.' Several interviewees, including T-bo, Mame McCutchin, Feedbuck, Natalia Tsarkova, Joshua White, John Christopher Morton, Marc Scarpa and Greg Lindsay also supplied research materials such as email tranches, prospectuses, video tapes, film footage or audio recordings. One of the things I love most about my work is its constant reminder of how generous people can be when piqued by an idea.

Equally valuable to me were the authors and journalists who'd been this way before. Here I'd make special mention of Casey Kait and Stephen Weiss, whose joyous oral history of the Silicon Alley boom, *Digital Hustlers* (from which I've quoted on occasion with the authors' blessing), looks more important now than it would have seemed to most people at the time, and to Michael Indergaard, whose painstaking academic assessment of the New York tech sector, *Silicon Alley: The Rise and Fall of a New Media District*, often felt like a raft of sober fact in a sea of hyperbole and contradiction. For their varied contemporaneous writings on the social implications of cyberspace in the 1990s, Doug Rushkoff, Doug Coupland, William Gibson and Michael Lewis have my deepest appreciation, while getting to grips with the economics was made not just bearable, but exciting by the likes of James Cramer, Bob Woodward and Maggie Mahar – whose *Bull! A History of the Boom, 1982-1999*, is as brilliant a blend of clear-eyed analysis and readability as I've ever encountered. Hundreds of articles from *New York* magazine, *The New York Times*, *Crain's New York Business*, *Barron's*, *The Wall Street Journal*, *The Village Voice*, *The New Yorker*, *Vanity Fair* and *Silicon Alley Reporter* brought those years back to life. We allow these kinds of journalism to wither at our peril.

Closer to home, a number of friends and experts read all or parts of the book and offered invaluable comment and criticism, among them Colin Midson, my agent Deborah Rogers and Mohsen Shah at RCW, Caroline Brindle, Trevor White, Jerry Colonna, Natalia Tsarkova, Dr James Watson from the Economics Department at the University of East Anglia and my great friends Simon Hattenstone and Adrienne Connors: the flaws that remain are my own. In addition, Simon & Schuster brought me a fabulous copy editor in Katherine Stanton and proof reader Karl French, and my editor Mike Jones, without whose willingness to go to bat for this book it might well never have happened; whose calm assurance and forbearance in the face of a writer from the Douglas Adams school of deadline ('I love deadlines. I like the *whooshing sound* they make as they fly by!') is more greatly appreciated than he knows.

Lastly, a word for the people who had to live with all this.

Thanks to my mum Elisabeth Smith and David Knight for encouragement and the occasional use of their home as a writing bolthole, to Lotte and Isaak for their patience and willingness to endure sacrifice and to my much 'uncomplainingly' cherished New York family the Capozzolis for their hospitality and support. Most of all, thanks to my wife Josie, whose boundless enthusiasm and intelligence and ability to share her partner with something as jealous and absurd as a book is worth all the love in the world. Whenever I was lost or had doubts, she was the one I went to: more than anyone, this is for her.

Bibliography

Akerlof, George A. & Shiller, Robert J., *Animal Spirits: How Human Psychology Drives the Economy, and Why It Matters for Global Capitalism*, Princeton: Princeton University Press, 2009

Amis, Martin, *Money: a Suicide Note*, London: Jonathan Cape, 1984

Andersen, Kurt, *Turn of the Century*, London: Headline, 1999

Anon, *Tales from the Thousand and One Nights*, London: Penguin Classics, 1955

Auster, Paul, *The New York Trilogy*, London, Faber and Faber, 1988

Banks, Michael A., *On the Way to the Web: the Secret History of the Internet and Its Founders*, Berkeley, Apress, 2008

Berlin, Leslie, *The Man Behind the Microchip: Robert Noyce and the Invention of Silicon Valley*, New York: Oxford University Press, 2005

Biggs, John, *Black Hat: Misfits, Criminals, and Scammers in the Internet Age*, Berkeley: Apress, 2004

Blair, Jayson, *Burning Down My Master's House*, Beverly Hills: New Millennium Entertainment, 2004

Bockris, Victor, *Lou Reed: the Biography*, London: Vintage, 1995

Bockris, Victor, *Warhol*, London: Penguin, 1990

Borges, Jorge Luis, *Labyrinths*, London: Penguin, 1970

Bradbury, Ray, *Fahrenheit 451*, London: HarperCollins, 2008

Brand, Stewart, *Clock of the Long Now: Time and Responsibility – the Ideas Behind the World's Slowest Computer*, New York: Basic Books, 2000

Brand, Stewart, *II Cybernetic Frontiers*, New York: Random Press, 1974

Brand, Stewart, *Whole Earth Software Catalogue*, New York, Doubleday, 1984

Burrough, Bryan & Helyar, John, *Barbarians at the Gate: the Fall of RJR Nabisco*, London: Jonathan Cape, 1990

Capote, Truman, *Breakfast at Tiffany's*, London: Penguin, 1961

Card, Orson Scott, *Ender's Game*, London: Century Hutchinson, 1985

Carroll, Lewis, *The Hunting of the Snark*, London: Penguin, 1967

Cassidy, John, *Dot.Con: the Real Story of Why the Internet Bubble Burst*, New York: HarperCollins, 2002

Castells, Manuel, *The Rise of the Network Society*, Oxford: Blackwell, 2000

Cellan-Jones, Rory, *dot.bomb: the Strange Death of Dot.Com Britain*, London: Aurum, 2001

Cervantes, *Don Quixote*, London: Penguin, 2000

Chomsky, Noam, *Media Control: the Spectacular Achievements of Propaganda*, New York, Seven Stories Press, 2002

Conrad, Joseph, *Heart of Darkness*, London: Penguin Classics, 2007

Conway, Flo & Siegelman, Jim, *Dark Hero of the Information Age: in Search of Norbert Wiener, the Father of Cybernetics*, New York: Basic Books, 2006

Coupland, Douglas, *Generation A*, London: William Heinemann, 2010

Cramer, James J., *Confessions of a Street Addict*, New York, Simon & Schuster, 2003

Davies, Paul, *The Eerie Silence: Are We Alone in the Universe?*, London: Allen Lane, 2010

Davis, Deborah, *Party of the Century: the Fabulous Story of Truman Capote and His Black and White Ball*, New York: Wiley, 2006

DeLillo, Don, *Underworld*, New York: Simon & Schuster, 1997

Dibbell, Julian, *My Tiny Life: Crime and Passion in a Virtual World*, London: Fourth Estate, 1999

Doidge, Norman, *The Brain That Changes Itself*, London: Penguin, 2008

Dyer, Geoff, *But Beautiful*, London: Abacus, 1998

Dyson, Esther, *Release 2.0*, New York: Broadway, 1997

Dyson, George B., *Darwin Among the Machines: the Evolution of Global Intelligence*, New York: Basic Books, 1998

Easton Ellis, Bret, *American Psycho*, London: Picador, 1991

Ferguson, Charles H., *High St@kes, No Prisoners*, New York: Times Books, 1999

Farmelo, Graham, *The Strangest Man: the Hidden life of Paul Dirac, Quantum Genius*, London, Faber and Faber, 2009

Ferrato, Donna, *Love & Lust*, New York: Aperture Foundation, 2004

Fitzgerald, F. Scott, *The Great Gatsby*, London: Penguin, 1994

Fleckenstein, William A., *Greenspan's Bubbles: the Age of Ignorance at the Federal Reserve*, New York: McGraw Hill, 2008

Galbraith, John Kenneth, *The Economics of Innocent Fraud: Truth for Our Time*, London: Allen Lane, 2004

Gelatin, *The B-Thing*, Koln: Verlag Der Buchhandlung Walther Konig, 2001

Gibson, William, *Burning Chrome*, New York: Arbor House, 1986

Gibson, William, *Neuromancer*, London: Victor Gollancz, 1984

Gladwell, Malcolm, *Outliers: the Story of Success*, New York: Little, Brown, 2008

Haden-Guest, Anthony, *The Last Party: Studio 54, Disco, and the Culture of the Night*, New York: William Morrow, 1997

Hafner, Katie & Lyon, Matthew, *Where Wizards Stay Up Late: the Origins of the Internet*, New York: Simon & Schuster, 2006

Harkin, James, *Cyburbia: the Dangerous Idea That's Changing How We Live and Who We Are*, London: Little, Brown, 2009

Horn, Stacy, *Cyberville: Clicks, Culture, and the Creation of an Online Town*, New York: Warner Books, 1998

Huxley, Aldous, *Brave New World*, London: Vintage Classics, 2007

Indergaard, Michael, *Silicon Alley: the Rise and Fall of a New Media District*, New York: Routledge, 2004

Janowitz, Tama, *Slaves of New York*, New York: Crown, 1986

Johnson, Stephen A., *Interface Culture*, New York: Basic Books, 1999

Joyce, James, *Finnegans Wake*, London: Penguin, 1992

Kait, Casey & Weiss, Stephen, *Digital Hustlers: Living Large and Falling Hard in Silicon Alley*, New York: HarperCollins, 2001

Kansas, Dave, *The Wall Street Journal Guide to the End of Wall Street As We Know It*, New York: Collins Business, 2009

Kaplan, Philip J., *F'd Companies: Spectacular Dot-com Flameouts*, New York: Simon & Schuster, 2002

Kirkpatrick, David, *The Facebook Effect*, New York: Simon & Schuster, 2010

Kirtzman, Andrew, *Rudy Giuliani: Emperor of the City*, NewYork: William Morrow, 2000

Kotkin, Joel, *The New Geography: How the Digital Revolution is Reshaping the American Landscape*, New York: Random House, 2001

Kurlansky, Mark, *The Big Oyster: a Molluscular History of New York*, London: Jonathan Cape, 2006

Kurzweil, Ray, *The Singularity is Near: When Humans Transcend Biology*, London: Duckworth, 2005

Lacey, Sarah, *Once You're Lucky, Twice You're Good: the Rebirth of Silicon Valley and the Rise of Web 2.0*, New York: Gotham, 2009

Ledbetter, James, *Starving to Death on $200 Million: the Short, Absurd Life of The Industry Standard*, New York: Public Affairs, 2003

Leibovich, Mark, *The New Imperialists: How Five Restless Kids Grew up to Virtually Rule the World*, Paramus: Prentice Hall Press

Lessard, Bill & Baldwin, Steve, *Netslaves 2.0: Tales of Surviving the Great Tech Gold Rush*, New York: Allworth Press, 2003

Lewis, Michael, *The Future Just Happened*, London: Hodder and Stoughton, 2001

Lewis, Michael, *Liar's Poker: Two Cities, True Greed*, London: Hodder and Stoughton, 1989

Lewis, Michael, *The Money Culture*, New York: Penguin, 1992

Lewis, Michael, *The New New Thing*, London: Hodder and Stoughton, 1999

Lewis, Michael, *Panic: the Story of Modern Financial Insanity*, London: Penguin, 2008

Mahar, Maggie, *Bull! A History of the Boom, 1982-1999*, New York: HarperCollins, 2003

Malmsten, Ernst, *boohoo: a dot.com story from concept to catastrophe*, London: Random House, 2001

Markoff, John, *What the Dormouse Said: How the Sixties Counterculture Shaped the Personal Computer Industry*, New York: Penguin, 2005

McCann, Colum, *Let the Great World Spin*, London: Bloomsbury, 2009

McLuhan, Marshall & Fiore, Quentin, *The Medium is the Massage: an Inventory of Effects*, London: Penguin, 1967

McLuhan, Marshall, *Understanding Media*, London: Routledge and Kegan Paul, 1964

McInerny, Jay, *Bright Lights, Big City*, New York: Vintage, 1984

Mezrich, Ben, *The Accidental Billionaires: Sex, Money, Betrayal and the Founding of Facebook*, London: William Heinemann, 2009

Mills, Nicolaus (ed.), *Culture in an Age of Money: the Legacy of the 1980s in America*, Chicago: Foundation for the Study of Independent Social Ideas, 1990

Minsky, Marvin, *The Emotion Machine: Commonsense Thinking, Artificial Intelligence, and the Future of the Human Mind*, New York: Simon & Schuster, 2006

Mitchell, Joseph, *Up in the Old Hotel*, New York: Vintage, 2008

Mnookin, Seth, *Hard News: Twenty-one Brutal Months at The New York Times and How They Changed the American Media*, New York: Random House, 2004

Motavalli, John, *Bamboozled at the Revolution: How Big Media Lost*

Billions in the Battle for the Internet, New York: Penguin, 2002

Murray, Janet H., *Hamlet on the Holodeck: the Future of Narrative in Cyberspace*, New York: Free Press, 1997

Naughton, John, *A Brief History of the Future: the Origins of the Internet*, London: Weidenfeld & Nicholson, 1999

Negroponte, Nicholas, *Being Digital*, London: Vintage, 2000

Noble, David F., *Progress Without People: in Defense of Luddism*, Chicago: Charles H. Kerr, 1993

Orwell, George, *1984*, London: Penguin, 2008

Palahniuk, Chuck, *Fight Club*, London: Vintage, 1997

Palmer, Sue, *Toxic Childhood: How the Modern World is Damaging our Children and What We Can Do About It*, London: Orion, 2006

Palmer, Sue, *21st Century Boys: How Modern Life Is Driving Them Off the Rails and How We Can Get Them Back On Track*, London: Orion, 2009

Prebble, Lucy, *Enron*, London: Methuen Drama, 2009

Pynchon, Thomas, *Inherent Vice*, London: Jonathan Cape, 2009

Rees, Martin, *Our Final Century: the 50/50 Threat to Humanity's Survival: Will the Human Race Survive the Twenty-first Century?*, London: Arrow, 2004

Rheingold, Howard, *The Virtual Community: Homesteading on the Electronic Frontier*, Cambridge: MIT Press, 2000

Ross, Andrew, *No-Collar: the Humane Workplace and Its Hidden Costs, Behind the Myth of the New Office Utopia*, New York: Basic Books, 2003

Roszak, Theodore, *The Making of a Counter Culture*, Berkeley: University of California Press, 1995

Rotolo, Suze, *A Freewheelin' Time: a Memoir of Greenwich Village in the Sixties*, New York: Broadway Books, 2008

Runyan, Damon, *Broadway Stories*, London: Penguin, 1993

Rushkoff, Douglas, *Bull*, London: Hodder and Stoughton, 2001

Rushkoff, Douglas, *Children of Chaos: Surviving the End of the World as We Know It*, London: HarperCollins, 1997

Rushkoff, Douglas, *Cyberia: Life in the Trenches of Hyperspace*, London: Flamingo, 1994

Rushkoff, Douglas, *Playing With the Future: What We Can Learn from Digital Kids*, New York, Riverhead Books, 1996

Salmon, Christian, *Storytelling: Bewitching the Modern Mind*, London: Verso, 2010

Schwartz, Sherwood, *Inside Gilligan's Island*, New York: St Martin's Press, 1988

Scott, Allen J., *The Cultural Economy of Cities: Essays on the Geography of Image-Producing Industries*, London: Sage, 2000

Seabrook, John, *Deeper: a Two-year Odyssey in Cyberspace*, London: Faber and Faber, 1998

Sennett, Richard, *The Corrosion of Character: Personal Consequences of Work in the New Capitalism*, London: Norton, 1999

Shields, David, *Reality Hunger: a Manifesto*, London: Hamish Hamilton, 2010

Shiller, Robert J., *Irrational Exuberance*, New York: Crown, 2006

Shirky, Clay, *Here Comes Everybody: How Change Happens When People Come Together*, London: Penguin, 2009

Soros, George, *The Bubble of American Supremacy*, London: Weidenfeld & Nicholson, 2004

Spector, Robert, *Amazon.com: Get Big Fast*, London: Random House Business Books, 2000

Standage, Tom, *The Victorian Internet*, New York: Walker, 1998

Tallis, Raymond, *Why the Mind is Is Not a Computer: a Pocket Lexicon of Neuromythology*, Exeter: Imprint Academic, 2004

Thurber, James, *The Years With Ross*, London: Penguin, 1963

Vidal, Gore, *The Last Empire: Essays 1992-2001*, London: Abacus, 2003

Warhol, Andy, *The Philosophy of Andy Warhol*, London: Penguin 2005

Washington, Irving, *Knickerbocker's History of New York, Complete*, Hamburg: Tredition 2011

Wolff, Michael, *Burn Rate: How I Survived the Goldrush Years on the Internet*, New York: Simon & Schuster, 1998

Weinberger, David, *Everything is Miscellaneous: the Power of the New Digital Disorder*, New York: Holt, 2007

Winston, Robert, *Bad Ideas?: an Arresting History of Our Inventions*, London: Transworld, 2010

Wishart, Adam & Bochsler, Regula, *Leaving Reality Behind: the Battle for the Soul of the Internet*, London: Fourth Estate, 2002

Wolfe, Tom, *The Bonfire of the Vanities*, London: Jonathan Cape, 1988

Wolfe, Tom, *The Electric Kool-Aid Acid Test*, New York: Farrar, Straus and Giroux, 1967

Wolfe, Tom, *The New Journalism*, London: Picador, 1975

Woodward, Bob, *Maestro: Greenspan's Fed and the American Boom*, New York: Touchstone, 2000

Yeats, W. B., *Selected Poems*, London: Penguin, 1991

Zukin, Sharon, *The Cultures of Cities*, Oxford: Blackwell, 1996

Zukin, Sharon, *Loft Living: Culture and Capital in Urban Change*, New Brunswick: Rutgers University Press, 1989

Zukin, Sharon, *Point of Purchase: How Shopping Changed American Culture*, London: Routledge, 2005

Index